BASIC TEACHING FOR
SLOW LEARNERS

PETER BELL

Basic Teaching
for
Slow Learners

MULLER EDUCATIONAL

First published in Great Britain 1970
by Muller Educational, a division of
Frederick Muller Ltd., Fleet Street, London, E.C.4

COPYRIGHT NOTICE

© *Peter Bell 1970*

Printed and bound by
The Garden City Press Limited
Letchworth, Hertfordshire

SBN: 584 10851 6

Contents

Introduction

BRITAIN is facing an 'educational explosion' resulting from a rapidly increasing school population and demands for more and better education. This fact has implications for the teaching of children with learning difficulties. It has been estimated that by 1970 there will be one million slow learners in British schools.[1] This startling claim does not seem to be unrealistic nor has it been disputed.

Who are these 'slow learners'? They are children, who, for various reasons, fall behind in their school work and require special teaching. These children were officially described as educationally subnormal (E.S.N.) over twenty years ago. Unfortunately this term was never really understood and was rarely applied to children in ordinary schools. Many of the benefits of the broad classification were lost because the needs of large numbers of children were ignored and the term not only became associated with children in special schools but also was considered offensive by many parents and teachers. The term 'slow learner' is becoming more widely used and throughout this book will be regarded as interchangeable with 'educationally subnormal', 'backward' or 'less able'.

At the present time slow learners are provided for in a number of ways. A minority are in residential or day special schools but the greater proportion remain in the normal school, some being catered for in special classes, others receiving a measure of remedial tuition, while many appear to be given no special consideration. In recent years there has been a rapid expansion in the provision of day special schools but the development of a proper system of special classes in ordinary schools has not been pursued with the same vigour. There are special classes in some primary schools and remedial departments in many secondary schools but special educational facilities in ordinary schools are often inadequate. Overall planning seems to be non-existent and there is a consequent lack of continuity both within schools and between primary and secondary stages. Too much depends on the interest or whim of the headteacher. This is frequently demonstrated by the setting up of a remedial class which is subsequently disbanded at the first sign of staffing difficulty. All too often, at the secondary level, the burden rests on the shoulders of one interested teacher. Can she be expected to cope with the problems of literacy in the first and second years and still support those who need guidance in the third and fourth years?

To provide a properly integrated system of special schools and classes, where children are taught in groups of not more than twenty, we should be urgently considering training 50,000 specially selected teachers. The prospect of finding enough teachers who are willing to teach slow learners, let alone training such large numbers, is a daunting one. Efforts are being made to provide some guidance by means of in-service training, short courses and summer schools. During the last decade there has been an increase in more specialised courses of longer duration which lead to additional qualifications. Unfortunately there are probably fewer than 600 teachers receiving such specialised training each year. This hardly covers the wastage from special schools alone, due to retirement, marriage or movements to other jobs. Inevitably there are going to be many more teachers who will have to teach slow learners without any special training. This book is intended to provide practical advice for such teachers. It is a primer on a wide variety of topics relating to slow learners but, essentially, it contains a general outline of a special curriculum. We must take into account both the abilities and the needs of children and basic teaching for slow learners should not merely be a matter of reading and arithmetic with a watered-down version of normal school subjects. Special Education demands a different curriculum which recognises the personal, social and occupational needs of individual children. The first priority is to recognise that children are individuals and to appreciate that there are no homogeneous classes of backward children. Accordingly, no writer can prescribe a teaching programme to suit all slow learners in all situations. Ultimately, only the teacher, who knows her pupils, can plan the most appropriate scheme of work. What follows then, is merely an account of activities which have proved successful with some slow learners. Individual teachers must adopt, adapt and improve these methods according to the needs of the children in their care. An essential consideration, therefore, is to make a careful study of each child and so some guidance is given on assessment, testing and diagnostic procedures. Following assessment we can consider the suitability and relative importance of various teaching techniques. There is considerable scope for developing suitable courses for slow learners and the methods and activities described here should be regarded as seminal. Some indication is given where further reading may enlarge upon the ideas and practices described here. Special education is not only concerned with teaching but should be a co-operative venture where several professions work together. Later chapters suggest how teachers may gain the support and advice of other experts and seek the co-operation of parents.

REFERENCES

1. Segal, S. S., 'The Teaching – Learning Process' in *Forward Trends*, Summer, 1966.

NOTE:
Numbered references in the text refer to source material listed at the conclusion of each chapter.

CHAPTER 1

Diagnosis—'A Suitable Case for Treatment?'

CONSIDERABLE progress has been made in special educational treatment in recent years. Notable advances have been made in the provision of a variety of specialist services. Within the schools there has been a clarification of the aims of special education and improvements in the broad content of the curriculum. In marked contrast less effort has been expended in the diagnosis and treatment of individual difficulties. Yet progress in this area would seem to be of the utmost importance both in the placement and education of slow learners.

Diagnosis has been interpreted in various ways. In one sense diagnosis has been simply descriptive. This applies to the ascertainment of educationally subnormal pupils. Ascertainment is the procedure whereby backward children are first discovered and then examined to decide which form of special education seems appropriate to their needs. This process could be improved.

A challenging but much more promising approach is in the developing field of differential diagnosis. Here we see a much more detailed examination of a child in an attempt to uncover particular strengths and weaknesses which may be significant in planning individual educational programmes. Essentially this calls for inter-professional team work with teachers, psychologists, doctors, and social workers contributing to a proper case study. Ideally education ought to assume a dominant role in any such structure, for case-studies which become clinical exercises, unrelated to educational procedures, are largely a waste of time.

There are thus various themes to be explored where diagnosis at different levels offers a distinct contribution.

1. The discovery of all children with learning difficulties.

2. A more detailed assessment of children with a view to proper placement.

3. A differential diagnosis which seeks to determine the significance of specific handicapping conditions in order to plan individual treatment.

SURVEYS AND SCREENING PROCEDURES

Diagnosis as discovery is haphazard and subject to extreme variations from one area to another. If we are to make proper provision for slow learners and to use existing services to the best advantage, then surveys must be carried out to ascertain the extent of 'backwardness' in each authority.

At the present time children thought to be backward are referred for assessment not only by teachers but from many other sources including school medical officers, parents, probation officers and magistrates. If there are some advantages in this practice there are clearly serious shortcomings. The early detection of difficulties by parents and medical practitioners is welcome, but referrals which arise when children are in serious trouble are usually too late. Links between delinquency and backwardness are given undue emphasis and external pressures may upset placement priorities. However, major disadvantages arise when an authority has no idea of the total numbers of E.S.N. children and therefore not only does not make the necessary provision but may also strain existing facilities. Lack of knowledge about the nature and incidence of school failure leads to guesswork in the planning and siting of special schools. Thus, with monotonous regularity, special schools report that they have long waiting lists. Selecting children for admission to special schools is unsatisfactory when the list does not include all those who are most in need of this treatment. Forward planning is thus impossible and promises to parents are likely to be upset by unexpected additions to the list. The waiting lists are too long and special classes and remedial services are inadequate. Thus many children are admitted to special schools who should be educated in ordinary schools.

A survey or screening process need not be a difficult undertaking. Many Local Education Authorities have established the procedure of testing whole age groups in junior schools. Commonly, this takes the form of testing all the seven to eight year age range, after they have been given one or two terms to settle down in the junior school. A simple non-verbal intelligence test and a reading test may be given. Ideally, attention should then be directed to giving immediate help in school to all retarded readers. Dull children who are also experiencing particular difficulty in school may be referred for a more detailed examination.

Unfortunately a screening process has been abandoned by some authorities. Undoubtedly it has been abused, for many schools used the information to stream children, and selection at 11 + became selection at 7 +. Dull children could be written off, or neglected by subconsciously assigning them to a 'waiting list' for special schools. Dangers still exist that teachers may acquire fixed expectations of a child's progress from an inadequate test given at an early age. This must be overcome by educating teachers to an awareness of these failings.

SURVEYS USING TEACHERS' ASSESSMENTS

An alternative to wholesale testing is to ask teachers to make a return of the numbers of children whom they personally assess as falling into various categories. For example—

1. Children of very limited intelligence who need education in a special school.

2. Children of limited intelligence who might benefit from tuition in a special class.

3. Children of average or above average intelligence who need special help because they are seriously retarded in basic subjects.

4. Children with social or emotional problems.

Like the test screening process, a survey based on teachers' assessments needs following up by visits to the schools. It is not unknown to find schools that fail to make a return, teachers who misinterpret categories, and the headteacher who has 'no backward children in *my* school!'

INTERNAL SCHOOL SURVEYS

If the local education authority fails to initiate surveys, head-teachers of primary schools might find it valuable to conduct their own screening process.* A preponderance of backward readers or dull children should lead to a request for additional teaching staff or the expansion of local remedial services. Test scores may well provide strong supportive evidence for an appeal to the education office, school managers or child guidance service. Joint action by two or three schools in an area may be even more effective.

EARLY DIAGNOSIS

Currently there is considerable emphasis on the early diagnosis and treatment of retarded children. This is reflected in the American literature[1] and in their 'Headstart' programmes for disadvantaged children (special nursery schools). The realisation is growing that pre-school experiences are vital to later learning and that 'lack of early meaningful experience' is often later translated into 'lack of ability'. We are failing to stretch our educational resources to include 'special provision' for selected pre-school children but there are some developments which show a trend towards some practical solutions.

Some local authorities lead the way, by admitting severely subnormal children to their junior training centres from the age of three years. Diagnostic and Assessment Units are being attached to many day special schools for children between the ages of five to seven years who are obviously in need of special educational treatment. Although the diagnostic functions of

*Using selected group tests from Charts 1 and 2, Chapter 3.

many of these units are primitive, they are already providing evidence of the need for infant classes in special schools.

THE 'AT RISK' REGISTER

To progress to a proper consideration of the needs of many pre-school age children better use has to be made of the 'at risk' register. This is kept by local health authorities and contains information about the birth, growth, development and ailments of babies. Much of the data is compiled by Health Visitors who attend mothers following the birth of a baby. The 'at risk' element of the register notes mishaps in pregnancy, difficulty at birth, and post-natal troubles. A close correlation has been established between pre-natal, natal and post-natal difficulties and observable handicaps in later life.[2,3] If 'special' nursery schools are ever established the 'at risk' register could form a main feature of a selection procedure. Even now, if this information were passed on to schools it might lead to early preventive treatment in the formative years. It could be of immense value to those perceptive infant school teachers who already note distinct variations in the skills which children have already acquired before they enter school. The information would certainly add to the validity of details about the early medical history of children who are later assessed as being in need of special educational treatment.

ASSESSMENT FOR SPECIAL EDUCATIONAL TREATMENT

The second stage of diagnosis deals with the more detailed assessment of a backward child who has been referred for examination because he is thought to be in need of special education. This is often categorically referred to as ascertainment. It has unfortunately acquired a formal, legal aura and school medical officers have assumed a dominant role in the procedure. Ascertainment should mean discovery in a much wider sense, for Local Education Authorities have a duty to 'ascertain' *all* children who are educationally subnormal.

This second part of the procedure involves the collation of

information about a child's psychological and educational status, his home background, school history and the results of a thorough medical examination. The information is recorded on the official forms 2.H.P. and 3.H.P. which are supplied by the Department of Education and Science. (H.P.—Handicapped Pupils.)

Form 2 H.P. has three sections and ends with the School Medical Officer's recommendation to the Local Education Authority. Part I gives a child's general history, name, date of birth, parents, school attendance, social history, home conditions etc. Part II provides details of Intelligence Tests and observations. Part III is the report of an examination by the Medical Officer and includes a personal history, physical examination, general knowledge, interests and observed capabilities, social and emotional characteristics.

Form 3 H.P. is a 'Report by a Headteacher on a backward child'. Section A gives a general history. Section B deals with Attainments which are to be indicated by responses to various questions under headings, Speech, Reading, Writing, Number, Art and Crafts and Physical Education. Sections C, D and E cover respectively, Interests, Progress, Behaviour, and Disposition. Section F allows for additional information. A graded word reading test is printed on the back of the booklet.

CURRENT FAILINGS

Many experienced special school teachers are dissatisfied with this procedure. It is common to find schools who receive these children but are not allowed access to information. This is a deplorable situation which teachers concerned should seek to rectify. When headteachers do receive confidential information about the nature of a child's difficulties, they frequently complain that it is limited or out-of-date. The psychological examination often gives little more than a mental age and an I.Q. If a Stanford-Binet test has been given, the latest revision (1960 Form L-M) should be used. Ideally before admission, a child should also be tested on the W.I.S.C. and some interpretation of results should be attempted. These two tests are described in the following chapter.

Information from previous schools is frequently at variance with the Special School teachers' assessment of a child on admission. Comments about home background may be guarded or speculative. A revision of forms 2 H.P. and 3 H.P. is overdue and information from 'restricted' tests such as the Illinois Test of Psycholinguistic Abilities (I.T.P.A.) and Vineland Social Maturity Scale ought to be available.

CASE STUDY AND THE TEACHER'S ROLE IN DIAGNOSIS

Schools should make their own case studies of children. Some form of record card is advisable. Ideally it should contain an extensive educational assessment, plus mental, physical and social data. A diagnostic assessment coupled with advice for teachers would be valuable. An excellent example of this type of record is provided by Tansley.[4] This information could profitably be supplemented by teachers' observations which might be embodied in an anecdotal report.

It is unfortunate that cumulative record cards for children, introduced on a large scale in the post-war period, have largely proved ineffective. We should learn from our failures. It is important to recognise that record keeping for its own sake has little value and may prove burdensome for teachers. Their purpose and value must be clearly demonstrated and entries must be selective. Some time might usefully be saved by abandoning the ritual of weekly forecasts or records of work. This could well be replaced by selective reports on individual children, who have particular difficulties, and be accompanied by a reappraisal of individual treatment. Less frequently assessments of educational attainments or social adjustment may be called for.

Educational assessments need to be much more comprehensive and searching.

Primarily there is a need to use more up-to-date tests and the use of diagnostic tests should be given a high priority.

Diagnostic tests in the basic subjects are readily available and are not difficult to administer. Particular reference will be made later to the claims of the Neale Analysis of Reading Ability and the Standard Reading Tests (Daniels and Diack). If these tests have their limitations, only extensive and continuous use from the practitioner in the classroom will lead to a demand for more refined techniques.

Diagnostic tests in reading and arithmetic commonly seek to break down subject areas into specific sub-skills which need to be taught. Although they can more accurately pinpoint specific weaknesses in a subject there are many other contributory factors or underlying psychological difficulties which may not be exposed. So, attitudes and interests, motivation, sensory and perceptual weaknesses remain to be examined.

Readiness for reading may be studied more scientifically through the use of the Harrison-Stroud Reading Readiness Profiles. Certain children appear to need closer study by examining perceptual and language development. Currently, there is considerable interest in the Marianne Frostig Development Test of Visual Perception as a screening test for young children who may need special training in various aspects of visual perception. It has the merit of an associated teaching programme.

Assessments of the level of vocabulary and verbal ability may be obtained from the Mill Hill Vocabulary Scale and the English Picture Vocabulary Tests. A more sophisticated test for diagnosing difficulty in the understanding and use of language is provided by the Illinois Test of Psycholinguistic Abilities.

Attitudes and interests need to be uncovered and the child's reactions to, and impressions of previous schooling may be checked. In the absence of suitable tests these factors are probably best left to the teacher to discover through informal discussion or enquiry. They are important but often seem to be neglected in practice. Schonell (1942) drew attention to the effective use of remedial reading material in relation to children's interests many years ago. His schedule D published in *Backwardness in the Basic Subjects*[5] might be re-examined.

American writers have also laboured the point and Blair[6] commented at length on techniques for assessing attitudes and interests.

Increasing attention is being paid to retarded motor development as a characteristic of many E.S.N. children. Tansley[4] has outlined a programme of activities for the treatment of acute reading disability, and pays considerable regard to children who reveal neurological abnormality and perceptual motor disturbance. Teacher's observations can either supplement tests or be an effective substitute. Children's gross bodily movements in physical activities can be revealing. Balancing, kicking, skipping, climbing, throwing and catching should be watched. Observation in P.E. or music and movement may also show up those children who are lacking in rhythmical ability, or whose spatial orientation may be questioned because of inability to move in the right direction, face the right way, or to know left from right. Lack of body awareness may be suspected when children cannot touch a knee or an elbow without first watching another child. Some of these difficulties may be due to language deficiencies or limited physical activity in earlier years. These problems may be difficult to resolve but they should not be ignored.

Aspects of social and emotional development may call for examination. Rutter's Behaviour Questionnaire is useful as a screening process and gives measures of neurotic or anti-social behaviour. The Bristol Social Adjustment Guides (U.L.P.) detect unsettled and maladjusted behaviour and show patterns of maladjustment in areas such as Hostility to Adults and Children, Withdrawal and Depression which may provide clues to providing guidance and help. The picture may be filled out by Sociometric Tests and teacher's observations.

A measure of social maturity may be provided by Lunzer's 'Manchester Scales of Social Adaptation' (N.F.E.R.) which is now available. A useful guide is provided by Gunzburg's Progress Assessment Charts (N.A.M.H.). Form 2 (for young people with the I.Q. range 55–80+) gives a check list and a diagrammatic chart of development in four areas—self-help, communication, occupation and socialisation.

A recent guide for use in child and family case-work is provided by the Systematic Interview Guides.[7] As the title suggests the guides bring system into the method of interviewing the mother about her child's early development. Guide 1 deals with the birth, health, physique and behaviour up to five years. Guide 2 deals with the pre-natal period. Although these guides may prove most useful for child care, welfare and social workers, the advantages of receiving comprehensive and comparable data could prove invaluable to teachers. The manual will aid teachers in the early detection of children who are vulnerable in health, social adjustment and educational failure.

On the basis of a careful assessment of the strengths and weaknesses of individuals a more realistic educational programme may be devised which should approximate more closely to their needs. It would not be unexpected to find groups of children who could benefit from special activities. Groups of children are already formed for remedial reading. An examination of individual difficulties may suggest different treatment. It is time for speech therapy, language development, remedial physical education and social education to appear on the timetable.

CONCLUSION

If we are to begin to see all slow learners receiving special educational treatment appropriate to their needs then we must assign a significant role to diagnostic techniques. As yet there are few educators in Britain who actively subscribe to the view hat differential diagnosis is important for differential treatment. It would be foolish to anticipate that the widespread introduction of more sophisticated testing and evaluation will be a panacea for all our failures. Some cautionary notes must be sounded.

It is clearly stated in Chapter 2 that testing has no merit in itself unless it leads to action. This stricture can be applied even more firmly to diagnostic tests. Diagnosis should lead to treatment. This is precisely the burden of Peter's book *Prescriptive Teaching*.[8] He defines his terms of reference thus (p.42).

Prescriptive teaching is a method of utilizing diagnostic information for the modification of educational programs for children with problems. It accomplishes this purpose by determining the educational relevance of the child's disability, and devising teaching procedures to yield desirable changes in the child's academic progress, emotional condition, and social adjustment.

Peter points to the dangers of diagnosis which is not school centred. He draws attention to the proliferation of diagnostic services which are available for American teachers. Referrals to clinics and centres he regards as 'essentially roads away from education'. Prescriptive teaching is seen as a 'road back' so that medical, and psychological findings are implemented in the classroom.

A clear and practical demonstration of differential diagnosis in relation to the teaching of reading has been outlined by Tansley[4] operating with a residential school population (E.S.N.) who had already been discovered and assessed. Tansley outlines a comprehensive reading programme which will have a general application to large numbers of his pupils. In the second part of his book, on the Remedial Teaching of Reading, a diagnostic programme is outlined which is linked to the remedial treatment of acute reading disability.

Explicit in this chapter has been the desirability for greater involvement by teachers in diagnostic procedures and this theme is substantiated by Gulliford.[9] He suspects that many teachers are a little uncomfortable about adopting a diagnostic role. They see diagnosis as the function of the specialist or the 'expert'. Gulliford considers that teachers are in fact continuously diagnosing and are frequently very good at it. Clearly his notion that teachers' observations and insights may be undervalued merits attention.

REFERENCES

1. Kirk, S. A. *et al.*, *The Early Education of the Mentally Retarded.* University of Illinois Press, 1958.
2. Stott, D. H., 'Physical and Mental Handicaps following a Disturbed Pregnancy', *Lancet*, 1959.
3. Barker, D. J. P. & Edwards, J. H., 'Obstetric Complications and School Performance', *Brit. Med. Jo.*, 16th July 1967.
*4. Tansley, A. E., *Reading and Remedial Reading.* Routledge & Kegan Paul, 1967.
5. Schonell, F. J., *Backwardness in the Basic Subjects.* Oliver & Boyd, 1942.
*6. Blair, G. M., *Diagnostic and Remedial Teaching.* Macmillan, New York, 1956.
7. Stott, D. H., *Systematic Interview Guides.* U.L.P., 1968.
*8. Peter, L. J., *Prescriptive Teaching.* McGraw-Hill, 1965.
9. Gulliford, R., 'Educationally Subnormal', in *What is Special Education?* Assoc. Spec. Educ., 1966.

FURTHER READING

Books marked * above and also the following:

Delacato, C. H., *Diagnosis and Treatment of Speech and Reading Problems*, Chas. C. Thomas, 1963.

Gardner, K., 'A Time for a Fresh Evaluation' in *Special Education*, Vol. LV, No. 3, 1966.

Kephart, N. C., *The Slow Learner in the Classroom*, Merrill Books, 1960.

National Union of Teachers, *The Ascertainment of E.S.N. Children.* N.U.T., 1962.

Williams, P. & Gruber, E., *Response to Special Schooling*, Longmans, 1968.

Wolfensberger, W., 'Diagnosis Diagnosed', in *Jo. Ment. Subn.*, Vol. XI, Pt. 2, Dec. 1965.

CHAPTER 2

Testing and Evaluation Techniques

TESTING and assessment have long been accepted as essential ingredients of educational practice. Unfortunately teachers' skills in testing techniques have not always kept pace with modern developments. It is evident that many schools are using out-of-date tests, that tests are often badly administered and that the purpose of testing is often obscure. Three important points ought to be kept in mind.

1. Testing has no merit in itself. There is no point in using a test unless it leads to action, decision or to the posing of further questions.

2. Standards and objectives have changed in schools and many older tests have out-lived their usefulness.

3. No tests can assess a pupil's present abilities or attainments with absolute accuracy. Equally they are not infallible predictors of future progress.

Test constructors have become dissatisfied with many earlier products. With much improved techniques at their disposal, they are now designing better tests and are becoming much more stringent in their attempts to 'test the tests' before they are passed on to the consumer.

This chapter draws attention to some important tests which have been produced during the last fifteen years. Space does not permit appraisal of earlier tests which, if not already known to the reader, are either out-of-date or do not satisfy rigorous standards of test construction. Tests which are not normally available to teachers are omitted or given a brief mention with references for more detailed study if required.

Tests are often listed under various categories; intelligence tests, attainment tests, personality tests and miscellaneous tests of specific abilities. Within each category there are usually individual and group tests, involving oral or written responses. Some tests have special claims as diagnostic instruments.

INTELLIGENCE TESTS

Many teachers wish to make some assessment of the mental ability of their pupils. This practice is being strongly questioned at a time when theories about the nature and constancy of intelligence are changing and many writers suspect that teachers' expectations are important factors in educational progress. Pupils' aspirations and self-concepts, motivation, interest and attention may all be more valuable attributes to excite examination. Good teaching should have regard to these factors which may affect progress to a remarkable degree. It is unfortunate that there are very few tests in these areas.

Awareness of the dangers of assessing a child's intelligence with any certainty and a healthy mistrust of the 'magic I.Q. figure' are the first signs of wisdom in a 'test-conscious' teacher.

INDIVIDUAL INTELLIGENCE TESTS

Early developments were concentrated on individual intelligence tests, i.e. where one child at a time is examined with a series of standardised questions. Since Binet and Simon's early work in Paris at the turn of the century, the individual test has stimulated considerable research and further development. Evaluation and revision have led to certain tests being widely used. They now offer high standards of validity and reliability. The best known and most used individual tests are the Stanford-Binet Scale of Intelligence and the Wechsler Intelligence Scale for Children.

THE STANFORD-BINET SCALE OF INTELLIGENCE

This test may sometimes be referred to as the Terman-Merrill as well as the Stanford-Binet. It is the outcome of various revisions of Binet's early work. An extensive adaptation of the test was completed in 1916 by Lewis M. Terman and Maud A. Merrill at Stanford University, U.S.A. This version was completely revised in 1937 and two parallel forms (L & M) were made available. A third revision (Form L-M) was issued in 1960. The test covers a wide age range, from two to eighteen years, and may take from one to two hours to administer. It cannot be described briefly and adequately. While noting that it is not suitable for untrained personnel, paradoxically, teachers should be alert to note whether 'trained' testers are using the 1960 revised version. It is reported in many quarters that not only is the 1937 version still in use, but correction tables, which have been produced in the intervening period, are not always being applied. Specially interested teachers might well read the test manual[1] or read a shorter description and appraisal of the test by Anastasi.[2]

WECHSLER INTELLIGENCE SCALE FOR CHILDREN (W.I.S.C.)

This test, first produced in 1950, is designed for use with children between the ages of five and fifteen years. The W.I.S.C. has frequently been used as an alternative to the Stanford-Binet and is increasingly being preferred. It has some special advantages in providing three measures of intelligence—a Verbal I.Q., a Performance I.Q., and a Full Score I.Q. In addition comparisons may be made between results obtained on the various sub-tests by any individual. The pattern of scores on the sub-tests may have implications for diagnostic assessment. Suggested interpretations of various strengths and weaknesses remain to be proven but a mood of optimism prevails. The recent provision of Scottish Norms for the W.I.S.C.[3] may encourage a more widespread use of this test in the United Kingdom.

GROUP TESTS

For teachers who wish to use an individual test, and this is advisable with young and distractable children, the group tests, which are listed below, can be administered individually. The

Raven's Progressive Matrices is one test which is often given as an individual test. It should be noted that this is only sampling one aspect of ' intelligence' and even when supplemented with the Crichton Vocabulary Scale, cannot provide either the measure of general intelligence provided by some other tests or the opportunity of examining contributory factors. A more useful test, designed for the non-specialist, is contained in Valentine's book *Intelligence Tests for Children*.[4] This is intended for children between the ages one-and-a-half to fifteen years.

Few teachers have the time to embark upon extensive individual testing of intelligence and group tests provide an alternative. It should be remembered that these are a poor substitute for a properly administered individual test like the W.I.S.C. They should therefore be regarded as a rough assessment, useful mainly as a screening process prior to recommendation for an individual test. Occasionally they may provide additional information as part of a more detailed study of a child or may be used to check on an out-of-date or questionable test result.

Group tests are mainly of the pencil and paper type and are generally classified as Verbal or Non-Verbal Tests. Obviously Verbal Tests, which use written questions, are unsuitable for poor readers who will obtain low scores irrespective of their mental ability. Unless a child has a reading age of at least nine years it is pointless to give him a verbal test. It is for this reason that Non-Verbal tests have been developed. These tests often make use of pictures and shapes which are presented to children with oral instructions. The sub-tests attempt to parallel Verbal Reasoning tests by including items to test powers to see relationships, similarities and differences, and to test abilities to make analogies.

Even so, it is apparent that Verbal and Non-Verbal tests are not measuring the same abilities. It has been noted that good readers do not always obtain the same scores on both types of tests. Indeed some children who perform well on verbal tests may receive lower scores on a non-verbal test. Obviously, pictures and shapes involve an element of spatial or practical ability (note the 'performance' element in the W.I.S.C. test). Reading ability correlates more highly with verbal scores (and the verbal elements of general intelligence tests). Non-verbal intelligence does not correlate highly with reading attainment. It is therefore unwise to attempt to predict reading potential from such tests or to make too much of discrepancies between a reading age and a mental age obtained from a non-verbal test.

Bearing these strictures in mind it must also be noted that some verbal tests do include 'non-verbal' items (e.g. Cotswold Junior Ability Tests). It is fair also to say that in giving instructions to children, when administering non-verbal tests, a verbal element is introduced through the understanding of the spoken word. A notable example in this respect is Young's *Non-Readers Intelligence Test*.[5] This is an 'orally presented' test which contains no pictures or shapes. It requires children to select an initial letter (from a choice of four) to indicate the correct word needed to answer the testers' question. Four sub-tests involve riddles, classification, analogues and opposites. The handbook, marking template and answer sheets are relatively inexpensive.

The following chart (Table 1) provides a guide to recently published intelligence tests. Addresses of publishers are listed at the end of this chapter. It is advisable to purchase a specimen set and study the teachers' manual before making extensive orders.

ATTAINMENT TESTS

Reading. There has been a move away from the word recognition type of test which tests children's ability to read a string of isolated and unconnected words. Developments first led to the introduction of tests using sentences, whereby children are able to make use of contextual clues. These are usually accompanied by questions to test comprehension (a prime example is the Holborn Reading Scale[6]). Latterly a further progression can be seen in the Neale Analysis of Reading Ability which makes use of graded short 'stories'. This test is more akin to the real

Table 1 *Intelligence Tests* (Group or individual)

Name of Test	Date	Age Range	Time	Author	Pub.
VERBAL TESTS					
Carlton Intelligence Test No. 1	1962	10-12 yrs.	45 mins.	H. C. Carlton	U.L.P.
Cotswold Junior Ability Tests. A	1961	9.4-10.6 yrs.	35 mins.	C. M. Fleming	Gibson
B.	1954	8.0-10 yrs.	35 mins.	C. M. Fleming	Gibson
C.	1954	8.4-9.9 yrs.	35 mins.	C. M. Fleming	Gibson
D.	1957	8.4-9.9 yrs.	35 mins.	C. M. Fleming	Gibson
F.	1961	9.4-10.6 yrs.	35 mins.	C. M. Fleming	Gibson
Maddox Verbal Reasoning	1960	9.5-10.5 yrs.	45 mins.	H. Maddox	Oliver & Boyd
(N.F.E.R.) Primary Verbal. 1.	1962	8-10½yrs.	30 mins.	D. A. Pidgeon	Newnes
(N.F.E.R.) Primary Verbal. 2.	1959	9-11½ yrs.	35 mins.	V. Land	Newnes
(N.F.E.R.) Primary Verbal 3.	1962	10-12 yrs.	35 mins.	T. N. Postlethwaite	Newnes
(N.F.E.R.) Secondary Verbal. 1.	1960	11-13½ yrs.	40 mins.	V. Land	Newnes
(N.F.E.R.) Secondary Verbal. 2.	1966	13.6-15 yrs.	45 mins.	V. Land	Newnes
Manchester General (Senior 1)	1952	13-14 yrs.	45 mins.	S. Wiseman	U.L.P.
Ability Tests (Senior 2)	1959	14-15 yrs.	60 mins.	S. Wiseman	U.L.P.
NON-VERBAL TESTS					
Carlton Picture Intelligence Test. (A & B—parallel forms)	1962	6.3-7.0 yrs.	32 mins.	W. K. Carlton	U.L.P.
Deeside Picture Test	1957	6½-8½ yrs.	25 mins.	W. G. Emmett.	Harrap
(N.F.E.R.) Picture Test 1	1961	7.0-8.1 yrs.	22 mins.	J. Stuart	Newnes
Non-Readers Intelligence Test	1964	6.9-8.11 yrs.	60 mins.	D. Young	U.L.P.
(N.F.E.R.) Non-Verbal Test No. 5	1958	8-11 yrs.	20 mins.	D. A. Pidgeon	Newnes
(N.F.E.R.) A.H. 4	1966	10 yrs. +	30 mins.	A. W. Heim	N.F.E.R.
Raven's Progressive Matrices—coloured	1958	5½-11 yrs.	untimed	J. C. Raven	H. K. Lewis
Raven's Progressive Matrices—A.B.C.D.E.	1956	8-14 yrs.	untimed	J. C. Raven	H. K. Lewis

reading situation and each passage is illustrated with an appropriate picture. As each passage increases in difficulty, the interest level is also raised so that story content may be tied to increasing chronological age.

Another development in the testing of reading attainments can be seen in the provision of group reading tests. This move relieves teachers of the time-consuming burden of the individual test. Those tests which involve usable sheets or booklets will prove to be more expensive than the old re-usable test card. To balance this expense some account must be taken of the cost of a teacher's time and some consideration of how to make best use of her skill. The modern tendency to provide marking keys or templates is also a time saver. A realisation of the potentialities of group tests may lead to products being more competitively priced.

The production of individual tests is now largely confined to those tests which can claim to have some diagnostic value. Children experiencing difficulty in learning to read need a much more detailed examination than can be gained from word recognition tests. The Neale Analysis of Reading Ability has some claims as a diagnostic instrument. In addition to providing separate scores to measure Accuracy, Comprehension and Rate of Reading, supplementary tests are supplied to test names and sounds of letters, auditory discrimination and ability to blend syllables. A record sheet may be completed for each child to guide testers in assessing specific errors and attitudes to reading during the test situation. Although this tends to be a lengthy procedure it may have additional benefits by training a teacher to be more observant while hearing children read. Transfer of this skill to the normal reading lesson may increase the number of perceptive teachers who can adequately judge a child's reading ability and pinpoint his difficulties by observing his attempts to read a passage from one of a series of graded reading books.

A comprehensive battery of reading tests is provided in the book *Standard Reading Tests*.[7] There are twelve tests which are intended not only to assess present reading levels but to

Table 2 *Reading Tests*

Name of Test	Date	Reading Age Range	Type	Author	Pub.
Group Reading Assessment	1964	6·3–11·7 yrs.	Word recognition and sentence reading	F. Spooncer	U.L.P.
Group Reading Test	1969	6·0–10·1 yrs.	Picture-Word matching. Sentence	D. Young	U.L.P.
Southgate Group Reading Test 1 (Parallel versions A.B.C.)	1959	6–7½ yrs.	Word selection	V. Southgate	U.L.P.
Test 2 (Parallel forms A & B)	1962	7–8·11 yrs.	Sentence completion	V. Southgate	U.L.P
(N.F.E.R.) Sentence Reading Test 1	1956	7·6–11·1 yrs.	Sentence completion	A. F. Watts	Newnes
'Standard Reading Tests'. 1. Test of Reading Skill	1958	5–9 yrs.	*Battery of Tests* Individual oral sentence	J. C. Daniels & H. Diack	Chatto & Windus
12. Grading Test of Reading Experience		6–14 yrs.	Sentence completion (indiv. or group)		
Tests 2 to 9	1958		Diagnostic		

20

Test	Year	Age	Description	Author	Publisher
Neale Analysis of Reading Ability. (3 parallel forms.)	1958	6–12 yrs.	Individual graded passages. Supplementary tests and record sheets for diagnostic use	M. D. Neale	Macmillan
(N.F.E.R.) Reading Comprehension I	1967	10–12 yrs.	Comprehension (3 apsects)	E. L. Barnard	Newnes
(N.F.E.R.) Secondary Reading Tests 1, 2, 3	1966	11–15 yrs.	vocabulary, comprehension, continuous prose	S. M. Bate	Newnes
Manchester Reading comprehension test	1959	13·6–15·2 yrs.	comprehension passages	S. Wiseman & J. Wrigley	U.L.P.

provide a more detailed diagnosis of reading difficulties at various levels. Test 1 is the key test. According to results on this test, children are assigned to reading standards (numbered 0 to 6). Further tests are indicated for the various standards. Diagnostic tests are as follows: 2. Copying abstract figures; 3. Copying a sentence; 4. Visual Discrimination and Orientation; 5. Letter recognition; 6. Aural discrimination; 7. Diagnostic word recognition; 8. Oral word recognition; 9. Picture-word recognition; 10. Silent prose reading and comprehension.

The battery ends with a graded spelling test and the graded Test of Reading Experience. This is a sentence reading test and the authors generously permit teachers to duplicate copies of this test and use it as a group reading test, without infringement of copyright.

Acknowledgement must be made to the extensive battery of reading tests developed over twenty years ago by F. J. Schonell.[8] Failure on the part of teachers to make full use of his diagnostic tests through an excessive preoccupation with the Graded Word Reading Test has led to the neglect of valuable test material and has hampered the refinement and development of improved diagnostic techniques.

OTHER TESTS ASSOCIATED WITH READING DIFFICULTIES

Increasing recognition of the need for more refined instruments to examine difficulties underlying progress in reading has led to a renewed interest in readiness tests, a belated acknowledgement of the related factor of language development, and practical attempts to evaluate visual perceptual deficiencies in relation to reading problems. A brief outline of some interesting tests covering these aspects is given below.

Harrison-Stroud Reading Readiness Profiles U.S.A., 1956 (obtainable from N.F.E.R. Test Agency).
Suitable for children over the age of six years. Comprises six sub-tests: 1. Using symbols; 2. Visual discrimination; 3. Using oral context; 4. Auditory discrimination; 5. Using oral context and auditory clues; 6. Naming letters.

* *

This can be used as a group test but the booklets are expensive. A specimen set is well worth purchasing for closer inspection. An enterprising teacher may decide to try out the test on a group of children who are experiencing difficulty in the early stages of reading. Some benefit may come out of this experience by leading to a comparative evaluation of the merits of published *Reading Readiness* books[9] as indicators of specific difficulties.

Readiness for phonic teaching should not be overlooked and attention is drawn to Bragg's *Test of Phonic Readiness*.[10]

VOCABULARY TESTS

English Picture Vocabulary Tests. M. A. Brimer and L. M. Dunn, 1963, from N.F.E.R. Test Agency.
Test 1: 5·0 to 8·11 years. Test 2: 7·0 to 11·11 years.

Crichton Vocabulary Scale. J. C. Raven, H. K. Lewis, 1958: 4½ to 11 years.

Mill Hill Vocabulary Scale. J. C. Raven, H. K. Lewis, 1943: 4½ years to adult.

ILLINOIS TEST OF PSYCHOLINGUISTIC ABILITIES (I.T.P.A.).

J. J. McCarthy and S. A. Kirk, 1961, from N.F.E.R. Test Agency.
Restricted for use by qualified psychologists. Measures nine aspects of using and understanding language. (See Chapter 3 for further details.)

TEST OF VISUAL PERCEPTION

Marianne Frostig Developmental Test of Visual Perception, U.S.A., 1964, available from N.F.E.R. Test Agency.
Suitable for ages three to eight years. Individual or group. A useful test for differentiating between various sub-skills of visual perception, of significance to reading. Comprise five sub-tests: 1. Eye–motor co-ordination; 2. Figure–ground

discrimination; 3. Form constancy; 4. Position in space; 5. Spatial relations.

NUMBER READINESS, ARITHMETIC AND MATHEMATICAL TESTS

There are very few suitable tests in this field. A chart of more recent British tests is appended—Table 3.

SPELLING TESTS

A detailed account of testing attainments in spelling is given in Chapter 6, on Spelling.

PERSONALITY TESTS

Tests of character and personality are concerned with 'non-intellectual' aspects of behaviour; emotional and social adjustment, motivation, attitudes and interests.

In spite of the fact that there are many hundreds of tests in this area, few tests have acquired the precision and reliability which we have come to expect from tests of attainment and intelligence. This largely remains a field for the expert and many tests are best left to the trained child psychiatrist.

To leave personality tests to the experts is not to suggest that we should ignore the problem altogether. The importance of social and personal adequacy has been mentioned elsewhere. The necessity for devising a curriculum to take these factors into account carries with it the need to evaluate progress in this area. All the techniques open to the psychiatrist cannot be described adequately in a short space. It is proposed therefore to examine a limited number of tests which can be of practical use to teachers.

Children's Behaviour Questionnaire, M. Rutter, 1967, available from Department of Child Development, Institute of Education, University of London.

Two forms. Scale A—for completion by parents.
Scale B—for completion by teachers.

Name of Test	Date	Age Range	Description	Publisher
N.F.E.R.				
Number Test I	1966	10½–12½ yrs.	understanding four number processes	Newnes
Junior Maths Test C.1	1966	9·3–10·8 yrs.	understanding maths, graphs, fractions, time, area	Newnes
Junior Maths Test C.3	1966	9·3–10·8 yrs.	understanding maths, graphs, fractions, time, area	Newnes
Junior Maths Test B.1. (Oral)	1965	8·6–9·8 yrs.	understanding maths, fractions, graphs, volume, area	Newnes
Staffordshire 1. Arithmetic Tests: 2.	1958	5·8–10·0 yrs. 10·2–15·6 yrs.	mechanical arithmetic	Harrap
N.F.E.R.				
Mech. Arith. 1C. 1D	1952	8–9 yrs.	four rules of number, money, weight, time, measurement	Newnes
Mech. Arith. 1A. 1B.	1952	8–10 yrs.	four rules of number, money, weight, time, measurement	Newnes
2A. 2B.	1958	7–8½ yrs.	four rules of number; addition and subtraction s. d.	Newnes
Arithmetic A1, A2	1963	8½–10 yrs.		
Progress B1, B2	1962	9–10·8 yrs.	mechanical and problem arithmetic	Newnes
C1, C2	1952	10–11·6 yrs.		
Wirral Mech. Arithmetic Tests 1A, 1B	1962	7–8 yrs.	mech. arith. (new version of Schonell's Essential Arith. Tests)	Oliver & Boyd
2A, 2B		8–9 yrs.		
3A, 3B		9–10 yrs.		
4A, 4B		10–11 yrs.		
7 Plus Assessment, Arithmetic	1957	7–8 yrs.	subtest on four rules, number and money (mechanical and problem)	U.L.P.

This is a short test of twenty-six questions which are easily answered by ticking appropriate statements. It appears to be very useful for screening or survey purposes in the preliminary identification of emotional instability in children aged seven to thirteen years. It is claimed that this test will pick out signs of behavioural disorder and differentiate between neurotic and anti-social tendencies. Full details of standardisation, scoring and interpretation are reported in the *Journal of Child Psychology and Psychiatry*, Vol. 8, 1967 (Pergamon Press).

Bristol Social Adjustment Guides, D. H. Stott, U.L.P., 1956.

These guides are intended to uncover unsettled and maladjusted behaviour. A delinquency predictor is also available. Three versions of the guide are produced: (*a*) The Child in School (*b*) The Child in the Family (*c*) The Child in Residential Care.

The guides are simple to complete and only require the underlining of a number of statements which may best describe a particular child. Using a transparent template the relevant items can be transferred to a diagnostic form. This will then show the extent of behaviour problems and give some indication of its nature.

Manchester Scales of Social Adaptation, E. A. Lunzer, 1966, available from N.F.E.R.

This test provides a measure of social maturity. It is laid out in two parts: (*a*) social perspective (*b*) self-direction. Although this test is still in the experimental stage and may be revised, it does seem to offer a reasonable alternative to an American test, the Vineland Social Maturity Scale, which is not readily completed by teachers.

Progress Assessment Charts, H. C. Gunzburg, N.A.M.H., 1965 (See Chapter 10—'Social Education').

A GUIDE TO TEST SOURCES

A number of organisations and educational publishers specialise in the production of tests. Some produce separate test catalogues, others have sub-sections within their educational catalogues. A list of the major British test suppliers is appended below.

National Foundation for Educational Research (in England and Wales) (N.F.E.R.) Test Agency, The Mere, Upton Park, Slough, Bucks.
Test Agency Catalogue—mainly Tests of foreign origin. Tests are marked to indicate the degree of skill which is required to administer them. Some are not available to teachers and will only be supplied to psychologists.

Newnes Educational Publishing Co. Ltd., Tower House, Southampton Street, London, W.C.2.
Catalogue *Educational Guidance in Schools* lists tests produced by N.F.E.R.

University of London Press Ltd., St. Paul's House, Warwick Lane, London, E.C.4.
Separate catalogue of intelligence, attainment, personality and aptitude tests. Lists books on testing and psychology.

G. G. Harrap & Co. Ltd., 182 High Holborn, London, W.C.1.
Supply catalogue of mental, attainment and temperament tests and books on testing.

Macmillan & Co. Ltd., 4 Little Essex Street, London, W.C.2.

Methuen & Co. Ltd., 11 New Fetter Lane, London, E.C.4.

Oliver & Boyd Ltd., Tweeddale Court, Edinburgh I.

Robert Gibson & Sons Ltd., 2 West Regent Street, Glasgow C.2.

H. K. Lewis & Co. Ltd., 136 Gower Street, London, W.C.1.

REFERENCES

1. Terman, L. M. & Merrill, M. A., *Stanford-Binet Intelligence Test* (1960 *Revision, Form L-M*). Harrap, 1961.
*2. Anastasi, A., *Psychological Testing* (Chapter 2). Macmillan, New York, 1961.

3. Scottish Council for Research in Education, *The Scottish Standardisation of W.I.S.C.* U.L.P., 1967.
4. Valentine, C. W., *Intelligence Tests for Children.* Methuen, 1958.
5. Young, D., *Non-Readers Intelligence Test.* U.L.P., 1964.
6. Watts, A. F., *Holborn Reading Scale.* Harrap, 1948.
*7. Daniels, J. C. & Diack, H., *Standard Reading Tests.* Chatto & Windus, 1959.
*8. Schonell, F. J., *Diagnostic and Attainment Testing.* Oliver & Boyd, 1960.
9. Grassam, E. H., *Getting Ready for Reading.* Ginn.
   McKee, P., *Getting Ready.* Nelson.
   Schonell, F. J., *Reading Fun.* Oliver & Boyd.
10. Bragg, H., 'Readiness for Phonics in Dull Children', in *Special Education* Vol. LI No. 2 1962. Also reported in Tansley (1967).

FURTHER READING

Books marked * above also the following:
Burt C., *Mental & Scholastic Tests*, Staples Press (4th edit.), 1962.
Cronbach, L. J., *Essentials of Psychological Testing*, Harper & Row, 1961.
Evans, K. M., *Sociometry & Education*, Routledge & Kegan Paul, 1962.
Jackson S., *A Teacher's Guide to Tests*, Longmans, 1968.
Kellmer Pringle, M. L., *Social Learning and its Measurement*, Longmans, 1966.
Nunnally, J. C., *Educational Measurement & Evaluation*, McGraw Hill, 1964.
Northway, M. L. & Weld, L., *Sociometric Testing*, Univ. of Toronto Press, 1957.
Vernon, P. E., *Intelligence & Attainment Tests*, U.L.P., 1960.
Vernon, P. E., *Personality Tests & Assessment*, Methuen, 1953.
Whilde, N. E., *Application of Psychological Tests in Schools*, Blackie, 1955.

CHAPTER 3

Language Development

THE importance of language should be self-evident. In school it is the major medium of instruction and communication. On leaving school the need to understand and converse with adults is inescapable. Social contacts depend on speech to a large extent. This is clearly demonstrated in school where inhibited speech is often associated with the isolate and the withdrawn child.

The poverty of social interaction amongst slow learners who have left school has been documented in a number of follow-up studies. Whereas a high percentage manage to gain employment the pattern of their leisure hours is often a drab one. Few join clubs and the majority are passive spectators of television, cinema and the football match. Limited powers of conversation may well restrict social contacts and limit leisure time pursuits.

THE LANGUAGE PROBLEMS OF THE E.S.N.

The neglect of language and communication skills in education is deplored by numerous writers. Failure to give due regard to language development for slow learners will undermine progress in every activity in the curriculum.

Few characteristics can be applied to all slow learners. Some form of verbal inadequacy or language deficiency can be detected in the majority of these children. Delayed speech development is common, particularly amongst duller pupils, and this factor has been recognised for at least thirty years

(Burt, 1937). Lack of parental stimulation in the early stages of learning to talk is also evident. Cashdan[1] in his preliminary study of the child-rearing practices of parents of subnormal children is already adding to our knowledge of parent/child language interaction. In addition to confirming that inadequate parents do not stimulate conversation, he suggests that late talkers may discourage some parents who receive little response to their approaches. The effects of delayed speech may become cumulative for parents may discontinue 'baby-talk' at a point when the child is ready to respond. Later such 'slow-starters' are also deprived of many of the nursery rhymes and stories which they ought to hear at mother's knee and in the early stages of infant school life. Because of their physical size late-talkers may thus be denied verbal experiences which should be related to their stage of maturity rather than their chronological age.

The early pre-school years are critical for the development of many skills. Language is a significant skill and is associated with sensory, motor, perceptual, and social and emotional development. Whereas it is important to understand that neglectful, ignorant or even over-protective parents may be contributing to language deficiences, it serves no useful purpose to apply universal blame to the home environment for there are other factors to consider.

Many children have sensory or neurological impairment to a greater or lesser degree which can affect their ability to hear or to interpret sounds or to be able to express themselves. The psychological components of language are complex and may be related to environmental, emotional or physical factors. The study of many of these deficits is in its infancy and experts tend to reach agreement only in stating the uncertainties of their findings.

SPEECH DEFECTS

Agreement is more readily reported on obvious defects and disabilities than in the determination of causes and effective treatment. Speech defects are common amongst E.S.N. children in special schools and the high incidence of such defects has been reported in numbers of studies. Figures quoted vary according to the criteria adopted by the investigators as to what constitutes a speech defect. Both Sheridan[2] and Tansley[3], from surveys of separate E.S.N. school populations, quote figures of the order of 20% of girls and 40% of boys with speech defects, ranging from mispronunciations to complete unintelligibility. Many headteachers of special schools would agree that 20–30% of their pupils are in need of speech therapy.

The prevalence and nature of this particular handicap calls for action. Reference has been made elsewhere both to the need for securing the services of a speech therapist and for supportive work by the class teacher. With the chronic shortage of speech therapists many teachers will have to accept responsibility for some speech training. The effectiveness of a teacher may not approach that of a speech therapist qualified by lengthy and specialised training but much may be achieved following the study of a number of books specifically written for teachers. (See further reading list—Anderson (1953), Beasley (1956), C. Sansom (1965).)

The language of many dull children is poor and thin. Vocabulary is limited and sentences are often short and grammatically incorrect. Some children may be quite garrulous but their conversation is often irrelevant, repetitive and lacking in qualities of abstraction. Others seem conscious of their inability to express themselves clearly and neither question nor respond to questions in the manner of normal children. Slow learners must be encouraged to ask questions and to ask for help when they do not understand.

STUDIES OF LANGUAGE

Reference has been made in the chapter on mathematics to a number of vocabulary studies of normal and educationally sub-normal children (Burroughs, Mein and O'Connor, Brooks). An interesting account of an investigation into the basic spoken vocabulary of E.S.N. children has been given by Scriven[4]. Using extensive tape recordings of the free and spontaneous conversation of fifty children in a day special school, he has listed 2,300 different words used by the pupils out of a total of over 70,000 running words of conversation. The 'quality' of the speech was striking—63% of the different words were nouns, 18% adjectives, 4% adverbs, 4% pronouns and proper nouns and 2% prepositions and conjunctions. Almost all the nouns used were 'referents'. This is a term which Chase[5] applies to words which label objects or real situations. It is clear that more abstract words are not used e.g. 'courage', 'truth', and 'faith'.

Evidence from Scriven's study also confirms that simple sentences were used extensively, compound sentences occurred less frequently and complex sentences had a very restricted usage.

ASSESSMENT OF LANGUAGE DEVELOPMENT

Generalisations about language deficiencies can only prod teachers to examine the specific problems of their own pupils.

The teachers' own observations are important and general comments i.e. 'never speaks unless spoken to', 'cannot repeat simple instructions', etc. can build up a general picture of a child. Tape recordings may be useful and, once children become accustomed to seeing one in the classroom, recordings can be made and later analysed. Cheap portable, cassette tape recorders are manufactured by a number of firms. The type with an unobtrusive stop/start control on the hand microphone is an asset. Obviously the direct confrontation in the classroom may not be as revealing as informal conversation in the art room, the playground or over school dinner.

LANGUAGE TESTS

At the present time there are few suitable measures of language attainments. Growing interest in language development will certainly lead to better forms of assessment and this movement would be encouraged if a more active concern was demonstrated from the classroom.

Watts in his book *Language and Mental Development of Children*[6] supplies both a 'Vocabulary Test for Young Children' (four to eight-and-a-half years) and an 'English Language Scale' (four to nine years) which calls for sentences of increasing complexity in response to pictures.

J. C. Raven has devised (*a*) the Crichton Vocabulary Scale (1958) (four-and-a-half to eleven years) and (*b*) the Mill Hill Vocabulary Scale (1943) (four-and-a-half years to adult, two parallel forms). These tests complement the Progressive Matrices (*a*) Coloured (*b*) A, B, C, D, E (published by H. K. Lewis) but could be used separately.

An American test has been revised by M. A. Brimer and L. M. Dunn (1963) to produce the English Picture Vocabulary Test (N.F.E.R. Test Agency). Test 1 is for children aged 5·0 to 8·11 years and Test 2 for ages 7·0 to 11·11 years. These tests demand the identification of pictures and provide measures of vocabulary and verbal ability.

Specimen sets of all these tests are inexpensive and could usefully be tried out in schools to give teachers practical experience in assessing their suitability.

THE ILLINOIS TEST OF PSYCHOLINGUISTIC ABILITIES (I.T.P.A.)

A more promising test which diagnoses difficulties in understanding and using language has been devised by McCarthy and Kirk.[7] This test, for children between the ages of two-and-a-half to nine years has been 'standardised' in Illinois, U.S.A. In spite of disadvantages due to 'Americanisms' and restriction to use by trained personnel (N.F.E.R. Test Agency) it merits extensive trial.

Briefly, this test seeks to examine how a child understands or responds to what he sees and hears. He receives messages visually and auditorally. He can display understanding by vocal or motor responses (words or gestures). These are the two 'channels of communication—input and output'.

The complex ways in which humans acquire language are examined at two 'levels of organisation'.

(a) The automatic—sequential level which involves memory of linguistic symbol sequences which are at a simple automatic level.

(b) The representational level which is a cognitive level where meaning is given to linguistic symbols.

Three psycholinguistic processes are tested—decoding, association and encoding. These are interdependent.

1.   Decoding involves the ability to extract meaning from the visual and auditory stimuli.

2.   Association is the internal manipulation of linguistic symbols leading to:

3.   Encoding, which is the ability to express ideas in words or gestures.

It can be seen from this simplified account of a rationale of linguistic processes that this is a complex theoretical and speculative view of human communication. Obviously, attempts at differential diagnosis of specific disabilities in language functions will remain at an experimental level for many years. The exciting prospect of being able to plan effective remedial programmes on a more scientific basis demands that teachers actively encourage the use of this test and experiment with remedial programmes.

Language programmes based on the I.T.P.A. have not been fully reported in the literature but work is in progress both in the U.S.A. (Smith, J. O., Peabody College; Bateman, University of Illinois; Minskoff, University of Yeshiva) and in Australia (Hart, Apelt, Swan and Perrott).

TEACHING METHODS

The breaking down of linguistic processes through a careful analysis by means of tests such as the I.T.P.A. opens the way to a structured, formal teaching method whereby individual progress is obtained through a carefully graded, step by step approach. Some teachers may feel that this is a sterile approach somewhat akin to traditional grammar lessons and that any skills acquired in this manner may not transfer to general conversation or encourage the desire for self-expression. More informal approaches where language arises naturally from interesting activities may be considered more productive of progress. There seems no good reason why both formal and informal approaches may not be attempted.

Frequent references have been made in other chapters to activities which may promote discussion naturally. It is often noted in E.S.N. schools that children who are sewing or painting will talk more freely about their personal problems. When the hands are busy and a sympathetic ear is present conversation may flow more easily. The direct confrontation in the classroom may only cause children to shrivel up. Many intelligent adults need a passport to conversation. The cocktail party or even the bridge club may be a vehicle for social intercourse.

FIRST-HAND EXPERIENCE

Expeditions and visits as outlined in *Units of Experience* provide the necessary first-hand experiences which can lead to discussion. Camps and day-trips are not just holidays for deprived children, but should provide real opportunities for all-round development. Children display unsuspected abilities in a different setting and the tense and the timid can become alive.

In school-time, short visits to stores, shops, supermarkets, churches, should be regularly undertaken. The nature walk is traditionally a respectable outing, but even a walk down the street or round a housing estate can provide many opportunities for observation and discussion.

CLASSROOM DISCUSSION

Confinement to the classroom need not stifle conversation. The 'backward' class in an ordinary classroom often stands out with its wealth of stimulating pictures and displays. Collections of specimens and items both ordinary and unusual can be exploited. A 'junk' table composed of small items discarded by parents and teachers can stimulate a variety of oral activities. A tobacco pouch, the inside of a broken clock, a shelf bracket, a butter dish or a discarded toy can all be identified and described. Their functions, shapes and material can be examined and classification, the use of collective nouns and the richer use of adjectives may be encouraged.

Classrooms full of charts, pictures, colourful picture books, scrap books and displays are not uncommon. Unfortunately we often fail to make the best use of them. Backward children need guidance and practice in attending to the classroom stimuli. A child guide for the visiting adult or a group from another classroom is only one of many ideas which a resourceful teacher may use to cause children to consider, reflect and re-examine the contents of a stimulating classroom.

STORIES

Story-telling should be frequently employed at every age. The use of gestures and dramatic presentation aids understanding and may incidentally lead to an interest in reading. Older children with some reading ability will find pleasure in a story from their own readers and will read it themselves with fresh interest and insight. Most children will ask to hear favourite stories again and the same is true for popular plays, poems and jingles. Repetition is very necessary and if this can be linked to children's choice it should be profitable.

DRAMATIC ACTIVITIES

Drama and puppetry have special claims to loosen tongues and stimulate imagination. Puppetry is often effective with children who are normally reluctant to talk. This purposeful activity is well-known to teachers and is described adequately in a number of books. Play reading from books has no value for slow learners and free drama or the dramatisation of stories is to be preferred. Excellent suggestions for dramatic activities are provided by Bruford (1948) and Tansley and Gulliford (1960).

There are many excellent oral activities to be seen in different schools. The following suggestions can only be listed briefly but should be sufficient to start readers thinking. (a) The morning assembly can be taken once a week by different classes in turn. (b) 'Radio Hopwell' makes use of a tape-recorded interview of children giving an account of the week's events.* The tape recorder is still not used sufficiently, yet modern, portable battery recorders could safely be handled by children working in small groups. (See also Stapleton, M.)[8] (c) Internal telephone systems can be used to advantage. The experience of 'phoning the school from outside, and taking incoming messages is essential for older children. (d) News time is no new feature in schools, but better results are often gained from small groups round the teacher's desk. (e) The teacher's accounts of items from the front page of the newspaper can be used to encourage older children to listen to the T.V. news. (f) Lecturettes can be given by dull children if they have pets or a hobby to describe. They may also describe something as they actually do it, or explain how they made a cake or a stool.[9]

PSYCHOLINGUISTIC ABILITIES

The following programme is primarily intended as a guide for those who have I.T.P.A. profiles on individual children. Where this test has not been given the programme itself may provide a rough and ready screening process. Children who are unable to respond readily to the first two items in any section should be given further practice. An awareness of the psycholinguistic processes may encourage teachers to be more systematic in general language training procedures.

The suggestions given under the different headings should provide a starting point to develop other ideas. It can be seen that:

1. Groups may be formed where children have similar difficulties.

*With acknowledgements to Hopwell Hall School, Ockbrook, Derby

2. Many activities can be combined into games which will have a dual function, e.g. 'Follow my leader' can include visual motor association and visual—motor sequential. If children are asked what teacher did—auditory vocal automatic ability may be added.

3. Additional activities and frequent revision will be necessary for many pupils.

4. Obvious links will be seen with work in other lessons— e.g. pre-number activities, pattern work in art, movement and music, P.E.

5. Opportunities should be seized in the last few minutes of a lesson to recall the sequence of activities.

6. Many items of apparatus from educational suppliers may be utilised to fill out a particular programme and provide practice for individual children.

A. *Auditory decoding*—the ability to understand what is heard. Demonstrated by answering questions—simply by Yes or No, or carrying out a simple instruction.

e.g. (*a*) Do you come to school on a bus?
         Do you ride a horse to school?
    (*b*) Put your hand up when I say something you can eat.
         'Bread, coal, tyres, toffee, raisins, stones', etc.
    (*c*) *Shopping.*
         Can you buy stamps at the post office?
         Can you buy bicycles at the newsagents?
         What do you buy at the butchers?
         I sell sugar—Who am I?
    (*d*) Am I a teacher?
         Are you a boy?
         Is this your sister?
    (*e*) Is ice hot?
         Is it cold in winter?
    (*f*) Has a car got wheels?
         Does a bicycle fly?
         Does a train run on rails?

(g) What sound does a bee make?
Make a noise like a sheep.

(h) Does a car run on the road or under the road?
Do you get into bed before you go to sleep or after?

(i) I sit down? I am walking to the door? etc. (with actions).

B. *Visual decoding.* The ability to identify similar objects, i.e. matching and simple classification. Thus either a horse may be matched to an identical horse, or a brown horse to a black one, or a dining chair may be matched to an armchair.

Various card games are useful—snap, domino cards, matching words, shapes, etc. Matching—pictures to objects; name cards to children; name cards to objects. Puzzles from comics —'How many cats can you find in this picture?' Visual discrimination cards—find the one that is different. 'Find one like this' (Teacher shows object, shape, picture). Children point to pictures or shapes. Party games—e.g. finding a partner with the same picture or shape.

C. *Auditory—vocal association*—the ability to extract relationships from what is heard, e.g. analogies, opposites, similes.

Opposites—'big' and 'little'—using pictures or objects.
The elephant is big. The mouse is . . . ?
This jar is little. This jar is . . . ?
Find something big. Find something small. Similarly with hot—cold, heavy—light, day—night, rough—smooth, etc. Also—as green as . . . ? as white as . . . ? and—Fish swim in water. Birds fly in the . . . ? etc.

D. *Visual Motor Association.* To be able to relate things seen, e.g. sorting objects and pictures—classifying by size, shape, colour and function.

1. Cards with pictures—hammer and nail, shirt and tie, key and door, etc.

2. Objects—egg and egg cup, cup and saucer, knife and fork, screw and screwdriver, bat and ball.

3. Picture matching—red hat—red dress; big hat—big head.

4. Simple jig-saws, e.g. figure cut into three strips—match head, body and legs.

5. Pictures of cars—classify by make.

6. Pictures of shops—match goods.

7. Pictures or small model of house—match furniture and fittings to rooms.

8. Flannelgraph—basic scenes, city, river, countryside, etc. —place buses, trees, animals, boats, etc., appropriately.

9. Sorting and matching big circles, small circles.

10. Jig-saw—insert shapes.

11. 'Follow my leader' game.

E. *Vocal encoding*—Ability to describe objects.

1. Tell me about this—to increase number of ideas expressed, e.g. shape, size, function, material.

2. Use visible objects—boys, girls, teachers, books, desks. Use actions.

3. Use more abstract or remembered objects or actions. Coming to school, the local shop.

4. Use pictures, children (*a*) describe (*b*) interpret actions, i.e. what people are doing or saying.

5. Children bring their own toys or pictures to describe.

6. Children tell a story about a picture.

7. Game 'O'Grady says' or 'Simple Simon says' (vocal encoding for the child leader).

8. Radio or T.V. commentator—describing scene from window.

F. *Motor Encoding*. To be able to express ideas in the form of gestures.

1. Using objects—demonstrate use in mime—spade, toy gun, decorator's paint brush. Guide child to increase range of actions, e.g. dip brush in tin, wipe off surplus paint, paint wall.

2. Mime actions—shopping, crossing the road—simple charades of domestic or personal actions. Encourage other children to develop and elaborate.

3. Use pictures to stimulate mime.

4. More complicated characters.

5. Game 'O'Grady says' or 'Simon says'. Teacher gives orders and children carry out actions.

6. Road plan (model or marked in playground), children make and obey signals, policeman, traffic lights, 'Halt' sign, etc.

7. Obey instructions, first involving one action then two or more.

G. *Auditory—vocal automatic*—Ability to use language which is common to the extent of being automatic—the grammatical use of plurals, change of tense, comparison of adjectives.

Actions, questions, and answers to establish facility in these areas, e.g. Here is one pen, here are two . . . ?

Describe boy walking—walked, sit, sitting, sat, jump, jumping, jumped, etc. This stick is long, this one is . . . , this one is . . .

As above, using pictures and objects.

Naming objects, giving plurals, comparing size. Find the biggest leaf, etc. Which is the biggest train? Which will carry the most people.?

H. *Auditory—vocal sequential*—The ability to reproduce a series of symbols produced auditorily.

1. Repetition of simple poems.

2. Repetition of numbers presented orally.

3. Repeating lists of items.

4. Naming four objects from left to right, repeating when hidden.

5. Completing a spoken sentence with an obvious ending. Tom dived into the . . . He swam to the . . .

6. Game 'I went to market'—'and I bought an orange', next child repeats, and adds another item.

I. *Visual —motor sequential*—The ability to reproduce a series of symbols presented visually.

1. Sequence of shapes presented for a few seconds are to be reproduced in the same order. Increase number of shapes gradually.

2. Similar procedure for colours, pictures, letters, words, or objects (e.g. traffic at lights—car, van, lorry, car, sequence).

3. Imitate a series of gestures or actions in the correct order, e.g. close the door, take a book, sit down at a desk.

4. Arrange a series of pictures in the correct order to portray a simple story.

5. Completing a visual pattern, e.g.

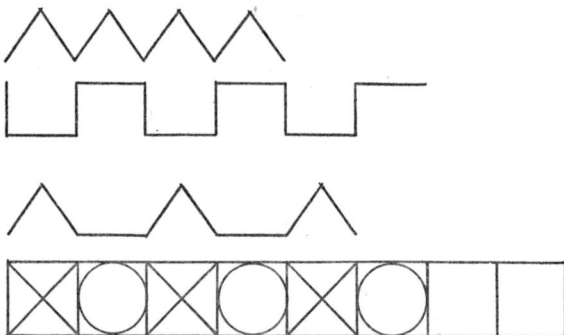

6. Teacher draws sequence on blackboard—shapes or pattern. Erases. Children reproduce sequence.

REFERENCES

1. Cashdan, A., 'Child Rearing Practices and the Development of the Handicapped Child', in *The Spastic School Child and the Outside World* (ed. Loring & Mason). Heinemann, 1966.
2. Sheridan, M. D., *The Child's Hearing for Speech*. Methuen, 1948.
3. Tansley, A. E., *The use of test data and case history information as indications for the educational treatment of E.S.N. children*. M.Ed. thesis. Univ. of Leeds, 1951.
4. Scriven, E., 'A Study of the Spoken Vocabulary of E.S.N. children', in *Special Education*, Vol. LI, No. 1, March 1962.
5. Chase, S., *The Tyranny of Words*. Methuen, 1950.
6. Watts, A. F., *Language and Mental Development of Children*. Harrap, 1944.
7. McCarthy, J. J. & Kirk, S. A., *Illinois Test of Psycholinguistic Abilities*. Experimental edition. Univ. of Illinois, 1961.
8. Stapleton, M., 'Experimenting with a Tape Recorder' in *Special Schools Journal No. 46*, 1957.
9. Percival, A. & Bryan, B., *Talking About*. Methuen. A series of books for class use and to provide ideas for the teacher.

FURTHER READING

Anderson, V. A., *Improving the Child's Speech*, O.U.P., New York, 1953.

Apelt, W., 'Language Development with Senior Children' in *Special Schools Bulletin* (Australia), Vol. VII, No. 1, 1965.

Atkinson, J. K., 'Reading Improvement through Psycholinguistic Remediation', in *Slow Learning Child*, Vol. 14, No. 2, Nov. 1967.

Beasley, J., *Slow to Talk*, Bureau of Publications, Teacher's College, Columbia Univ., New York, 1956.

Board of Educ. City of New York, *Speech for the Retarded Child*, Teacher's Handbook.

Bruford, R., *Speech and Drama*, Methuen 1948.

Dawe, H. C., 'A Study of the Effect of an Educational Program upon Language Development and Retarded Mental Functions in Young Children' in *Jo. Exp. Educ.*, 1942.

Gulliford, R., 'Teaching the Mother Tongue to Backward and Subnormal Children', *Educational Research*, Vol. II, No. 2, Feb. 1960.

Hart, N. W. M., 'Differential Diagnosis of Psycholinguistic Abilities' in *Special Schools Bulletin* Vol. V, No. 2, 1963.

Lewis, M. M., *Language in School*, U.L.P., 1942.

Lewis, M. M., *How Children Learn to Speak*, Harrap, 1957.

McDonald, J. L., 'The Teaching of Language to older E.S.N. Children', *Special Schools Journal* No. 47, 1958.

McKee, P., *Vocabulary Development*, 36th Yearbook, Nat. Soc. Study. Educ. Pub. Sch. Publishing Co., 1937.

O'Connor, N. & Hermelin, B., *Speech & Thought in Severe Subnormality*, Pergamon, 1963.

Reid, J. F., 'Talking, Thinking and Learning' in *Reading*, Vol. I, No. 1, March 1967.

Renfrew, C. E., 'Speech Problems of Backward Children', in *Speech Pathology & Therapy*, April 1959.

Sansom, C., *Speech in the Primary School*, A. & C. Black, 1965.

Tansley, A. E. & Gulliford, R., *The Education of Slow Learning Children*, Routledge & Kegan Paul, 1960.

Watts, A. F., *Language and Mental Development of Children*, Harrap, 1944.

CHAPTER 4

Failure in Reading

CONSIDERABLE effort has been expended over many years in searching for the best method of teaching reading. Yet irrespective of claims for particular methods or media it seems evident that no single method proves successful with all children. We may ask why this is so. It is due to deficiencies in the method, in the children or in the teacher? Clearly there are many methods which yield satisfactory results with large numbers of children. Many remedial teachers suggest there is nothing special about the methods they adopt and that they are merely following a systematic approach as opposed to earlier inefficient or even non-existent methods. Even so, remedial teachers have their failures, and apparent success with some children is often short-lived. Instead of looking for methods of teaching reading we should be examining methods of learning used by children. We might consider the possibility that although teachers may be using one method, some children may be learning by another.

If this is true we must take into account not only children's deficiencies but also their strengths. A main feature of a remedial programme must be to cater for individual differences. We should be asking 'Which is the best method for this particular child?' or 'How can I prepare this individual to learn this particular skill?'

Viewed in this way, reading is not solely a question of method but rather method related to individuals. Fortunately many children appear to learn with any method and this probably is a factor in the successful use of mixed methods. Many remedial teachers find that they have to use 'trial and error' in determining which method is best for a particular child. This is good sense but it must be tempered with caution for children who are exposed to a further period of failure may develop negative attitudes towards reading and a poor self-image of their own ability to master the skill. So, the period of 'trial' must be foreshortened and there may be a need for the temporary removal of the pressure to read books.

Some form of assessment and diagnosis is essential. Although standardised testing should play a part in this procedure, information from records and other sources will be required and teacher's observations and insights may be vital. If we accept that individual difficulties require individual treatment, teachers should be prepared to vary approaches. Some general points which are common to the needs of many backward readers should be borne in mind.

1. Begin at the child's present reading level or below.

2. Do not expect children to attempt tasks for which they are unprepared.

3. Build up a child's self-confidence. Praise and encouragement are necessary. Success is the antidote to failure and the child himself must see signs of progress.

4. Use children's special interests. Build an interest in reading; use a wide variety of books and supplementary materials, give children an element of choice.

There are four aspects to any good reading programme.

(a) Preparation for reading.

(b) The acquisition of a basic sight vocabulary.

(c) The development of word attack skills.

(d) Reading for meaning.

These are neither separate stages nor do individual children pass through them in a logical order. It is better to regard them as being overlapping and even running alongside each other. For example, reading for meaning cannot be tacked on at the end of a programme which teaches mechanical word recognition skills. Meaning must be emphasised from the beginning.

Clearly, too, this aspect may involve preparation and some children may need a programme of language development and a variety of experiences which will stimulate ideas and enrich their vocabulary.

Preparation for reading does not mean waiting, but should be an active period associated with reading skills at various levels. At many points in the development of reading a child will need preparation for the next step. This is one of the maxims of remedial reading, that no child should be expected to attempt a task for which he is unprepared.

Some pre-reading activities may well precede a formal introduction to books. Not all children will need these experiences but it should never be taken for granted that they have mastered all these fundamental skills.

1.   Reading stories to children is not just an activity to be undertaken with infants. It is appropriate at every age and stage. It would be naive to assume that every non-reader will be stimulated to want to read by hearing stories but there are essential links with reading in the exposure to spoken words, ideas and concepts. Habits of listening must be encouraged and the growth of a listening vocabulary is important. The enjoyment of stories may be enhanced by careful choice of material and dramatic presentation by the teacher. Children's reactions should guide a discerning teacher in the choice of stories, and dramatisation may test comprehension to enrich meanings and avoid undue emphasis on question and answer.

The television and the tape recorder may be powerful aids and children themselves should be given opportunities to tell simple stories or to recount experiences.

2.   Collect magazines, newspapers, pictures, advertisements. Use for discussion and spotting interests.

3.   Collect wrappings, labels, names of packets. Classify and label on wall charts or in large scrap books.

4.   Introduce interesting objects into the classroom for discussion.

5.   Label common objects. Vary with colours and materials,

e.g. door—wood—brown. Change frequently and let children apply them.

6. Command cards—'open the door'; introduce humorous activities.

7. Drawing and painting pictures—add captions.

8. Use classroom and environment for shape discrimination.

9. Opportunities for basic skills, using pencil (scribbling, shading, tracing); using scissors, glue, rule. Observe motor co-ordination. Encourage conversation, group projects.

10. Reading readiness work books.

11. Wall stories, with pictures of shared experiences, in sequence, with appropriate captions.

12. Special activities to develop left to right orientation, visual and auditory discrimination and memory.

Many classrooms are alive with stimulating material relating to these activities. The important factor is to make good use of this material. Use it, refer to it, give much practice in various ways. When interest flags, remove it.

ACTIVITIES TO DEVELOP LEFT–RIGHT DIRECTION

The left to right sequence in reading and writing is something a child must learn. Following this order is not a natural tendency, but because many children learn this order incidentally it is possible to overlook a minority of children who have not acquired this facility. There is, therefore, a need to check that slow readers do read across the page from left to right and that individual words are sounded out from left to right. Ask the children to point to a title, to find the first page in a book, to indicate where they should begin to read a line or start to 'sound out' a word. Other indications of this difficulty may be given by a tendency to make reversals or omissions, to lose their place, or to sound from cues in the middle or at the end of a word.

Explanation followed by training can be profitable. For some children 'overlearning' may be necessary to establish the habit.

1. *Tracing* in left to right direction; follow arrows.

2. *Joining dots*/numbers.

3. *Writing patterns* (e.g. Marion Richardson).

4. *Duplicated exercises*

(*a*)

Show how the mouse gets the cheese. Variations with dog chasing cat, boy kicking ball, car going into garage, etc.

(*b*)

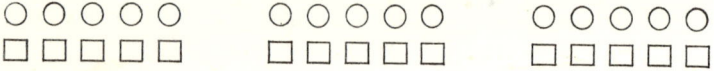

Starting at the left put a dot in each circle, and a cross in each square.

(*c*)

Join dots to make bridges, fences or railway lines.

5. Following words in passage read by teacher, follow individual letters in word (large print) as teacher sounds letters.

6. Following sequence of pictures in comics.

7. Re-arranging pictures to tell a story, e.g. child getting out of bed, washing, having breakfast, going to school. (This activity is also important for children who have sequencing difficulties.)

8. Similar activities in Reading Readiness Workbooks.

9. Activities to establish knowledge of left and right.

DEVELOPING VISUAL DISCRIMINATION

The ability to detect similarities and differences has an important part to play in word recognition. Confusion between letters and words is the most significant factor, and deficiencies may be revealed by careful observation of children reading, by examining the results of appropriate sub-tests from intelligence tests, tests of Visual perception (Frostig), diagnostic reading tests (Daniels and Diack), or reading readiness tests (Harrison-Stroud). Specific training can be given to encourage the development of visual discrimination.

1. Reading Readiness Workbooks.

2. Games which involve matching similar shapes, pictures, symbols, letters, words, e.g. Symbol snap—Cards with six sets of circles, squares, triangles, etc. Rules as for snap. Dominoes, using pictures, symbols or ordinary dominoes.

3. Simple jig-saw puzzles.

4. Duplicated sheets of exercises for identification of:

    (a) Similar geometric shapes—simple and more complex.

    (b) Common objects with slight differences. e.g. Clock faces with different times shown, missing figures, digits. Use similar ideas from non-verbal intelligence test items.

    (c) Letters and small words.

        e.g. Put a ring round the letter or word that is exactly like the one on the left.

b	p	b	d	q
N	W	M	N	Z
has	hat	his	here	has

    (d) Finding a given letter in a sentence.

e	see the little red hen

    (e) Finding a given word in a sentence. (Newspaper cuttings are useful.)

    (f) Pairs of words listed in different orders. Draw lines to connect the pairs.

DEVELOPING VISUAL MEMORY

Some form of memorisation of words and letters is required in word recognition. It is commonplace to meet backward readers who quickly forget words.

Some memory training activities are described below but teachers must watch for evidence that the effects transfer to reading skill. It is as well to remember that there may be other causes and remedies for this difficulty. Visual discrimination activities may help some children. Many may require additional help through other sensory channels. In some cases it is helpful to try a kinaesthetic approach (Fernald)—tracing a word or letter and sounding it until it can be reproduced from memory. Writing is clearly an aid and following the shape of sandpaper letters (Montessori) may be necessary for some children at certain stages.

Another important factor is to ensure that children see a word repeated many times. Although this is normally taken into account by authors of reading schemes, new words being introduced gradually and then repeated many times, repetitions are frequently inadequate for many slow learners. Supplementary readers, apparatus and workbooks may be necessary. Jogging a child's memory and ensuring that he understands the nature of the task may be helpful. Thus before reading a new page, ask him to recall new words seen last time, or to look back at the last page to spot new words or difficult words. If a child fails to remember a word, the teacher may ask 'Have you seen this before? Can you find it?' Teaching techniques may be faulty. A well-known failing of 'look and say' methods is that children do not 'look'.

ACTIVITIES

1. *Kim's Game.* A number of objects, exposed for thirty seconds, are covered and one is removed. Children guess which is missing.

2. *Memory Flash Cards.* Teacher displays large card with symbol, letter or word for ten seconds. Children either find a similar card from their own individual set, or reproduce by drawing or writing. In cases of special difficulty resort to tracing with a finger in the air or on the desk.

3. *Finding Missing Parts.* Drawings and pictures with

missing items, e.g. chair with three legs, dog with one ear. Collect puzzles of this type from children's comics or items from non-verbal intelligence tests.

4. *Observation and Memory Games.* Child leaves room; remove prominent item, re-arrange furniture, or children change positions. Child returns to note change.

5. *Pairs.* Pack of cards with sets of two or four like pictures or shapes. Place face down, spread out at random. Children follow each other, to turn up two at a time. Like pairs are collected.

ACTIVITIES TO DEVELOP AUDITORY MEMORY AND DISCRIMINATION

Teachers of backward children appreciate the difficulties that many children have in detecting similarities and differences in sounds and in being able to recall sounds. Special difficulties are highlighted in phonic work by inability to blend sounds. Tests which pinpoint these problems may be found in Daniels and Diack's *Standard Reading Tests* and Bragg's *Test of Phonic Readiness*. (See Chapter 2).

ACTIVITIES

1. Games like 'What can you hear?' Children sit still with eyes closed and listen to the sounds around them. Say what they heard. Indentify common sounds—running water, tapping, bell, whistle, etc. Lead up to sounds requiring finer discrimination. Use tape recorder.

2. Rhythmic activities. Children listen with eyes closed whilst teacher taps on desk. Children count taps or repeat pattern of sound.

3. Telling which words begin with the same sound, e.g. Mother, milk, ball, moon, man.

4. 'Odd man out.' Naming word that does not begin with the same sound as the others.

5. Similar activities as 3. and 4., listening for endings which do or do not sound alike.

6. Rhyming activities. Recognising rhymes from teacher's

list of words; supplying words to rhyme with given word; completing orally very short rhymes begun by the teacher.

> Jack and Jill
> Went up the . . .

7. Telling which pair of sounds are alike. Increase in difficulty to similar sounds, e.g. m, n, m.

8. Games like 'I Spy'. It may be necessary to begin by restricting choice to five or six objects which are clearly visible (on a table) and which have been identified by name beforehand. Variations—'I Spy something that beings with the same sound as *d*esk' or 'I Spy something that ends with the same sound as boo*k*'. Link with usual symbol—initial consonant on card.

A detailed account of training perceptual abilities is given in *Reading and Remedial Reading* (Tansley 1967) and teachers who have to deal with cases of severe reading disability should read this book. In the visual field Tansley stressed the value of training in form perception, eye–hand–eye motor co-ordination, visual copying, completion and closure, visual rhythm, visual sequencing in addition to visual memory and discrimination.

BUILDING UP A SIGHT VOCABULARY

'Sight words' are those which can be recognised instantly without contextual clues or the need for analysing words phonetically. A basic sight vocabulary is a limited number of words which seem to be of special help to the beginner in reading because of their frequency in the reading, spoken, or written vocabularies of children. Many years ago Dolch produced a list of 220 words which were said to form over 50% of the running vocabulary of children's primer reading books in America.[1] Lists of this type have proved very useful to authors who were seeking to control and grade the vocabulary of children's books. Equally they are of importance to teachers who wish to know where to concentrate children's efforts most effectively.

A more recent, British list contains 300 'Key Words'[2] and

these are said to form three-quarters of all the vocabulary in children's books. Many of the words which occur most frequently are short, common words like A, AS, AND, AT, ARE, HAD, HAVE, HIM, HIS, IN, IS, IT, OF, ON, ONE, THE, THAT, THEY, etc. Clearly, instant recognition of these words will greatly aid a child's reading progress. Unfortunately the words are not nouns and therefore difficult to explain and illustrate, and because they are short, often similar in appearance and without clear meaning, children find them hard to learn. As they are such important helper words children should memorise them at an early stage. Various games and activities should be devised to provide plenty of practice. It is important to remember that many dull children may need as many as 100 repetitions of a word before it is remembered.

ACTIVITIES

1. *Graded Lotto.* Divide 'key words' into fifteen groups in order of frequency. Use one group of words to make up a set of six cards. Each card may contain nine words but no two cards will be alike. Groups of up to six children can play 'Lotto'.

2. *Collector's Progress.* A variety of games may be devised where children 'win' the words they can read. They may retain cards in a matchbox marked 'words I know' or on a key-ring which takes punched cards. Individual word ladders, may be kept to 'climb'. A simple 'word album' is another novel device.

3. *Flash cards.* This is an aid which many teachers use. Unfortunately it is an activity which is not always used effectively. It is not enough to provide words in large letters on cards and ask individuals in a group to read them. More active responses are required from each individual. An investigation by Roberts[3] suggests that the use of flash cards is justified. It seems clear that her teaching method was important. The teacher had one set of words and the children another. They were required to find a card like one displayed by the teacher, listen to her pronounce the word and say the matching word themselves. Thus children were looking, listening and saying

with a degree of individual involvement. Clearly this method can be extended and it would seem reasonable to give children practice in using the same words in sentences.

4. *Card and Dice Games.* Simple games may be devised by the teacher, e.g. two dice, one with words, one with numbers. Throw dice; move marker along track only when the word can be read.

5. *Use of film strips or slides.* Words which are projected on to a screen, in semi-darkness, may well help some children to focus their attention on a word with an increased attention span. Responses may well be required using other practice material.

WORD ATTACK SKILLS

To become an independent reader a child needs techniques for working out the meaning and pronunciation of words for himself. Much discussion, argument and research has been centred on the problems of when, and how, to develop competence in word study skills. Phonics are only one aspect of word recognition and children may need help in using structural and context clues. General agreement about the benefits of direct phonic instruction should not obscure the fact that some children are not ready for phonics until considerable experience has been gained in the use of whole words. Many children can make progress using look and say, sentence or story methods, whilst they are still developing auditory skills. It is essential, therefore, to make sure that each child is ready for phonic instruction. Observation of a child's reactions to a 'trial' teaching situation may supplement the use of tests of auditory discrimination (mentioned earlier), and both Bragg's *Test of Phonic Readiness* and the *Learning Methods Test* devised by R. Mills[4] are useful predictors.

Phonic work should not be an isolated activity. Many matching word and picture games may merely occupy children if they do not relate the activity to reading. Some children need to be told that letters stand for sounds, that combinations of letters can make words which have meaning. Children must

hear sounds and words, they must say them, they must associate
the spoken sound with the visual symbol.

The 'penny will drop' for many children following explanation and some practice. Few need to follow a phonic scheme
to the bitter end, until every rule has been taught and every
double consonant or digraph has been learned. A careful step-
by-step approach in the early stages is perhaps the most
important means of enabling most children to deduce other
rules as their reading progresses. Above all one must avoid
dangers of children developing the habit of 'sounding out'
words past the time when they should have been committed to
memory.

The teaching of phonics is complicated by irregularities and
inconsistencies in the English language and by variations in
children's experiences and abilities which affect their own
individual methods of word attack. The multiplicity of rules
creates problems in teaching, for children need to learn all the
principles at once yet can only learn one at a time. For example,
when we teach the short vowel 'a' they inevitably seem to read,
on the next page, words like; ALL, EAT, CAR, TAKE, AGAIN, SAID,
PLAY, ARE, HAVE, WAS, SAW.

Thus, the following steps in phonic instruction, though they
may appear to have a logical order, must be modified in practice.
Teachers may devise exercises, use books and published
apparatus for all steps, but the guiding principle should be to
give practice where and when it is needed.

1. *Single consonant sounds.* These consonants which normally have only one sound (b,h,j,l,m,p,t,v) should be learned
first, (*a*) as initial consonants (*b*) at the end of words (*c*) in the
medial position. e.g. *b*at   so*b*   a*b*out
                        *b*all   tu*b*   ba*b*y

Follow up with other consonants.

2. *Substitution of initial consonants.* Teaching 'word families'
is a useful practice. Moving from the identification of the
common element in 'man' and 'ran' children make words like
'can', 'ban', 'pan', 'span', 'plan'. There are a number of 'word

families' which will bring in many words which occur frequently in early reading material.

e.g. words ending in:

-ake, -all, -am, -ame, -an, -and, -arm, -as, -at, -ate, -eat, -ell, -en, -est, -et, -ick, -in, -ing, -it, -ot, -un.

3. *Substitution of final consonants.* Exercises may be given as:

*ca*t	*ru*n
*ca*p	*ru*g
*ca*n	*ru*b

Some children find it easier to add final consonants when saying *ca*—t but find c—a—t more difficult to blend.

There are many exercises of types 2 and 3 in basic reading schemes and in a number of phonic work books (e.g. *Sounding and Blending* (Gibson)).

4. *Initial Consonant Blends* frequently cause difficulty. There are two types—consonant digraphs which have special sounds—th, sh, ch, wh. These are often met at an early stage in reading in a number of key words like: this, that, which, when, she, children, etc. There are many other consonant blends which are more readily formed by fusing the two sounds.

bl, br, cl, cr, dr, fl, fr, gl, pl, pr, sc, sk, sl, sm, sn, sp, st, sw, scr, spl, spr, str, tr, tw.

Some of these sounds may be studied as they occur at the ends of words e.g. fi*sh*, chur*ch*, fro*st*, '*ck*' may be included, e.g. sa*ck*, ro*ck*, etc.

5. *Vowel Sounds.*
   (*a*) Short vowel sounds—tap, top, tip, etc.
   (*b*) Long vowel sounds—make, may.
   (*c*) Double vowels—digraphs, e.g. ee, oo, ea, ou, ow, ai, oa, au, aw, ew, ie, ei, and dipthongs oi, oy.

6. The final 'e' rule—mak*e* hop*e* tub*e* etc.
7. The effect of 'r' and 'l' on vowels, e.g. ar or ur ir er all.
8. Soft 'c' and 'g'—usually before e, i, or y, e.g. city, germ.

9. Silent letters. *K*nife, *w*rite.

    w —*w*rite, s*w*ord, ans*w*er.

    k —*k*nife, *k*now, *k*nee.

    b —com*b*, bom*b*, lam*b*, clim*b*.

    h —sc*h*ool, g*h*ost, Jo*h*n.

    u —g*u*ess, b*u*ild, bisc*u*it.

    c —s*c*ent, s*c*issors, s*c*ene.

    g —*g*naw, *g*nome, si*g*n.

    n —hym*n*, Autum*n*.

    o —c*o*untry, c*o*usin, y*o*ung.

    gh—sli*gh*t, si*gh*t, li*gh*t.

    s —i*s*land.

10. *Double consonants.*

    ll, ff, bb, ss, pp, dd, nn, tt, rr, gg, zz.

11. Long vowel sounds at the end of words, e.g. my, try, fly, go, so, no, me, he, she.

AIDS TO PHONICS

There are many published aids which teachers may profitably use. A wide variety of books are listed in the next chapter and these include reading schemes which adopt a phonic approach, e.g. *Royal Road Readers*, and phonic series which may be used in conjunction with other readers, e.g. *Sound Sense* (Arnold); *Step Up and Read* (U.L.P.); *Sounding and Blending* (Gibson) and *Sounds and Words* (U.L.P.).

Apparatus which can be linked to various stages is obtainable from the major educational suppliers, Philip and Tacey, E. J. Arnold, Galt, E.S.A. A relatively new source of reading materials is the Remedial Supply Company[5] who produce a phonic scheme using tape recordings and workbooks.

Classroom organisation is of paramount importance if teachers are to cater for individual differences and apparatus which children can learn to use and then operate on a 'self-help' basis is particularly valuable. Two items are notable in this way, one is Stott's *Programmed Reading Kit*[6] (W. & R. Holmes) and, for teachers with limited funds at their disposal, the construction and use of easily-made apparatus is described in Moxon's book *A Remedial Reading Method.*[7]

Structural analysis.

Teachers should be alert to the possibilities of helping children who are failing to recognise familiar units or parts of words, i.e. prefixes, suffixes, endings, or compound words.

Endings—Look for children who do not see car in cars, or knowing walk cannot read walks, walked, walking.

Common Suffixes— -able, -ande, -ant, -en, -er, -ful, -hood, -ible, -ion, -ish, -ism, -less, -ly, -ment, -ness, -ory, -ous, -tion, -ty, -y.

Common Prefixes— a-, ab-, ad-, be-, com-, de-, dis-, en-, ex-, in-, pre-, pro-, re-, sub-, un-.

Compound Words— After—noon, foot—ball, some—thing.

CONTEXTUAL CLUES

At every reading level the ability to use contextual clues often marks out a good reader from a poor one. Children who will not 'guess' at a word or who insert words which could not possibly belong may be suspected of a weakness in this direction. There are several kinds of context clues which call for experience, the understanding of moods, definitions and familiarity with synonyms, comparisons, opposites and common expressions. It may happen that inability to deal with opposites for example, may be the exercise needed rather than training in the use of context. Words at the beginning of sentences or stories cause particular difficulty. Even if little training can be given, teachers who are aware of the problem, may give help to children during the course of oral reading practice. Explain to the child that he can guess the word by thinking about the rest of the sentence. The child may re-read the sentence or look at the words which follow. The teacher may read the sentence for the child. Other aids to identification should be stressed, i.e. use of pictures, or initial letter of the word. This difficulty again draws attention (*a*) to the need for care in the selection of reading material which introduces new words gradually and (*b*) to the importance of encouraging children to search for meaning in reading material.

READING FOR MEANING

We may not always achieve our highest aims in teaching reading for comprehension and enjoyment. Although, in Britain, we learn that average standards in reading have risen significantly since 1959[8] the criteria of progress were limited to simple tests of reading. It would appear from other evidence that only a small percentage of the population could be considered as avid readers. An examination of the reading habits of adults suggests that few buy books and that the increase in the use of public libraries is due to the enthusiasm of less than 50% of the population.

It would perhaps be more appropriate to consider our aims and to review our methods in the light of what use children make of their reading in later life.

LEVELS OF READING FOR SLOW LEARNERS

Three levels of attainment in reading have been identified as worthy goals for children of limited ability.

1. Reading for Protection.
2. Reading for Information or Instruction.
3. Reading for Pleasure.

1. *Reading for protection* has often been associated with the needs of children of low intelligence (approx. I.Q. 50 or below) or those children who, late in their school life, have made very little progress in reading. The words which are taught to these children comprise the simplest sentences and notices which they are likely to meet at work or in the street. Such words as DANGER, BUS STOP, LADIES, GENTLEMEN and CAFE are obviously useful and important for them to know.

Teachers can easily make up their own lists to include local examples. It would be wrong to assume that only a few words are necessary or that teaching them will be easy or entirely mechanical. The following list is by no means comprehensive and is included merely to indicate the scope of the project and to encourage further thought.

List of Socially Useful Words

ADDRESS	EXIT	NO ENTRY	RING
AGE	FIRE ALARM	NO SMOKING	ROAD (Rd.)
AVENUE (Av.)	FIRE ESCAPE	NOTICE	SHUT
BANK	FISH & CHIPS	ON	SIGNATURE
BUS STOP	GENTLEMEN	OFFICE	SILENCE
BY REQUEST	GENTS.	OFF	STAMP
CAFE	HALT	OPEN	STOP
CHOCOLATE	HOSPITAL	PAY HERE	STREET (St.)
CLOSED	HOT	PLEASE	SURNAME
COLD	ICE CREAM	POISON	TEA
CROSS NOW	KEEP LEFT	POLICE	THANK YOU
CROSS HERE	KEEP OUT	POST OFFICE	TOILET
DANGER	KEEP OFF	PRESS	UP
DATE	LADIES	PRIVATE	VACANT
DOCTOR (Dr.)	LAVATORY	PROHIBITED	WAIT
DOWN	MEN	PULL	WAY IN/OUT
ENGAGED	MILK	PUSH	WET PAINT
ENQUIRIES	Mr./Mrs.	PUBLIC	WOMEN
ENTRANCE	NO	CONVENIENCE	YES

From this short list it can already be seen that many words can be grouped together around certain topics and this should suggest appropriate teaching techniques. A fundamental requirement is that the words should be presented many times in different situations. It is essential that meanings are grasped and that words are not associated with any one setting or one printed form. Work can begin in school with a liberal use of labels and notices. Opportunities must be taken to move out of school to observe and respond to signs. Practice in the classroom may follow the pattern of word recognition activities using flash cards and games like Lotto. Mime and dramatic play can be used to aid memory and fix meanings. A stock of wall charts may be built up using large pictures which call for the insertion of signs at suitable points.

2. *Reading for Information and Instruction.* Whereas there is no compulsion in adult life to read books for pleasure there will be many occasions when there is a need to obtain information or to follow written instructions. For this reason classrooms should contain items like telephone directories, railway and bus timetables, newspapers and television programmes. Children should be encouraged to study these and some assignment cards will both give them practice in seeking information and opportunities to follow instructions. Any attempt to link reading with real life situations brings into play the Utility Motive, for children are more likely to see the purpose and relevance of the activity. Opportunities for this type of activity often arise naturally in other subjects of the curriculum.

There are many occasions when adults read for specific information. The following list gives a number of suggestions where children may practice their skills. The list can be extended and the items themselves suggest appropriate apparatus and materials.

Recipes, directions on tinned foods.
Instructions for making or assembling objects.
Newspaper reports, weather, T.V. programmes, advertisements, shopping bargains, gardening hints.
Telephone directory, timetable, dictionary.
Notices, indexes.
Holiday guides, maps, routes.

3. *Reading for Pleasure.* Ultimately we must hope to introduce children to the pleasure and enjoyment which can be gained from reading books. This may be difficult to achieve with some slow learners whose early experiences of failure may still cloud later achievements.

To encourage the desire to read, points should be borne in mind throughout the reading programme.

(a) Fluency is important. Children who read easily are likely to read often.

(b) Develop a meaningful vocabulary.

(c) Arouse and sustain an interest in books and reading.

The following activities are related to these points:

1. Provide plenty of easy books, which use simple words, sentences and ideas. Supplement with special interest books (e.g. Junior True Books—Muller).

2. Use pictures to teach words, meanings and concepts. Use at different levels: e.g. Street scene—young children—bus, car, etc.; older children—vehicles, pedestrians. Expand meanings of words—give daily practice.

3. Use salesmanship. Read interesting items from news-papers, magazines every week. Recommend books in library, read extracts from books—leave at interesting point for child to finish. Announce and display new books.

4. Introduce to library books, do not restrict choice, but be prepared to give guidance. Allow quiet times for browsing and reading from library shelves.

5. Allow time for children to discuss, to raise questions about books they read.

6. Initiate questions and discussion, not to test memory but to encourage imagination, to try to picture situations, and interpret authors meaning, e.g. Which part of the story did you like best? find exciting, humorous, etc? Do you know anyone like the people in the story? What would you feel like if . . . ?

7. Draw pictures to illustrate stories.

8. Visit libraries, bookshops.

THE TOTAL TEACHING SITUATION

Teachers who have responsibility for several classes of slow learners or a special school may have to develop a reading scheme which takes into account factors other than individual differences in children. The teacher is an equally important variable in reading instruction. There are other factors which affect progress and indeed it seems reasonable to assume that unless the total teaching situation is taken into account optimum progress is unlikely to be achieved.

Narrow concentration on the teaching of reading as an isolated skill is unlikely to produce startling results. Considerable emphasis has been laid in this book on the need for planning a full and varied curriculum for slow learners. Other chapters show the importance of language development, units of experience, practical and leisure training and the contribution of parents. A reading scheme which ignores the contribution of other educational activities is a restricted one.

Ultimately this is why it is impossible to supply a neat and perfect reading scheme for others. Every teaching situation is different. The children are individuals and teachers have varying skills, and personalities. The material resources for learning also differ greatly. One must, therefore, consider books, apparatus, technical aids, building, neighbourhood and the availability or lack of specialist advice and services.

It is impossible, briefly, to supply examples which will illustrate how different factors influence reading progress but the interested reader may like to examine an article by Vera Southgate[9] in which she draws attention to the phenomenon 'Reading Drive'. She extends inferences which research workers have already observed in experimental situations (the Hawthorne effect) whereby experimental groups will always show a measure of improvement over a control group due to the psychological effects of receiving extra attention. Mrs. Southgate suggests that in some experiments such factors as the supply of new books, training of teachers, and parental involvement all combine to form a 'reading drive' which is bound to effect improvement.

We may well feel that this has lessons for teachers using other methods and that improvements in reading attainments may be secured if teachers discuss methods and adopt common procedures. Supplies of new books or apparatus may also foster enthusiasm.

A popular cliché states that many children learn in spite of the teacher. Equally it might well be said that many succeed because of the teacher. Certainly the teacher is the vital factor in ensuring progress for slow learners. Far too little is known about the subtleties of interaction between teacher and pupils. Is it personality or a special blend of teaching skills that enable one to teach a child where another has failed? One encouraging feature of special education is to see so many teachers who are sufficiently mature to recognise that they may not be the best teacher for a particular child.

A reading scheme for a school may have to be devised to take into account the strengths and weaknesses of the teaching staff. Inexperienced teachers find some schemes more difficult to operate than others. They may be much more secure and effective working with a system which relies largely on a published reading scheme. Individualised reading whereby a wide variety of books are used and children have some responsibility for their own progress requires much more skilful handling. The implications for a headteacher are far-reaching. Teachers must be trained within their own schools in order to make the most of the reading scheme and to ensure co-operation and continuity. The school approach to reading then becomes a dynamic one, for as the staff progress and learn together the reading scheme may change and become much more geared to the needs of individual children through increased ability to carry out a diagnostic approach.

REFERENCES

1. Dolch, E. W., *Problems in Reading*. Garrard Press, 1948.
*2. McNally, J. & Murray, W., *Key Words to Literacy*. Schoolmaster Publishing Co., 1962.
3. Roberts, U., 'Word Recognition with six-year old children', in *Reading*, Vol. 2, No. 3, December, 1968.
4. Mills, Robt. E., *Learning Methods Test*. Mills Centre, 1514 E. Broward Blvd., Fort Lauderdale, Florida, U.S.A.
5. Remedial Supply Company, Dixon Street, Wolverhampton.
6. Stott, D. H., *Programmed Reading Kit*. W. & R. Holmes.
*7. Moxon, C. A. V., *A Remedial Reading Method*. Methuen, 1962.
8. Department of Education & Science, *Progress in Reading*. H.M.S.O., 1966.

9. Southgate, V., 'Approaching i.t.a. results with caution', in *Educational Research*, Vol. VII, No. 2, Feb. 1965.

FURTHER READING

Books marked * above, also the following:

Ablewhite, R. C., *The Slow Reader*, Heinemann, 1967.

Chall, J. S., *Learning to Read, the Great Debate*, McGraw Hill, New York, 1967.

Daniels, J. C. & Diack, H., *Royal Road Readers, Teacher's Book*, Chatto & Windus, 1954.

Diack, H., *In Spite of the Alphabet*, Chatto & Windus, 1965.

Diack, H., *Reading & the Psychology of Perception*, Skinner, 1960.

Dolch, E., *Psychology & the Teaching of Reading*, Garrard Press, 1951.

Fernald, G. M., *Remedial Techniques in the Basic Subjects*, McGraw Hill, New York, 1943.

Gattegno, C., *Words in Colour, Teacher's Guide*, Educ. Explorers Ltd., 1962.

Keir, G., *Adventures in Reading, Teacher's Companion*, O.U.P., 1951.

Morris, R., *Success & Failure in Learning to Read*, Oldbourne Press, 1963.

Moyle, D., *The Teaching of Reading*, Ward Lock Educ., 1968.

Ravenette, A. T., *Dimensions of Reading Difficulties*, Pergamon, 1968.

Roswell, F. G. & Natchez, *Reading Disability*, Basic Books, 1964.

Stott, D. H., *Roads to Literacy*, Holmes McDougall, 1964.

Tansley, A. E., *Reading & Remedial Reading*, Routledge & Kegan Paul, 1967.

CHAPTER 5

Choosing Suitable Reading Material for Backward Readers

MOST requests for advice about the teaching of backward readers begin with an enquiry regarding suitable reading books for a particular age group. An honest answer will almost certainly point to the fact that books are not always the best material to give to a reluctant reader. Yet to some extent this sort of reply is hair-splitting and is unlikely to be helpful to the enquirer. Accordingly, the writer intends to give a comprehensive list of current books, apparatus and other reading material which has been graded by reading age. These charts are printed at the end of this chapter. In addition some guidance is given about making the best use of a graded list and practical suggestions are made on how to assess new books.

Two important factors which ought to be taken into account when making an appropriate choice of books are the level of difficulty of a particular book and the interest age of the topic presented. Most teachers nowadays are well aware that one cannot encourage older children, who are just making a start in reading, to display much interest in an infant reader which may have a suitably simple vocabulary but in content and illustrations is obviously childish. This is easily recognised with older children but until recently little attention was paid to the fact that for those younger, backward children, who live on council estates or in rows of terrace houses, the upper middle class families depicted in many of our popular readers represent an alien world. Can they identify themselves with the professional home with its family of two adults and two children in their detached house, with garden, car and the inevitable ball and dog? Can Tom, Dick and Mary compete with popular television characters? Yet, though one may be critical about children's books, it is also necessary to appreciate that writing books on interesting topics, using a restricted vocabulary, is difficult. It is an exercise which might be recommended to any teacher of backward children.

Likewise, talking glibly about children's interests is one thing but identifying interests with any certainty is another. One is left with the feeling that their interests are sometimes as ephemeral as the heroes of television programmes appear to be. It is important to keep a constant enquiry afoot in an attempt to pin-point pupils' interests. Awareness of a child's particular interest however fleeting, may influence choice of books from time to time. It should also suggest topics for writing and other activities.

READING MATERIAL

A distinction ought first to be made between published material and the variety of 'Do-It-Yourself' apparatus which is the result of teachers' and children's efforts. Less attention will be given to the latter 'school-produce' as much of it is devised to suit individual children and situations and does not always have a universal application.

Published materials comprise books and apparatus. *Apparatus* is mainly confined to cards and games and is the concern of a small number of well-known educational suppliers. Names like Brown of Hull, Philip and Tacey, E.S.A., Galt and Arnolds are well known to teachers and most primary and special schools have elegant catalogues supplied by these firms. Copies are obtainable free of charge on request to bona fide enquirers from schools (addresses given at the end of this chapter) and the catalogues are well worth perusing to see if any reading apparatus is made to suit a particular need. The range of materials supplied has increased enormously in recent years and products are both durable, colourful and attractive to children. They offer an alternative to a teacher's material and may reinforce learning by presenting a child with a slightly different, more polished production. Apart from the intrinsic value of this type of apparatus, of course, teachers can be saved a deal of work by using this material. Some see disadvantages in commercially produced apparatus: and indeed it may not be as apposite as material the teacher prepares on the spot. It is liable to fall into disuse quicker than apparatus a teacher has made herself. Some is of doubtful value and difficult to relate to work in classroom, sometimes the vocabulary and pictures used are out of step with modern ideas. Care must be taken in selection.

BOOKS FOR BACKWARD READERS

Published reading books fall into several categories—Reading Schemes, Graded Series, Supplementary Readers and a miscellany of library books, workbooks, comprehension exercises and interest books.

BASIC READING SCHEMES

A basic reading scheme is usually planned to provide enough suitable reading material to lead a child with very little reading ability through the basic steps until he has sufficient skill to be able to read a wide variety of simple reading matter. In other words, such a scheme should start at a level where a child with a reading age of only five years can tackle the preliminary or introductory book. It should provide carefully graded books of increasing difficulty, often with parallel books and small supplementary readers to give plenty of practice and consolidate progress. A scheme may well continue until the child has reached a reading age of eight or nine years and is able to read a much wider range of books. A well formulated scheme may also include exercises to encourage comprehension, some vocabulary work and progressive phonic training (if the scheme is not basically phonic in its initial plan).

GRADED SERIES OF READERS

Graded series are seldom self-sufficient in the manner of a full reading scheme. They usually comprise several books which are linked together by a common theme or format and they are arranged in order of difficulty such that a child will have a higher reading attainment on completing the series. For example, in a series of ten graded books, Book One may be intended for a child with a Reading Age of seven years and Book Ten for someone with a Reading Age of nine years. One distinction that might be made between a series and a scheme is that few graded series start with a reading age low enough for absolute beginners to tackle.

SUPPLEMENTARY READERS

This type of book, as the title suggests, is mainly for use as an adjunct to other schemes. They provide further reading material at various stages and are intended to widen a child's reading experience, to consolidate learning at a particular reading level and to add variety and interest to the reading process. This function is paralleled at a later stage in reading by the use of library books. Supplementaries are occasionally isolated copies, sometimes a set of books, produced on one topic, all at approximately the same level of reading difficulty.

MISCELLANEOUS BOOKS

The categories outlined above may become less clearly defined in the future. Ideas about the teaching of reading are changing and many schools are placing less emphasis on the use of reading schemes.

Germs of new ideas may be seen in some of the miscellaneous books produced. There is an increase in the demand for simple reference or information books which include many topics and interests to appeal to much younger children, who are being encouraged to find things out for themselves. The need for backing up this type of approach with more mechanical exercises in spelling, grammar, vocabulary and comprehension exercises has long been recognised. The use of consumable workbooks in this field has been notable and this seems likely to expand to include more reading workbooks devoted to pre-reading activities, phonic activities of many kinds and the type of comprehension exercises which can be tied in with any basic reading series.

MAKING GOOD USE OF READING SCHEMES

Many schools use Reading Schemes very successfully. They have the merit of recognisable continuity and are usually numbered. Teachers can see children progressing logically through Books 1a, 1b, 1c and on to Books 2a, 2b and so on. Children have little difficulty in following a sequence like this, can gain the essential feeling of making progress and will usually know which book to move on to next.

Accordingly, many inexperienced teachers may find that a reading scheme can offer them much support. Most schemes include a teachers' manual which will give considerable help and may even present detailed lesson plans and suggestions for supplementary work. Regrettably not enough teachers buy the manuals which go with reading schemes and few read them to advantage. As a result schemes may not be put to their best use. Sometimes they are not used in the way the authors intended and this soon leads to dissatisfaction in the classroom. Most schemes will benefit from imaginative use but it is wiser first to absorb the author's ideas and then make adaptations to suit the particular needs of the children and any unusual school conditions. It seems reasonable to expect that improvements to the original model may best be achieved by the imaginative use of supplementary material and teacher-made-apparatus rather than by tampering with the main design.

There are still few suitable schemes for backward readers. Many of the well-known reading schemes in use in Britain were designed for infants. Their content is likely to be thought childish by older children, who may be sensitive to their reading failure and in need of something intrinsically more interesting to them. The fact that a child has already failed on one particular scheme and may need to be encouraged to make a fresh start with something new also limits the available choice.

Because of this limitation of choice, the need to find alternatives for some pupils, and the lack of sufficient material at certain levels in most schemes, many teachers of slow learners have taken to using a wide variety of reading books. Thus they may use books with a strong phonic element for one child who appears to need this approach. Another child may be attracted by some series which catches his interest. Others, who are plodding along making imperceptible progress, will need to read many books at the level of 'Book One' before they can move safely and without setback to the 'Book Two' stage.

In using a wide variety of reading books, teachers encounter a number of pitfalls. By abandoning the security of an established reading scheme where stages are clearly indicated the need to chart a passage through shoals of different books becomes paramount.

USING A GRADED BOOK LIST

The following charts have been devised to help teachers find appropriate reading material for children who are at different stages in learning to read. It is a useful guide for situations, described above, where a teacher feels that a child needs to read more books at the same level of difficulty before he is ready to move on to the next step. There are occasions like this for many children when they may need a period of consolidation or an opportunity to read books without constantly straining to 'decipher' new words. Often a backward reader may have completed a book to his own satisfaction but still has an imperfect grasp of a basic sight vocabulary or other skills which he should have learned at a particular stage. To keep him overlong on one particular book may well arouse undesirable attitudes to reading. It is sometimes wise to offer another book which may repeat the required experiences in another way. In addition some guidance is offered as to useful workbooks, exercises and phonic activities which can be used at different stages.

Regardless of the system adopted in any class the list also can help in remedial reading. One of the guiding principles in remedial work is to determine the child's reading age and then to provide material of commensurate difficulty or even slightly easier. For example, if on test, a child scores a Reading Age of six years and three months a glance at the section for R.A. six years to six years and six months will show a range of books from which to make a selection. Some of these may only appeal to young children. Others have a more obvious appeal to older children.

APPROPRIATE READING MATERIAL

Any frequent visitor to schools who pays some interest to the actual work children are doing and has an opportunity to hear children read will often find some child with a reading book which is too difficult for him. What is worse is that it is often easy to spot a child who has a reading book in front of him which he has been 'reading' for a long time without either pleasure or profit. Of course, teachers are busy, classes are large and individual attention is at a premium. Consequently it is much easier for a child to exchange a book, while teacher is occupied, and then to be 'working' at the wrong grade. This is more likely to happen in an informal setting where much more freedom of movement is permitted. Where children are given responsibility for selecting their own books in this way allowances must be made for mistakes.

Unfortunately this sort of thing seems to happen so frequently that it is important to draw the attention of teachers to this failing. It is essential for a child to be working with books which are not too difficult for him otherwise he may easily become discouraged. Attention to this one point would minimise many reading problems.

ORGANISING BOOKS AND APPARATUS

For effective individual progress in reading teachers must have some system which children can understand and operate with the minimum of aid. With numerous children ready and willing to act as 'teacher aides' it is obviously sensible both to make use of their talents and to recognise that there is some educational value in allowing children some responsibility for their own learning. To see the whole scheme which the teacher has devised may be a strong motivating force rather than just to have one small piece handed to him with little comment. In any discussion which follows it is implicit that children should be taken into the teacher's confidence. The system should be fully described to them and they should be trained to use it.

In the arrangement of books the Graded Book List can be useful. A common practice which has proved successful in many classrooms is to arrange the books on different shelves in the bookcase according to reading difficulty. Books are often given a colour coding or some other symbol whereby all can be easily guided to select reading matter at the appropriate level. Some of the coloured stars or spots, often used by teachers as merit awards, are very useful for marking books without defacing them. This system can well be carried over into the school or class library to help all children make sensible selections in library lessons.

Reading Record
Name:......John Jackson......................
Reading Score:.........54, 56,..................

Date	Book	Teacher
Feb. 22	Ladybird 2a	p.8 p.12
Mar. 9	Ladybird 2b	

In several schools this practice has been coupled with the use of a reading card for each child. Such a card can be duplicated easily on cheap coloured card. Apart from its use as a bookmark and a reading record, a colour coding system to match the books on shelves ensures that child, librarian, class teacher, headteacher or even supply teacher may readily see that the system is functioning.

Organising the use of apparatus is notably less successful, but here, too, the teacher must have some overall plan. Basically material needs to be graded, and should be made readily available to children either in low cupboards or open shelves. A link with the colours used in grading books may be helpful. Some indication of useful apparatus and its place in a scheme is given in the Graded Book List. Suggestions given are by no means comprehensive and are mainly confined to pre-reading activities.

A useful tip for this stage might be as follows. Assuming all reading books graded at a level below reading age five years are marked with a red symbol, then red circular adhesive discs may be used to number boxes of cards and apparatus from, say one to twenty. Children, issued with cards, marked with these numbers, can then tick off the appropriate number each time the apparatus has been used. It may not matter if a child selects a particular game many times, but some simple record helps the teacher to direct a child's attention to other activities from time to time.

Grading apparatus can be difficult unless the teacher builds up his stock gradually and takes care to relate it to each individual child's stage of reading.

As a cautionary note here it is well to appreciate that for duller slow learners the games skills involved in using some apparatus may need grading too. Children often need to be taught these skills and too great a variety of games skills in use at any one time can cause confusion.

Excellent examples of reading apparatus arranged logically and planned for children to use with the minimum of help from teachers are to be found in Moxon's *Remedial Reading Method* and Stott's *Programmed Reading Kit.* Teachers may learn much from reading about these methods and by trying them out with children.

Listed below are a number of other guides to the selection of books for backward readers which are inexpensive and well worth acquiring by interested teachers. Indeed they should form part of the staff library in most schools.

BOOK GUIDES

A Survey of Books for Backward Readers, University of Bristol Institute of Education, Publication No. 9, published by University of London Press, 1956.

A Second Survey of Books for Backward Readers, University of London Press, 1962.

(The above both contain extensive critical accounts of books based on teachers' reports, in addition to an appraisal of reading and interest ages, illustrations, methods, contents, style and other useful information regarding publishers and prices.)

Help in Reading, published by National Book League, 3rd edition, 1966.

(A concise catalogue relating to the N.B.L. travelling exhibition of books, but containing notes about books and materials for children. Also gives some guidance regarding books for the teacher on teaching and testing of reading.)

Words of Persuasion, A. Pullen, Cambridge University Press, 1962.

(An analysis and evaluation of more than 150 books.)

Books and Publications Recommended for use with Dull and Backward Children, Kent Education Committee, 1964.

(Advisory catalogue, part of a series designed to help teachers, acts as a catalogue to committee's educational exhibition. Brief Reviews by serving teachers, 2s. 9d. post free.)

Some Books and Apparatus for Backward Readers in the Primary School, Child Guidance Service, Leeds, 1959–61.

(*This list is continued on p. 92.*)

PUBLISHED READING BOOKS, APPARATUS AND MATERIALS FOR COMPREHENSION AND PHONIC WORK
(Graded according to Reading Age)

Reading Age below 4 years 6 months.

Reading Schemes	Activities and Apparatus	Supplementary Reading Books
Picture Books (Macmillan)	Sorting and matching exercises: objects shapes, pictures by colour, class and shape.	Colour Photo Books (E. J. Arnold).
Pre-reading material:	Listening for sounds; initial letters.	Before We Read (Interest, Animal and Helen books) (Oliver & Boyd).
Getting Ready for Reading (Ginn).	Acquisition of initial sight-vocabulary.	Fountain Picture Books (Ginn).
McKee: Pre-Readers (Nelson).	Left to right habits.	Photographic Books (Oliver & Boyd).
Reading for Fun and Happy Venture Pre-Reader (Oliver & Boyd).	Recognition of names.	
'Are You Ready—' Growing and Reading Scheme (Macmillan).	Encourage language growth, perceptual development, picture interpretation. auditory discrimination of sounds.	
Bluebird Scheme and Picture Books (Chambers).	Classify: labels: observe and remember.	
	Gay Way Introductory Pictures (Macmillan)	
	Look & See Cards (Macmillan)	
	Methuen Caption Books.	

Reading Age 4·6 to 5·0 years

Preparatory workbooks:	Matching picture-word; word-word.
Splash, Tuffy and Boots (Macmillan, N.Y.).	Copying sentence below child's picture.
Ladybird Keyword Reading Scheme, Books 1a, 1b, 1c (Wills and Hepworth, Ltd.).	Matching words to this sentence. 'I Spy' games.
Activity Reading Scheme, sets 1, 2, 3 (Macmillan).	*Oxford Junior Workbook I.* (O.U.P.)
Happy Trio Scheme (3 pre-readers) (Wheaton).	Recognition of letters and sounds. Listening for sounds.
Through the Rainbow. **Pre-readers** (Schofield & Sims).	Sequence of ideas.
	Follow directions (action-flash cards).
	Wall stories, charts, news.
	Book of Sounds.
	Programmed Pre-reading. (McGraw Hill).
	Gay Way Workbooks (Macmillan).
	Ladybird Workbook I.
	Wall pictures, Sentence cards and other supplementary material.
	Colour and Write (Gibson).
	Through the Rainbow—Conversation Pictures.

Before We Read (Interest, Animal and Helen Books) (Oliver & Boyd).

Macmillan *Picture Books.*

Progress Books, 1-3, reading and number (Longmans).

N.B. The names of publishers are given only after the first reference to a book in a series.

PUBLISHED READING BOOKS, APPARATUS AND MATERIALS FOR COMPREHENSION AND PHONIC WORK
(Graded according to Reading Age)

Reading Age 5·0 to 5·6 years

Reading Schemes	Comprehension, Workbooks, Phonic Activities	Supplementary Reading Books
Ladybird Keyword Books 2a, 2b, 2c (Wills & Hepworth).	*Play-Learn Reading Scheme* Books 1-3 (Harrap).	*Play-Learn Reading Scheme* Books 1-3 (Harrap).
Adventures in Reading, Book 1 (O.U.P.).*	Step up and read. Cards (U.L.P.)*	*Good Luck Series*, Book 1 (Macmillan).
New Age in Reading (4 Pre-readers) (E. Arnold).*	*Oxford Junior Work, Book 2.*	*Reading Through Interest*, Books 1-3 (Collins).
Happy Venture Introductory Book and Playbook.	*Adventures in Writing*, Book 1 (O.U.P.).*.	*Introducing Ginger* (Ward Lock).
Happy Venture Lib. Books 1-5 (Oliver & Boyd).	*Happy Venture* Introductory materials—workbook.	*Dr. Fobbins*, 1 (Macmillan).
Janet and John: Here We Go; Off to Play (Nisbet). or Book 1 (M.L.B. 1-5).	*Gay Way* Work Books, Book 1.	*Racing to Read*, 1 (E. J. Arnold).
Gay Way. Red Book. Red Stories, 1-8 (Macmillan).	*Ladybird* Workbook 2 and supp. material.	*Start Afresh Readers*, 1 (Hulton).
McKee Book 1 (Nelson).	*Looking at Words* (Rupert Hart-Davis).	*Gay Way Auxiliary Readers* (Red book).
Gates Readers: Come and ride (Macmillan).	*Happy Venture* Colouring book.	*Picture Book Readers* (Macmillan).
Beacon Reader, 1 (Ginn).	*Sounding and Blending* (Gibson).*	*Learning to Read*, 1-3 (Ladybird) (Wills & Hepworth).
	First Word Books (Macmillan).	*Progress Books*, 4 to 6.
	Programmed Reading (Sullivan Associates).	*Five Friends*, 1-4 (Arnold).
		Happy Trio, 1 (Wheaton).

Reading Age 5·0 to 5·6 years

Mike and Mandy, I (Nelson). *Through the Rainbow*.	*Colour Story Reading* (Nelson). *Adventures of Betty and Colin*, Apparatus I (Davis & Moughton).	*Kingsway Open Air Books*, I (Evans). *One, Two, Three and Away*, Books I and 2 (Hart-Davis). *Adventures of Betty and Colin*, Book I.

PUBLISHED READING BOOKS, APPARATUS AND MATERIALS FOR COMPREHENSION AND PHONIC WORK

Reading Age 5·6 to 6·0 years   (*See also overleaf*)
(Graded according to Reading Age)

Reading Schemes	*Comprehension, Workbooks, Phonic Activities*	*Supplementary Reading Books*
Ladybird Keyword Books 3a, 3b, 3c.	*Adventures in Writing*, Books 2 and 2a (O.U.P.).*	*Ginger Book* I (Ward Lock).
Mike and Mandy, Book 2.	*Over the Stile*, Book I (Black).*	*Racing to Read*, Books 2 and 3.
Oxford Colour Books, Red.*	*First Steps in Reading for Meaning*, Book I (U.L.P.).*	*Dr. Fobbins*, Book 2.
Adventures in Reading, Books 2 and 2a.	*Stott's Programmed Reading Kit*, 1st part (Holmes).	*Kingsway Open-Air Readers*, Books I to 3 (Evans).
Griffin Book I (E. J. Arnold).	Activities to identify words by first letter sound.	*Play-Learn Books*, 4-6.
New Age in Reading, Book 5.*		*Good Luck Work Book* I, and supplementary reader, *Game of Two's*.

*Books which may appeal to children of secondary age.

Happy Venture, Book 1, Playbook 1 (and Library Books 6-10).

Janet and John: Out and About (and M.L.B. 6-22).

Gay Way: Green Book and Green Stories 1-8.

McKee, Book 2. Platform Readers 'A'.

Gates Readers: This is Fun.

New Age, Book 5 (Red, Blue, Brown, Maroon, Green and Yellow).

Beacon Reader 2.

Through the Rainbow.

Royal Road Readers, Book 1, Part 1. First Companion Books.

Question Time Book, 1.

Step Up and Read (U.L.P.).*

Oxford Junior Workbooks, 3 and 4.*

Griffin Workbook A (E. J. Arnold).

First Phonic Workbook (Ginn).*

Looking At Words.

Ladybird Workbook, 3.

Colour and Write (Gibson).

Happy Venture Workbook, 1.

Adventures of Betty and Colin Apparatus 2.

Reading Through Interest, 4-6 (7-12 girls).

Ladybird Learning to Read, Books 4-6.

Gateway Readers, 1 (Evans).

Sea Hawk Introductory Books, 1 and 2 (E. J. Arnold).

Start Afresh, 2.

Reading With Rhythm: Set 1 (Longmans).

Cowboy Sam, 1, 2, 3 (E. J. Arnold).

Living Together (Pergamon).

Adventures of Betty and Colin, 2.

Five Friends, 5-8.

Happy Trio, 2.

Kenny Books, 1-3 (E.J.A.).

Kingsway Open Air, 2.

One, Two, Three and Away, 3, 4.

*Books which may appeal to Children of secondary age.

Reading Age 6·0 to 6·6 years   (See also overleaf)

Reading Schemes	Comprehension, Workbooks, Phonic Activities	Supplementary Reading Books
Ladybird Keyword, Books 4a, 4b, 4c	*Ladybird Book*, Workbook 4.	*Ginger Books* 3, 4.
Mike and Mandy, 3	*Over the Stile*, Book 2 (Black)*	*Racing to Read*, 5-8.*
*Oxford Colour Series** 2. Yellow	*Adventures in Writing*, 3*	*One, Two, Three and Away*, 5, 6.
Adventure in Reading, Book 3 and Supplementary Book 3a*	*Royal Road Readers*:* Book 1, Part 2.	*Dr. Fobbins*, 3, 4, 5.
McKee Books 3; Platform B.	Apparatus Set 3.	*McKee Platform B.*
Griffin Books, 2 and 3*	Miniature Books.	*Family Affairs*, Book 1 (Oliver & Boyd).*
Happy Venture, Book 2. Playbook 2 (and Library Books 11-15).	Question Time 2.	*Goodluck 2* and Workbook and Supplementary Reader.
Janet and John. I went walking or Book 2 (and M.L.B. 23-32).	*Sounds and Words*, 1* (U.L.P.)	*Sea Hawk*, Book 1.*
Gay Way. Blue Book Stories 1-8.	*First Steps in Reading for Meaning*, Book 2*	*Dragon Books* (E. J. Arnold)— A1, A2*
Gates; Tags and Twinkle; In came Pinky.	*I can help myself*, 1-4 (Wheaton).	*Modern Reading* Bk. 1 (U.L.P.).*
New Age, Book 6.* Red, Blue, Green, Maroon, Yellow.	*Gay Way* Work Book 1 (and Letters and Words).	*Cowboy Sam*, 3, 4.
Beacon Reader 3	*Sounds for Reading* 1* Practice Books 1, 2, 3 (Nisbet).	*Muller Easy Readers.*
	Step up and read (cards and Companion Books).*	*Reading with Rhythm*, Sets 2 & 3.
	Words in Colour (Educational Explorers)*	*Pathfinder* A (Oliver & Boyd).*
		Challenge Readers, 1, 2. (McDougal).*

Reading Age 6·0 to 6·6 years (continued)

Second Phonic Workbook (Ginn)*	Beginner Books (Collins).
Happy Venture Workbook 2.	Start Afresh Reader 3.
Think and Do Workbooks (Wheaton).	Easy Readers (Collins).
Adventures of Betty and Colin, App. 3.	Living Together.
New Dragon Workbooks (Arnold)*	Happy Trio 3.
S.R.A. Reading Laboratories, I, 1a, 1b, 1c.	Fell Farm Adventures (Blackie).*
	Ladybird, Learning to Read, 7, 8.
	Ben Books (Longmans).
	Adventures of Betty & Colin, 3.
	Five Friends, 9-12.
	Flamingo P.1. (Oliver & Boyd).
	Kenny Books, 4-7.
	Kingsway Open Air, 3.
	Nippers (Macmillan).

PUBLISHED READING BOOKS, APPARATUS AND MATERIALS FOR COMPREHENSION AND PHONIC WORK
(Graded according to Reading Age)

Reading Age 6·6 to 7·0 years.

Reading Schemes	Comprehension, Workbooks, Phonic Activities	Supplementary Reading Books
Ladybird Keyword Books, 5a, 5b, 5c.	Ladybird Book, Workbook 5.	Ginger Books 5, 6.
Mike and Mandy, Book 4.	English Work Books: Ridout; (1st Introductory Book) (Ginn).	Racing to Read, 9-12.*
Adventures in Reading and Writing, Book 4 (supplementary Book 4a).*	Kingsway Open Air, Book 2.	McKee, Platform (1-6).
	Tom's Day Work Book (Collins).	Dr. Fobbins, Books 6, 7.
	Sounds and Words, Books 2 and 3.	Dolphin A series (U.L.P.).*
		Gateway Readers, Book 2 (Evans).

Griffin, Book 4, 5.*

Oxford Colour Series, 3 (Blue).*

McKee, Book 4; Platform C.

Happy Venture, Book 3, Playbook 3 (Lib. Books 16-21).

Janet and John: Through the Garden Gate, or Book 3 (Blue Stories 21-28).

Gay Way Yellow Book, Yellow Stories 1-4.

Gates: The Painted Calf; Bruce and Barbara.

Beacon 4.

Space Age Readers, 1, 2 (Blond).*

Sound Sense, Books 1 and 2.*

I Can Think and Do, Books 1-6 (Wheaton).

Gay Way Work Book 2 (Looking at words).

Royal Road Readers: Books 2 and 2a; Second Companion Book; Question Time Book 3.

Ginger Puzzle Books.

Step Up and Read (cards and books).*

Sounds for Reading, 2 (Workbooks 1 and 2).*

Third Phonic Workbook.*

One, Two, Three and Away Workbook A.

Happy Venture Workbook, 3.

Reading for Meaning, 1, 2 (U.I.P.)*

S.R.A. Labs. 1a, 1b, 1c.*

Family Affairs, Book 2.*

Sea Hawk, Book 2.*

Tempo Book, 1, 2 (Longmans)*

Dragon Books, B1, B2, B3.*

Modern Reading, Books 2, 3.*

Start Afresh, 4, 5.

Reading with Rhythm, 4, 5.

Read and Play (Muller).

One, Two, Three and Away, 7, 8.*

Challenge Reader, 3, 4.*

Tim's Gang, 1, 2 (Hamish Hamilton).*

Living Together.

Beginner Books.

Adventures of Betty and Colin, 4.

Cowboy Sam, 5, 6.*

Day of the Week, 1-3 (Holmes).

Happy Trio, 4.

Kenny Books, 8-14.

Pathfinder, B, C.*

Wild West Readers, 1-4 (Wheaton).*

Nippers.

Tales and Adventures (Hulton).*

*Books which may appeal to children of secondary age.

Reading Age 7·0 to 7·6 years.

Reading Schemes	Comprehension, Workbooks, Phonic Activities	Supplementary Reading Books
Ladybird Keyword, 6a, 7a, 6b, 7b.	Ladybird, Book 6c, Workbook 6.	Sea-Hawk, 3, 4 (Library Books).*
Griffin, 6, 7.*	Get Ready for Bonfire Night (Ginn).*	Dragon Books, C1, C2, C3.*
Mike and Mandy, 5.	English Workbooks (2nd Introductory Book).*	Challenge Readers, 4, 5.*
Oxford Colour Books, 4 (Green).*	Royal Road Readers, 3, 3a; 3rd Companion Book, Question Time Book 4.*	Racing to Read, 12, 13-16.*
McKee, Book 5 (Platform D).		Tempo 3.*
Happy Venture Book 4; Playbook 4 (Library Books 22-27).	Sounds and Words, 4, 5.*	Cowboy Sam, 7-9.*
Janet and John: I Know a Story, or Book 4 (Pink Stories, 21-28).	Sound Sense, 3, 4.*	Tom's Day Reader.*
Gay Way, Violet Book (Violet Stories 1-4).	Tom's Day (Collins).	Pathfinder.*
New Age in Reading, 7 (Red, Blue, Mauve, Green, Brown, Yellow Books).	Reading to Some Purpose, 1 (Oliver & Boyd).*	Happy Trio, 5.*
Space Age Readers, 3, 4 (Blond).*	Gay Way, Workbook 3.	Gateway, 3.
Beacon Reader, 5.	Let's Make Something (E. J. Arnold).*	Flamingo, P.1.
	Step Up and Read, (U.L.P.).*	Bonfire Night Reader.*
	Programmed Reading (McGraw-Hill).*	Story Path to Reading, 1-3 (Blackie).*
	Words in Colour.*	Explorer Readers, 1 (Schofield & Sims).*
	Fourth Phonic Workbook.*	Betty and Her Friends, 1 (Warne).*
		Peter and His Football, 1 (Warne).*
		Burgess Books, 1a, b, c, d (U.L.P.).*
		Start Afresh, 6.

*Burgess Workbooks, 1A, 1B, 1C, 1D.**

*Adventure in Life Workbooks (Wheaton).**

*Happy Venture Workbook 4.**

*Reading for Meaning, 3, 4.**

*S.R.A. Labs. Ia, Ib, Ic, IIa.**

*D.A.T.A. Workbook 1.**

Easy Readers, 1-8 (Collins).

*Family Affairs, 3.**

*Wild West Readers, 5-9.**

*Go Readers, 1, 2 (Blond).**

*Micky, Book 1 (Blackwell).**

One, Two Three and Away, 9, 10.

Beginning to Read (Benn)

Read and Play.

Websters of Welford, Book 1 (Nelson).

*Scope Readers, 1, 2 (Oliver & Boyd).**

*D.A.T.A. series (Schofield & Sims).**

*Skipper Books (Hulton).**

*Adventure in Life, 1-4 (Wheaton).**

Springboard Books, 1-3 (Arnold).

Days of the Week, 4-7.

*Modern Reading, 4, 5.**

*Adventures in Space, 1-4 (R. Hart-Davis).**

*Teenage Twelve, 1, 2 (Gibson).**

*Peter Brown, 1 (U.L.P.).**

*Bandit Books, 1-3 (Benn).**

Reading with Rhythm, 5-18.

*Books which may appeal to children of secondary age.

Reading Age 7·6 to 8·0 years.

Reading Schemes	Comprehension, Workbooks, Phonic Activities	Supplementary Reading Books
Ladybird Keyword, 8a, b, 9a, b.	Better English, Introductory Book.*	Sea Hawk, 5, 6.*
Griffin, 8, 9.*	Highfield English Workbook (Nelson).*	Tempo, 4, 5, 6.*
More Adventures in Reading and Writing, Books 1-3 (O.U.P.).*	Sounds and Words, Book 6.*	One, Two, Three and Away, 11, 12.
Mike and Mandy, 6.	Sound Sense, 5, 6.*	Pathfinder, Book 2.*
Janet and John: Once Upon A Time, Maroon Stories, 31-39.	English Workbook, 1st book.*	Wide Range, Blue, Green. 1.*
Gay Way, Orange Book and Stories, 1-4.	Royal Road Readers, Books 4, 5, 6.*	Dragon Books, D1, D2, D3.*
Oxford Colour Reading Books, Grade 5 (Purple).*	Read and Do (Collins).*	Challenge Readers, 6, 8.*
Beacon Reader, 6.	Get Ready for London Express (Ginn.)*	Read and Do Reader.*
	Reading to Some Purpose, Book 2.	Reader: 'London Express' (Ginn).
	Step Up and Read, Book 3.*	Story Path to Reading, 4-6.*
	Programmed Reading.*	Explorer Readers, 2.*
	Fifth Phonic Workbook.*	Betty and Her Friends, 2.*
	One, Two, Three and Away, Workbook.	Peter and His Football, 2.*
	Burgess Workbooks, 2a, 2b, 2c, 2d.*	Burgess Books, 2a, b, c, d.*
	Reading for Meaning, 5, 6.*	Discovery Readers, 1-10 (Harrap).
	D.A.T.A. Workbook, 2.*	Dolphin Books, B series (U.L.P.).*
		Micky, Book 2.*
		Websters of Welford, 2.*

Using Your Reading, 1, 2 (Arnold).*

First Interest Books (Ginn).
They Were First (Oliver & Boyd).*
Magnet Readers (Wheaton).*
Scope 2.*
Adventure in Life, 5-8.*
Pattern Readers (Macmillan).
Go Readers, 3, 4.*
Bandit Books, 4-6 (Benn).
Teenage Twelve, 3, 4.*
Adventure Road to Reading (Hamilton).*
Flamingo, P.2.
Peter Brown, 2, 3.*
Modern Reading, 6.*
Inner Ring Books, 1, 2 (Benn).*
Wild West Readers, 9-12.*
Adventures in Work, 1-6 (O.U.P.).*
New Reading (Readers' Digest).*

*Books which may appeal to children of secondary age.

PUBLISHED READING BOOKS, APPARATUS AND MATERIALS FOR COMPREHENSION AND PHONIC WORK
(Graded according to Reading Age)

Reading Age 8·0 to 8·6 years.

Reading Schemes	Comprehension, Workbooks, Phonic Activities	Supplementary Reading Books
More Adventures in Reading, 4-6.*	Sound Sense Book 7.*	Challenge Reader, 7.*
New Adventures in Reading, 1-3 (O.U.P.).*	Ridout; 2nd Workbook.*	Inner Ring Books, 3, 4.*
New Age in Reading, 8 (Red, Blue, Brown, Green, Mauve, Yellow).*	Get Ready for Derwent Adventures*	Websters of Welford, 3.*
Mike and Mandy, Books 4, 7, 8.	New Adventures in Writing, 1-6.*	Ready Readers (Longmans).*
Griffin Readers, 10, 11.*	Book Builder, Books 1-43 (Methuen).*	True Adventure, 1-16 (Blackie).*
Oxford Colour Reading Books, Grade 6 (Grey).*	Royal Road Readers, Books 7, 8.*	Pathfinder Book, 3.
Ladybird Keyword, 10a, b, c; 11a, b, c; 12a, b, c.	Can you Solve It? (Odhams).*	Wide Range, Blue, Green II.*
Beacon Reader, 7.	Reading to Some Purpose, 3-5.*	Gateway Books, 4.
	Step Up and Read.*	Reader: Derwent Adventure.*
	Sixth Phonic Workbook.*	Story Path to Reading, 7-9.*
	Booster Workbooks, 1, 2, 3 (Heinemann).*	Adventure in Life, 9-12.*
	Burgess Workbook, 3a.*	Explorer Readers, 3.*
	Reading for Meaning, 7, 8.*	Micky Books, 3, 4.*
	S.R.A. Labs., 1a, b, c; IIa, b; IIIa.*	Betty and Her Friends, 3.*
	D.A.T.A. Workbook, 3.*	Peter and His Football, 3.*
	Using Your Reading, 3.*	Headway Readers (Evans).*
		Onward Readers (Cassell).*
		No. 5 Charles Street, 1-3. (Wheaton).*
		Pioneer Books, 1-4 (Harrap).*
		Sea Hawk, 7, 8.*
		Family Affairs, 4.*
		Wild West Readers, 10-12.*

Dolphin Book, C, D, series.*

Booster Books, 1, 2.*

Ann and Jenny, Books 1-6 (Ginn).*

It Really Happened (Johnstone & Bacon).

Anvil Books (Hamish Hamilton).*

Jets, red series (Cape).*

Adventure and Detection, 1-3 (O.U.P.)

Springboard Books, 4, 5, 6.*

Pattern Readers.

Forward Books (Methuen).*

Pegasus Books (Newnes).*

Modern Reading (U.L.P.).*

Scope 3.*

Tempo 7-10.*

Burgess 3a.*

Teenage Twelve, 5-7.*

Adventures of Bill and Betty, 1-6. (O.U.P.)*

Buckskin Books, 1-4 (Macmillan).*

Flamingo R.2.

Peter Brown, 4, 5.*

Adventures in Work, 7-12.*

*Books which may appeal to children of secondary age.

Reading Age 8·6 to 9 plus.

Reading Schemes	Comprehension, Workbooks, Phonic Activities	Supplementary Reading Books
More Adventures in Reading.*	Ridout: 3rd and 4th Workbook.*	Challenge Reader, 8.*
New Age Books, 9, 10 (Red, Blue, Brown, Green, Mauve, Yellow).*	Royal Road Readers, 9.*	Wide Range, Blue, Green III, IV.*
Simon and Dorothy Readers (Blond).*	Sound Sense, 8.*	Story Path to Reading, 10-12.*
	Step Up and Read.*	Betty and Her Friends, 4.*
Mike and Mandy, 9-12.*	Booster Workbooks, 4, 5.*	Peter and His Football, 4.*
Beacon Reader, 8.	Burgess Workbook, 4a.*	Booster Books, 3, 4, 5.*
Griffin Book 12.*	Reading for Meaning, 9-13.*	Forward Books, (Methuen).*
New Adventures in Reading, 4-6.*	Reading to Some Purpose, 6, 7.*	Jets, Blue series.*
	S.R.A. Labs. 1b, 1c, IIa, b, c, IIIa.*	Triumph Books (Warne).*
	Using Your Reading (4).*	Dolphin series, E, F, G, H.*
		Adventure and Detection, 4-6 (O.U.P.).*
		Pathfinder, 4, 5.*
		Websters of Welford, 4, 5.*
		Pioneer Books, 5-8.*
		Springboard Readers (E. J. Arnold).
		Spotlight on Trouble (Methuen).*

Reading Age 8·6 to 9 plus.

Bernard Ashley Books (Allman).*
Windrush Books (O.U.P.).*
Compass Readers, Space Readers, Magnet (Wheaton).*
Streamline Books (Nelson).*
True Adventure Series, 17-32.*
Pattern Readers.
Scope, 4.* *Peter Brown,* 6.*
Joan Tate Books (Heinemann).*
Burgess 4a.*
Titans-series, Ward Lock.*
Teenage Twelve, 8-12.*
Buckskin, 5-9.*
Flamingo, P.3, P.4, R.3, R.4.
Adventures in Life, 13-16.*

*Books which may appeal to children of secondary age.

A Selected List of Books for Less Able Children in Primary Schools, and

A Selected List of Books for Less Able Children in Secondary Schools, Derbyshire Education Committee, School Library Service, 1962.

(Compiled by teachers, these useful lists include basic reading books, additional activities, supplementary readers and library and reference books and an arithmetic section.)

University Institute Library Lists and book collections, at Reading, Hull.

Children's Reading, K. S. Lawson, University of Leeds Institute of Education. Paper No. 8, 1968.

(A recent, valuable guide to fiction and non-fiction school books, graded according to reading and interest age.)

CHAPTER 6

Spelling Can be Taught Successfully

WE are less inclined to make a fetish of excellence in spelling in school today. Outside schools, much more liberal attitudes are reflected in the tendency for employers to realise that a dictionary is just as important a part of a secretary's equipment as a shorthand notebook. People seem much more aware that intelligent adults are prone to occasional spelling errors and teachers themselves make innocent mistakes from time to time. But increased tolerance should not lead to the misguided assumption that some basic skills need not be acquired through instruction. Spelling is one skill which may be improved through good teaching.

Impressions from a number of schools suggest that there is a considerable reaction against formal spelling lessons. This is probably an attitude in keeping with much more informal approaches to teaching in many primary schools. Teachers have also realised that many children make some progress in spelling incidentally through reading, writing and other activities. Rejection of formal spelling lessons may have arisen out of dissatisfaction with the results of some out-moded practices. Where 'Spelling' was a distinct period on the timetable, lessons were often too long and concerned with rote learning of lists of words totally unrelated to other work. It is good to see the back of such old-fashioned practices at last. Yet it is evident that many children still have difficulties in spelling, and this is particularly true of slow learners. Complete reliance on incidental learning is inadequate for children with learning difficulties. They need systematic instruction in spelling and indeed many more children could improve their attainments in spelling if they were shown the best methods of teaching themselves to spell.

Spelling is important, for illiteracy is more easily displayed by the number and nature of spelling mistakes in a simple letter, whereas limited reading ability may pass unnoticed. Careless spelling impedes communication for reader and writer alike. School teachers are less inclined today to discourage their scholars' free writing by over-use of the red pencil on spelling errors. Improvement in spelling cannot simply be left to chance. It is equally possible that by helping some children to make their written work more readable they may thereby overcome a reluctance to put pen to paper. For reluctance to write may have arisen because they are only too well aware of their own weakness in spelling. Writing can become a painful experience when every word involves a mental effort. Having the ability to spell automatically may free the child's mind to concentrate on the content of his writing, to develop better forms of expression, or even to try to use new words.

To expect perfection in spelling from slow learners would be unrealistic, but it is certainly reasonable to try to eradicate errors in the spelling of common words and to make their written work much more intelligible. For example, it is not unusual to see 'night' spelled 'nite'. This is easy to read in context whereas other versions such as 'net' or even 'nit' are confusing, particularly when nearly every word on a line requires translation. In both cases help is urgently needed for, although 'night' is a difficult word to spell, it is a very common one.

Writing skills follow reading just as reading follows speaking. It is reasonable to expect some delay in learning to spell for children normally can read words before they can spell them. This difference between spelling vocabulary and reading vocabulary has been defined by Sir Cyril Burt as 'a period of orthographic latency'.[1]

It is perhaps most marked with those children in the beginning stages of learning to read and write. However, as skills develop, a wide discrepancy between Reading Age and Spelling Age should not be accepted as being either natural or irremediable.

The burden of this chapter is therefore to declare that slow learners and other poor spellers need some systematic teaching in spelling. Research suggests that spelling can be taught effectively and supports the ideas, that:

1. Children should be taught words which they commonly use in their writing.

2. Methods of teaching should be adopted so that children can learn for themselves how to tackle new and difficult words.

3. Sooner or later children must be able to work at spelling as individuals because children progress at different rates and find some words more difficult to learn than others.

4. Teachers should develop their own tests to assess progress and attempt to diagnose specific difficulties.

WHERE TO BEGIN

Before making drastic changes in methods of teaching spelling it would seem sensible to examine critically both the methods already in use and the progress being made in your class or school. This is probably good advice prior to introducing any curriculum change. It is not uncommon to find uneven progress due to individual teachers misinterpreting schemes of work which have some merit. One may also discover teachers who are intuitively adopting procedures which produce remarkable results. Good practice in one class may be the lever or the inspiration to encourage general acceptance of either modification or extensive revision of less satisfactory teaching methods.

The use of a standardised Spelling Test throughout the school is recommended as a first step. Then one can begin to ask questions about problems in spelling which are bound to be peculiar to each individual school and may be specific to different classes or groups of children.

In addition to using a standardised Spelling Test it is important to examine samples of children's written work. This is the acid test, for we are not teaching children to do well in spelling tests but to improve spelling in their daily work. Although it is unlikely that a child with a high Spelling Age will make many mistakes in his written work, it does not always follow that a child will spell 'automatically' when concentrating on the content of his written work. This can be more easily demonstrated from a teacher's own weekly test of the spelling programme where success is not always reflected in improved spelling in free writing. Teachers use many methods of teaching spelling. Some, it has been suggested, teach 'incidentally' relying on an observable association between reading and spelling attainment and often accepting minor deviations or severe spelling difficulties as irremediable, others teach daily lists of words and test weekly. Lists may be obtained from published texts or teachers may make up their own lists. Some lists appear to follow no particular pattern, others are grouped according to some phonic element, some centre on a topic like 'The Railway Station' and children supply words—porter, train, luggage, etc. A mixture of methods is often used. The more profitable aids to learning include attention to individual children's mistakes. Here we find children making their own spelling dictionaries and teachers producing wall charts which are gradually built up to include words commonly used in class alongside new words introduced in other lessons, words of local or special interest and sometimes words which cause particular difficulty. Undoubtedly there are also many activities of dubious value, but it is perhaps better to concentrate on more positive suggestions than to dwell on malpractices.

WHICH WORDS TO TEACH

There is a long history of attempts to produce spelling lists for schools. Teachers are familiar with Basic Sight Vocabularies in the teaching of reading. Key Words and the American lists by Dolch and Dale show us that a limited number of words are common to all reading matter and occur so frequently that they may usefully be taught in the initial stages of reading. However, these lists are derived from reading material and are not necessarily the same words which children want to write. Accordingly many attempts have been made to produce lists of words most frequently found in writing. Early investigators concentrated too much on the written products of adults. Even the popular Schonell's Essential Spelling List was in part derived from earlier studies of adult writing.

Some excellent research has been carried out to provide lists of words used by children. Many of these are American in origin and accordingly have some limitations for the U.K. Other studies by Arvidson[2] in New Zealand and the Scottish Council for Research in Education[3] have relevance to normal British children. They have less value for slow learners as they are far too long and certainly contain many words which are not common to an E.S.N. child's written vocabulary.

A survey of children's writing in Leicestershire by Edwards and Gibbon[4] though not designed as a spelling list, gives some idea of the words young children use.

Two limited surveys have been conducted into the written vocabulary of older E.S.N. children in day special schools. One experiment, carried out by Matthew[5] at the Claremont School, Wallasey, showed that eighty-five Key Words formed 67·5% of the written vocabulary of children aged twelve to sixteen years. A further 204 words were found to form an additional 19·1% of the total vocabulary. It might be concluded, therefore, that by learning 289 words thoroughly these youngsters could achieve 86·6% perfection in spelling.

A similar investigation by Bell and Ward,[6] in Chesterfield, sought to verify Matthew's findings and to discover if there might be differences due to regional use of vocabulary. A wider range of written work was examined to see how far this would influence the pattern of word usage.

Accordingly, some 10,000 words of written work were collected from E.S.N. children aged eleven to fifteen years. Written work included free writing, letters, diary work, set compositions and stories, and simple recipes written up by girls in Housecraft lessons. The full support of the school staff was enlisted in the examination of scripts and the tedious business of counting words. The survey was later extended to include another 6,000 words as a check that the initial study was sufficiently extensive.

The total written vocabulary of these children was found to be only slightly in excess of 1,200 words. Sixty-one words formed 60% of the children's written work—(Class 'A' words in list at the end of this chapter). A further eighty-one words comprised the next 7·75% of the total number (Class 'B' words). The next seventy-one words ('C' words) formed an additional 5·75% of the total vocabulary.

Although there were variations in the results of the two surveys it was found that there was a large measure of agreement on actual words common to both lists. Words not appearing at one level of frequency in the first survey came in at a slightly lower level of frequency in the other survey. Regional differences seemed too slight to be of any account and variations were attributed mainly to the selection of different types of written work for the word counts.

The general hypothesis could be sustained that, for all practical purposes, 213 words from the Ashgate List form over 70% of older E.S.N. children's written work. Having mastered this list it would seem sensible to continue with the remaining words from Matthew's 289 basic words for a spelling vocabulary.

In both surveys it was discovered, on extending the word count, that, although the total vocabulary might be increased slightly, the list of frequently used words did not alter. Other investigators have claimed that the most profitable approach to teaching spelling is to concentrate on words which the children actually use in their own writing and that a primary objective should be to give practice in those words which are most commonly used. Where teachers need convincing that such a list is applicable to their own pupils it would be a comparatively simple matter to type out the list in alphabetical order* and tick off words as they appear in samples of pupils' work. This might

* See list at the end of this chapter.

more profitably be attempted with younger slow learners to try to establish some order of teaching for different age groups. Matthew, in the Claremont investigation, does arrange his 289 words in ascending order of difficulty. The investigators in both experiments would not claim that their lists were ideal for every special school, nor should use of a basic list of this type stop children from learning other words, which they may learn through reading or writing activities, or many special words which they will want to use, and may like to record in their own spelling dictionaries.

A by-product of the survey is a clear demonstration of the paucity of the written vocabulary of E.S.N. children. It seems clear that they are unable or unwilling to use more than 1,500 different words in writing. This should have implications for language enrichment in other lessons.

METHODS OF TEACHING SPELLING

Many children do learn to spell words incidentally or indirectly through other experiences. Hildreth[7] summarises much of the American research in this field. She concludes that 'Teachers should not think of incidental learning and integrated teaching as excluding systematic, well-organised drill'. Fitzgerald[8] noted that 'systematic teaching of spelling should begin where incidental learning leaves off'.

In England, Nisbet[9] claimed that children are likely to learn to spell only about 4% of the words they read. Schonell (1942)[10] particularly stressed that the casual experience of words in reading lessons is, in the case of young and backward children, insufficient for recording permanent impressions.

More attention needs to be given to the systematic teaching of spelling not only to ensure progress but to show children how they can best teach themselves. This is particularly important. Sooner or later spelling will become an individual task, for it is rare to find a class where children make exactly the same mistakes.

Teaching spelling and indeed the study of the sounds of

which a word is composed must aid reading, particularly in the case of the weaker readers.

Daily short spelling of the type described below seems most effective. Once the pattern of testing and teaching is established, teachers will find a reduction in time spent on lesson preparation for spelling. Methods advocated here are not new and are compounded from a number of common points which emerge from the writings of a number of investigators. They seem to have a sound theoretical basis and are effective in practice.

1.   It is advisable to have a definite plan for the week so that children know what to expect and when to study words to be learned. This will help to cut teaching time to a minimum and children soon get into the habit of coming into the classroom and carrying out their own assignments in the first few minutes of a lesson period. Children should be convinced that the method used will help them to learn, and this will be invaluable for those children who are better spellers and may be working at a word list on their own.

2.   Children appear to have strengths and weaknesses in different sensory channels and there is general agreement that an approach which makes use of sight, hearing, speech and muscular sense will best allow for individual differences. In other words, visual, auditory, articulatory and kinæsthetic methods should be combined.

3.   Actual teaching in the initial stages is probably best carried out from the blackboard as a class lesson.

(a) The child sees the word, reads it correctly (from left to right), and notes the shape and any special characteristic.

(b) Clear enunciation by the teacher is important.

(c) The child must say the word clearly.

(d) The word may be traced in the air with the finger or written on the desk with the blunt end of the pencil.

(e) A vital step is then to demand immediate recall from memory. The word is covered up, and the child, being aware of this, will normally have attended well and can write the word correctly first time.

(*f*) The child checks his own version against the correct spelling. If correct, the word may then be written again two or three times.

(*g*) Ensure that the meaning and use of the word is known.

4. Further points which may be noted are—to limit the words to be learned to three or four per day; to revise words which seem to cause special difficulty, and to give children revision in the form of sentences which permit the word to be used in context.

TESTING SPELLING

Tests to evaluate progress in spelling can take various forms. A logical order for a testing programme would seem to suggest (*a*) Standardised Tests of Attainment in Spelling, (*b*) Diagnostic Tests, (*c*) Supplementary tests constructed by the teacher, (*d*) Tests carried out by children. In terms of practical value the order might well be reversed.

The child ought to be regarded as a tester. It is essential both to develop the habit of checking his own work and to give responsibility for testing his own progress. Further, because spelling lessons should progress from class teaching to group and individual work, class organisation is possible only if children are trained to test each other, as for example when they may be working in pairs.

SUPPLEMENTARY TESTS

Tests devised by the teacher are probably the most useful with weak spellers. A standardised spelling test ought not to be needed more frequently than as an annual check. It gives little indication to a child that he is making progress. Children with low attainments in spelling may make steady progress through the list of common words. If only a few of these words appear in the standardised spelling test he will get little satisfaction, and the teacher may be misled into underestimating real progress in actual work done.

Supplementary tests should therefore be devised to measure progress made in the actual words learned in the spelling lesson. Tests at weekly and termly intervals seem to be called for. In both cases it is important to give a pre-test and a final test.

(a) *Term Tests.* Consider the words which might usefully be tackled over the whole term. A conservative work load for beginners may be well based on three words per day, four days a week (testing on Friday?), thinking of a term as being two weeks less than the actual working term. This allows for the unexpected interruptions, or disturbances to school routine or may give time for some informal Spelling Games as revision— for example, Spelling Bees, Spot the Little Word in the Big One, Word Building, Simple Dictation, Spot the Mistakes, etc.

Make up a test from the words to be tackled. Use it at the beginning and the end of term to show actual progress made and where revision may be needed.

(b) *Weekly Testing.* The weekly assignment of words to be learned should be given as a test at the beginning of the week. Children can then see exactly which words need to be learned. At the end of the week the same test given again will show teacher and child the real progress which has been made. For no matter how well graded a spelling list is, in any class, some children will be able to spell some of the words before they are presented as the weekly assignment. Thus failure to pre-test may disguise individual progress. The boy with all spellings correct at the end of the week may have started at an initial advantage whereas another scoring two on the pre-test and nine later has measurably improved. This system, which some writers refer to as the Test-Study Method, is likely to be more economical, for time can be spent studying words which need to be learned. When learning methods are well established the better spellers need only to devote time to learning those words mis-spelled in the weekly pre-test or revising earlier words which caused difficulty. Initially, however, with slow learners it is desirable to establish the habits of learning through the multi-sensory approach described earlier using the complete weekly assignment for practice.

DIAGNOSTIC TESTING

Diagnosis of specific weaknesses in spelling is difficult, uncertain and time-consuming. A number of investigators have devoted considerable attention to diagnostic techniques, and it is fair to point out that until more remedial teachers attempt to follow out diagnostic procedures we can hardly expect to build up a body of knowledge to help evaluate the effectiveness of their proposals.

For the teacher who is determined and has time for remedial work with individual children it is essential to read further in some of the recommended books which deal with diagnosis in more detail. Study may be amply repaid by the satisfaction of seeing children directed to more efficient ways of learning and teachers may well gain additional insights which will help them guide better spellers towards independent methods of study.

Peters,[11] in a recent book, draws together evidence from research into spelling which underlines the difficulties of diagnosis and shows clearly some of the dangers of making assumptions on superficial evidence without real understanding. This is a short and readable book which includes an extensive bibliography for further reading. She quotes evidence to support the view that defects of sight and hearing need not be a handicap to learning. Attention is also drawn to Schonell's[12] claim that defective speech and faulty pronunciation may frequently be a cause of bad spelling. Peters' suggestion that perceptual disabilities may be partly accounted for by habitual lack of attention and that poor spellers do not look at the whole word strengthens the present writer's view that if the teaching procedures, outlined previously, are carried out properly the need for diagnosis may be eliminated in many cases.

Encouraging children to look at the whole word and to try to retain a visual image of it is vital. Usually when children appreciate that they are no longer permitted to copy a word letter by letter from the blackboard, because the word is covered up before being written, the need to attend closely to the word is increased. When some children still seem to be negligent in looking at the whole word additional strategies may be adopted, as, for example, asking them to close their eyes and to try to picture the word.

It follows then that observation by the teacher is part of diagnosis for, in this particular example, children who fail to write the word correctly at the first attempt may sometimes be seen to be inattentive, failing to follow the methods of learning thoroughly, or in need of extra practice through one sensory channel. Thus, many weak spellers may benefit from laying greater emphasis on the kinæsthetic approach. They may have to persist much longer until this step becomes habitual. Tracing, large writing and even raised letters (made in sandpaper or felt) can be utilised. Cards with words causing special difficulty can be made by writing the words in glue and sprinkling them with sand.

The kinæsthetic approach is, of course, also valuable for some children in the initial approaches of learning to read but we are assuming here that children who are non-readers will not be subjected to instruction in spelling. There would seem to be little point in teaching spelling until children have reached a Reading Age of six-and-a-half to seven years and are making attempts to write more than two or three sentences.

Motivation may be a very strong factor in promoting good spelling. Slow learners may often have a very poor self-image of their own capabilities. Unfortunate previous educational history has already labelled them as failures and they may easily continue to live up to this estimation of their worth. In spelling, as with many other subjects, they have to achieve success and be given experiences which will seem relevant and interesting to them. An examination of other educational experiences may be important here, for lack of opportunity to engage in interesting activities which involve writing will not help them to see the need for good spelling. To achieve success with some children it may be necessary to restrict their spelling to learning one word a day, with revision and over-learning until they are convinced that they can do it. Only then may the burden of work be gradually increased.

Some Diagnostic Spelling Tests can be of value. Schonell[13] has devised Regular and Irregular Word Tests and Visual and Auditory Discrimination Tests (S.4, S.5 and S.6).[10] Some insight into the nature of children's spelling mistakes can be gained from tests of this type. Familiarity with these tests may also give teachers sufficient confidence to make some diagnostic assessment purely from a study of a child's written work or from the weekly class test.

Patterns of error can be noted such as:

(*a*) Errors due to poor speech, e.g. 'muvver' for mother.

(*b*) Visual confusion, e.g. 'agian' for again.

(*c*) Phonetic spelling, e.g. 'skool'.

(*d*) Poor auditory discrimination, e.g. 'bill' for bell.

STANDARDISED SPELLING TESTS

The use of Standardised Tests of spelling has been advocated on the grounds that:

(*a*) Comparisons can readily be made with Mental Age and Reading Age.

(*b*) They act as a reliable check on progress.

(*c*) Children can be grouped for appropriate teaching.

(*d*) The level of attainment will help in the selection of words to be taught.

(*e*) Some diagnostic value arises from an examination of types of error made.

Some of these claims seem exaggerated in the light of the limitations of available tests. British tests can be listed briefly and are familiar to many teachers.

Schonell's Spelling Tests, S.1, S.2, in *Diagnostic and Attainment Testing*, Oliver & Boyd, 1950.

Burt's 'Graded Spelling Vocabulary Test' in *Mental and Scholastic Tests*, Staples Press, 1921.

Seven Plus Assessment, Lambert, C. M., U.L.P., 1951 (7-8 years).

Kelvin Spelling Test, Fleming, C.M., R. Gibson & Co., Glasgow, 1933.

'Standard Spelling Test', Daniels J. C. and Diack, H., in *Standard Reading Tests*, Chatto & Windus, 1958.

Many of these tests may be criticised on the grounds of age, reliability or inadequate standardisation data. Burt's test, which is now very old, relies on words which are dictated separately. Because these words are not embedded in an illustrative context, confusion may arise at various points where words, pronounced in isolation, may have alternative spellings (e.g. 'lesson', 'rough', 'raise', 'manner' and particularly 'to' which is the fourth word in the test.)

Schonell's tests, consisting of ten words for each year, are dictated, repeated in an explanatory sentence, and then dictated again. The two tests, which are intended to provide alternative versions, do not appear to the writer to produce comparable results. When applied to sixty children some time ago, there were more discrepancies than agreement between the two sets of results. Following this experience the annual progress check, in this particular school, was made by using only Test S.1.

Lambert's Seven Plus Assessment Test is restricted to use in seven to eight year range, and like the Kelvin Test is expensive to administer as test forms are required. No standardisation data is provided for Daniels and Diack's Graded Spelling Test but this test has the merit of being of more recent origin and may well be useful for teachers using the 'Standard Reading Tests'. The test has four lists of words, grouped according to levels of use and spelling difficulty. Marking and administration are easy and the groupings suggest some possibilities for diagnosis.

There would appear to be a need for a modern, well standardised Spelling Test. Some promising developments in America seem to indicate that alternatives to dictated word tests are likely to prove valid tests of spelling. Investigations are being carried out with multiple choice tests where children are required to pick out correctly or incorrectly spelled words, from written material. Until new tests are developed in Britain teachers can only select one of the above tests according to personal preference, bearing in mind their own particular purpose for using the test.

OTHER ASPECTS

Other educational experiences, both in and out of school, contribute to improvement in spelling. Simple spelling lessons using only the list given here may not always lead to the correct spelling of the same words in written work. Other aids are vital. One of these is the child's own individual spelling book which he builds up and includes words he has learned or wants to learn. Another essential aid is a simple dictionary. Children should be taught how to use a dictionary and encouraged to use it. It is not easy to find one suitable for slow learners. The colourful picture dictionaries designed for young children are worth having in the school but contain the wrong vocabulary. Junior school dictionaries contain too many words and include meanings. Slow learners often find these confusing and become discouraged. Simple Spelling Dictionaries are more appropriate for their use. Teachers may profitably examine the *Alphabetical Spelling Lists* (published by Wheaton), or *Words for Spelling* (published by Evans).

A wall dictionary is often a very good aid, particularly in the beginning, and as words are taught they can be added to separate sheets which can be hinged or made into a large book for class reference.

Having a good basic Spelling Scheme ought to lead to spelling lessons being linked with other work in reading, free writing, speech and handwriting lessons. Teachers are alerted to those words which reappear in other situations and these can be stressed. Phonic work often aids spelling. Children should be made to feel that good spelling is important and written work may be used to show the need for this. Letter writing offers a specially strong motive if this is a real situation where letters are being posted.

On these occasions when opportunities for free and interesting writing are given many teachers try not to hamper imagination by over-insistence on correct spelling. The basic list is useful here, for it is reasonable to insist on the correction of common words from the list and to expect that those words already learned in spelling lessons should be correct. Children can be encouraged to check their own written work, looking first for those words which they should know.

Quite often when doing written work, children ask for aid in spelling a word. This should be refused where words have already been taught and they should be referred to their own spelling books or dictionaries. With other words it is often a good plan to make them attempt the word on scrap paper. Many get words right first time in this way and are encouraged to think about the word themselves. Direct help by the teacher should be the last resort.

Finally, the need for revision must be stressed. These youngsters will not learn to spell correctly and automatically unless there is frequent revision and 'overlearning' particularly of words which they find difficult. It is probably at this point, where classroom organisation should allow for children to take some responsibility for their own individual assignments. They can select those words from their own individual dictionaries which from repeated entry and constant reference are seen to need revision. These words can be studied and working in pairs or groups, children should test each other while the teacher exercises overall supervision.

REFERENCES

1. Burt, C., *Mental and Scholastic Tests*. P. S. King & Son, 1926.
*2. Arvidson, G. L., *Learning to Spell*. Wheaton, 1963.
*3. Scottish Council for Research in Education, *Studies in Spelling*. U.L.P., 1961.
4. Edwards, R. P. A. & Gibbon, V., *Words Your Children Use*. Burke, 1964.
5. Matthew, G., 'The Problem of Spelling in the E.S.N. School', in *The Slow Learning Child*, Vol. 4, No. 1. Univ. of Queensland Press, 1957.
6. Bell, P. & Ward, C. J. B., *Ashgate School Spelling List*. (Unpublished) 1963.

*7. Hildreth, G., *Teaching Spelling*. Henry Holt & Co., New York, 1956.
 8. Fitzgerald, J. A., *The Teaching of Spelling*. Bruce Pub. Co., 1951.
 9. Nisbet, S. D., 'The Scientific Investigation of Spelling Instruction in Scottish Schools', *Brit. Jo. Ed. Psych.*, Vol. XI, Pt. 2, 1941.
10. Schonell, F. J., *Backwardness in the Basic Subjects*. Oliver & Boyd, 1942.
*11. Peters, M. L., *Spelling Caught or Taught*. Routledge & Kegan Paul, 1967.
12. Schonell, F. J., 'The Relation between Defective Speech and Disability in Spelling', *Brit. Jo. Ed. Psych.*, Vol. IV, Pt. 2, 1934.
*13. Schonell, F. J., *Essentials in Teaching & Testing Spelling*. Macmillan, 1949.

FURTHER READING

Books marked * above and the following:
 Horn, E., *Teaching Spelling*, Dept. Classroom Teachers, America Education Research Assoc., 1954.
 Freyberg, P. S., *Teaching Spelling to Juniors*, Macmillan, 1962.

Ashgate Spelling List (arranged alphabetically)

Word	Frequency	Class	Word	Frequency	Class
a	496	A	baby	10	C
about	32	B	back	66	A
after	42	B	bank	11	C
again	21	B	be	34	B
all	55	A	because	29	B
am	31	B	bed	35	B
an	22	B	been	27	B
and	933	A	before	14	C
are	76	A	better	10	C
around	10	C	big	18	C
as	22	B	blew	14	C
ask	20	B	book	14	C
at	112	A	boy	34	B
aunt	10	C	brother	44	B
away	21	B	bus	12	C

Word	Frequency	Class	Word	Frequency	Class
but	49	B	get	65	A
by	11	C	girl	29	B
			go	146	A
call	23	B	good	22	B
came	87	A	got	137	A
can	21	B			
car	42	B	had	160	A
cat	13	C	hand	10	C
catch	11	C	has	31	B
come	53	A	have	157	A
could	24	B	he	127	A
			help	10	C
dad	35	B	her	90	A
dance	20	B	him	69	A
day	33	B	his	63	A
did	40	B	holiday	13	C
dinner	36	B	home	77	A
do	48	B	hope	14	C
dog	16	C	hospital	11	C
door	16	C	house	54	A
down	64	A	how	10	C
family	13	C	I	628	A
farm	11	C	if	38	B
father	30	B	in	285	A
finish	12	C	into	36	B
first	18	C	is	75	A
fish	15	C	it	240	A
for	146	A			
found	18	C	just	18	C
four	17	C			
friend	34	B	kitchen	12	C
from	27	B			
front	10	C	lady	23	B
			last	19	C
gave	20	B	let	20	B

Word	Frequency	Class	Word	Frequency	Class
like	44	B	or	17	C
little	19	C	over	18	C
live	27	B	our	92	A
look	35	B	out	106	A
lot	29	B			
			people	10	C
made	23	B	play	18	C
make	21	B	please	14	C
man	70	A	police	46	B
married	14	C	policeman	31	B
me	91	A	pull	10	C
men	10	C	put	58	A
minute	10	C			
money	21	B	rabbit	13	C
morning	27	B	rain	13	C
mother	84	A	read	11	C
much	12	C	ready	23	B
my	322	A	right	11	C
			road	21	B
name	12	C	room	13	C
new	13	C	round	20	B
next	26	B			
nice	50	A	said	175	A
night	32	B	saw	30	B
no	16	C	say	12	C
not	83	A	school	63	A
now	22	B	sea	10	C
			see	49	B
of	139	A	seen	11	C
off	27	B	she	123	A
old	31	B	shop	21	B
on	163	A	sister	56	A
once	16	C	sit	10	C
one	90	A	sleep	11	C
o'clock	21	B	so	97	A
other	32	B	some	79	A

Word	Frequency	Class	Word	Frequency	Class
sometimes	11	C	walk	47	B
start	19	C	want	27	B
station	10	C	was	257	A
stay	13	C	wash	22	B
street	10	C	watch	12	C
			water	10	C
tea	31	B	we	371	A
teacher	20	B	week	22	B
that	70	A	well	18	C
the	913	A	went	224	A
their	11	C	were	57	A
them	38	B	what	32	B
then	185	A	when	171	A
there	106	A	where	34	B
they	119	A	while	20	B
thing	20	B	who	10	C
this	23	B	will	94	A
time	48	B	wind	14	C
to	525	A	window	23	B
told	27	B	with	104	A
too	26	B	work	50	A
two	47	B	woman	10	C
			wood	15	C
			would	56	A
up	86	A			
upon	12	C	year	22	B
us	43	B	yes	23	B
			you	158	A
very	76	A	your	30	B

213 words.

Class A. Words with a frequency of 50+. 61 words (total number 9,294). Approximately 60% of all words

Class B. Frequency of 20+. 81 words (total 1,201). Approx. 7·75%.

Class C. Frequency of 10+. 71 words.

CHAPTER 7

Essential Written Work

ENCOURAGING dull children to write can be a discouraging and disappointing exercise for the teacher. Equally it is an irksome task for the pupil who demonstrates his uneasiness with a pen by a marked reluctance to attempt written work of any kind. Reluctance to write must be expected from children who may have had difficulty first in using words and then in reading them. They are not predisposed to engage in another verbal activity which introduces the additional requirements of legible handwriting, ability to spell and a logical and grammatical form of expression which is more readily observed and criticised than oral communication.

A diet of exercises, grammar, punctuation and composition is not necessarily the answer. As in other aspects of the curriculum it is important to remember the poor background of many of these children and to realise that a limited vocabulary and lack of intelligible experience may severely restrict self-expression. Some fundamental deficiencies may be uncovered which stem from limited meaningful school experiences at an early age. Questioning will often reveal, for example, that many slow learners seem to have little knowledge of nursery rhymes and it takes little imagination to appreciate that contact with stories and fables may have been limited.

Emphasis is being directed to this factor because it is always possible to pay too much attention to written work, and ignore earlier and more fundamental activities. Assuming that we are neither expecting too much from a child nor trying to build on shaky foundations, some priorities have to be established in encouraging written work. It would seem more purposeful to concentrate on a very limited scheme directed towards functional writing. A programme which clearly reveals its social and utilitarian aims will tend to deal with written work which children regard as being relevant. Any scheme which is essentially restrictive is likely to be criticised as being less than educational in its fullest sense. There is some truth in this but this is one area where realism should prevail and progress is more likely to follow when initial targets are limited.

The first consideration in planning a minimum programme leads to the question, 'What are these youngsters likely to need to write when they are adults which can be taught in school and made to seem immediately relevant to children?'

Letter writing is an obvious asset. For many this will remain the major commitment involving writing. It is possible to imagine a number of situations in later life where various forms of letters will be needed. Writing absence notes to schools, letters of application for jobs, short communications to relatives on various occasions, are likely to be common.

Letters ought to be written frequently. Residential Special schools have something to offer here, for it is common practice to make the weekly letter home a part of lessons. This exercise is often effective, for, in addition to the purposeful nature of the task in maintaining home contacts, the letters tend to be rather repetitive and children become familiar with the form of the letter, addressing of envelopes and the writing and spelling of recurring words and phrases.

Day schools could adopt regular letter writing with some benefit. The activity should be real and letters, once written, should be posted. Pen pals in other schools offer one meaningful experience. Any other opportunities should be seized and children may write for brochures, catalogues and for information in response to offers or advertisements in newspapers. Letters of thanks to visitors or people who have helped the school, and to visiting sports teams, are not only motivating for the young writers, but often give greater pleasure to the recipient than a formal note of thanks from the teacher.

Teachers are sufficiently imaginative to see other opportunities for letter writing which arise out of day to day occurrences in school. The sick classmate, whether at home or in hospital, will welcome a shoal of letters and will maintain links with school. This by-product of the main aim of the exercise can be quite important, for, the longer a child stays away from school the more difficult it may become to face up to coming back.

From time to time an internal postal service can serve a useful purpose. Christmas-time is a good starting point and the exchange of Christmas cards needs little encouragement. On other occasions, when a class has mounted an exhibition, completed a project or needs audiences for a play or puppet show, letters of invitation can go out to other classes and to members of staff. A general interest in the 'post-box' soon leads to individual children taking some initiative and birthday cards and postcards from the seaside will appear. This activity can be encouraged if the school makes some arrangement whereby each child receives a card on his birthday. It is quite common to find that a number of children get no acknowledgement of a birthday. Young children, particularly, ought to be remembered.

Older children can be introduced to the idea of telegrams. This is a difficult exercise but the need for comprehension and brevity, related to cost, can be got over to children. Duplicated forms can be provided and imaginary situations set up between pairs of children or teacher and child where short messages can be exchanged, costed and criticised. This can become an amusing and enjoyable endeavour. Once or twice children should be allowed to fill in the official telegraph form even though it will not be possible to send it off.

Associated aids to letter writing can keep interest buoyant. Good examples of letters of different kinds should be displayed alongside correctly addressed envelopes. A collection of letters from the correspondence columns of local and national newspapers can be displayed and changed frequently. Business letters to the school are sometimes suitable for display. Many schools already do read letters aloud to the assembled school when the content directly concerns the children.

Some idea of the possibilities of letter writing have been given. Many slow learners will need practice over a period of years and varied types of letters ought to be attempted. If a regular personal correspondence can be established letter writing will naturally develop and take over many of the characteristics of the composition. There will be less need to look at its limitations for the content will include descriptions of visits and local events and details of home and school news.

FORM FILLING

Filling in forms is a feature of modern life. Some forms are extremely complex. Income tax forms are becoming more so and are a trial for intelligent people. Many such forms are complicated by cross-references, clauses with exceptions, and other qualifications which bemuse the reader.

Attainments in special classes will often range from children who cannot sign their own name to those who might well benefit from studying the intricacies of filling in forms like Driving Licence Applications. Any scheme should allow for individual differences and may have to provide a gradual introduction to the wide variety of forms likely to be encountered. A simple beginning may well include the completion of coupons from advertisements, particularly those in children's papers and comics. An extensive collection will quickly be brought to school from cereal packets, newspapers, mail order firms and other sources. This is one activity which children will soon take up and their own collection, assembled and discussed at school will act as a lively starting point for what could easily become a very dull topic.

Some system of graded form filling seems to be called for. Duplicated in school, a good supply of forms in the classroom can be available for those odd minutes between lessons to give brief but necessary practice. At the simplest level the form will only include name and address. Additional difficulties can be progressively introduced. So, the second form will call for a signature, next (BLOCK LETTERS) and (CAPITAL LETTERS) are introduced. Age and date of birth will cause trouble for some children. Father's occupation, nationality and other terms common to so many forms can be included one at a time. Some simplified versions of form filling for various purposes can now be undertaken. Questions about health, previous occupations, schools and references may be included according to whether one is dealing with imaginary applications for employment, passports, television and other licences, social security benefits, etc.

Following up this work, some contact with the real forms is required. The extent and nature of these forms can be formidable. Attention will inevitably become centred more on the implications of some features, as for example, questions about epilepsy on an application for a driving licence, or the small print on guarantees and hire purchase agreements. Some children will appreciate these intricacies, others may only begin to be aware that they will need to seek help and advice. So individuals may benefit from this study in different ways. The lesson can be repeated, to give additional opportunities for learning, by rearranging the forms in a number of ways.

SOME GENERAL POINTS

Facility in writing does not appear overnight and undoubtedly there are many simple written tasks which precede letter writing or free writing. In a special school the overall scheme will seek to develop writing skills progressively. Beginners will be encouraged to label books and objects and will write sentences under pictures. It is usual to find writing associated with reading books and simple questions will call for written answers to test comprehension. Slowly, with a great deal of oral work preceding the written, and through the provision of real experiences, the teacher will extend the vocabulary of the children and, by example, teach something of the correct use of words, grammatical usage and the idea of sentences.

In isolated special classes, with very dull pupils, or with children referred for remedial help at a late stage in school life, a teacher may have to work through many of these simple processes. There is a danger that through a desire to make work look attractive, or impatient with slow copying, a teacher may do too much for a pupil. For example, it would be wrong to write children's names for them on each new book, and to miss out some of the traditional school practices like putting name and date on pieces of work. More opportunities for signing and writing names are required, not less, and teachers could profitably introduce artificial requirements to precede many activities, e.g. signing for a borrowed football or receipts for the issue of new books and pencils.

The teaching of grammar and punctuation should be restricted. At most some attention may be paid to the sentence, full stop, capital letters, commas, apostrophes and speech marks, singular and plurals and common errors made locally in such matters as agreement between verbs and subject. Occasional lessons, duplicated work sheets containing 'deliberate' mistakes culled from children's work plus training children to correct their own and each other's work may help eliminate errors. Work books and textbooks of exercises have little value.

CREATIVE WRITING

Functional writing through the medium of form filling and letter writing need not occupy a great deal of time week after week.

Over and above this kind of exercise a well planned curriculum will naturally call for a certain amount of other written work. In Chapter 9, 'Units of Experience', it has been emphasised that activities and experiences should show the need for writing. Even when the curriculum is not correlated in this way, other subject teachers ought to be encouraged to create opportunities for children to write. Thus, the domestic science teacher following up the practical cookery lesson, will see that the recipe is copied up. Many girls leaving special schools now take away with them a housecraft book which is a personal record of their work. Built up from their own written recipes and duplicated hand-outs from the teacher, this type of booklet is more likely to be referred to later, and to be read and understood because it is firmly based on the girls' experience.

Drama and puppetry improvised by children can be written up and if typed or duplicated by the teacher, can be returned to the children and provide a pleasurable spur to reading, acting and further writing. Most of the traditional subjects lend themselves to writing and there is truth in the old adage that every teacher is a teacher of English.

Slow learners need opportunities to express themselves perhaps even more than normal children. Frustrations, feelings of failure, bottled-up emotions and the strains of adolescence are often revealed in their paintings or free drama work. Every child does not find emotional outlets through art, music or drama. Some slow learners may find that written expression provides them with a satisfying form of expression.

Many teachers who have been prepared to work with these youngsters, to stimulate ideas and give them time to arrange them, find evidence of sincerity in their free writing for it is devoid of any sophisticated attempts to impress.

The following examples are the uncorrected efforts of boys and girls aged twelve to thirteen years, at a day special school (E.S.N.).*

DANGER

Morning as come evray one geting up the day as come agan. We drawr are certens and open are windows. There is the sunshin Here to greet us wene we get up but last night I was closing my window and I saw a Gorilla I screamed it was Just looking at me I was fratend I head attractive noses comeing nere and bang in the night I herd a bang bang bang it went. I was shivering in fright I roshedt and got dresst. I ran down stais I saw this man who was hanging at my door. I ran out I bumpt into a pleas. I told him I never had Now TroBle No

* Reproduced by kind permission of the Headmaster and Staff, Ashgate Croft School, Chesterfield.

TroBle at ole, at ole, at ole, at ole (at all) and Then it comes, morning again.

WAR

The war is sad
The girl is all alone in the war
Bombs drop bombs all round
Why do the bombs drop on people?
The girl is crying
She does not know why the bombs drop down
She was sitting on the door step
She was still weeping on her dirty knees in the war.

The following poem about Bubbles was written by a very timid girl, whose attainments were very limited. Even in its brevity it has a certain charm and the young writer gained some pleasure and encouragement from the acceptance of her effort.

BUBBLES

The bubbles are light
The bubbles are light
On my fingers
My fingers will burst the bubbles.

Others will be sufficiently motivated to attend closely to spelling, punctuation and rhyme—as in:

THE GALE

Fierce raged the wintry wind,
    Whistling through the creaking trees,
The old man, struggling through the storm
    Held his hat and bent his knees.

There are many ways of stimulating children to write, and

individual children will respond to different stimuli. One will be moved by music, another will react to a painting or picture, others may respond to an animal or an interesting object which is brought into the classroom. All that is required is for the teacher to be willing to try a number of approaches and to accept stories and poems not critically but with a readiness to see qualities of freshness and personal involvement beneath the screen of mistakes in spelling, grammar and punctuation.

FURTHER READING

Few books on the teaching of backward or slow learning children devote many lines to written work. David Holbrook in *English for the Rejected* gives a heart-warming account of his approach to C and D stream children in a secondary modern school. Sympathy and an encouraging approach are evident in a book which charts the progress of a group of disturbed and backward children, through their written work.

One can hardly fail to shed rigid ideas about what constitutes acceptable writing after reading this book. This may lead to a wish to read other enlightened books which deal mainly with modern ideas on teaching writing to children generally. From here it is only a small step to see how ideas can be adapted for slow learners. Recommended books are listed below.

Beckett, J., *The Keen Edge*, Blackie & Sons, 1965; an analysis of poems by adolescents.

Clegg, A. E. (edit.), *The Excitement of Writing*, Chatto & Windus, 1964.

Holbrook, D., *English for the Rejected*, Cambridge Univ. Press, 1964.

Hourd, M. L. & Cooper, G. E., *Coming Into Their Own*, Heinemann, 1959. (Chapter 4, 'Tony' – verse writing and a backward child).

Langdon, E. M., *Let the Children Write*, Longmans, 1961.

Marshall, Sybil, *An Experiment in Education*, Cambridge Univ. Press, 1963.

Maybury, B., *Creative Writing for Juniors*, Batsford, 1967.

CHAPTER 8

The Question of Mathematics

TEACHERS are noticeably uncertain about both content and methods of teaching mathematics to slow learners. There are no easy answers to the questions they ask for little has been written on the subject and research directly related to the needs of slow learners is minimal. Indeed, A. A. Williams[1] goes so far as to suggest that our present level of knowledge is such that we are only at the stage of wondering which are the most important questions to ask. In a rational appraisal of current trends, Williams lists some of the questions which are frequently posed.

'Which, if any, of the bewildering array of structural materials now available are appropriate to our children's abilities and needs? When, and how, should it be introduced? What is Piaget getting at, and is it relevant? When are our dull children "ready" for arithmetic? Are there any suitable arithmetic books for backward children? How can we do social arithmetic when our backward children cannot read the problems?'

Other fundamental questions could well be added to this list. Do we need to teach any mathematics to slow learners? In what sense should we be more concerned with number and arithmetic rather than mathematics? Is there a place for 'modern maths'? What part does vocabulary play in learning maths? What is the essential content of a scheme for the less able?

Teachers themselves are in the best position to begin to answer these questions through their daily contacts with children. They must accept the challenge to experiment and the obligation to evaluate their methods. Some encouragement may be gained from the thought that much of the available published material has emanated from teachers.[2]

This chapter will be directed towards an attempt to answer some of the questions raised at the beginning. A scheme of work will be outlined to provide a broad framework for teachers to adopt and adapt to suit different children and situations. From the security of a scheme which is based upon our present knowledge the way ahead to further experiment may become clear.

THE ESSENTIAL CONTENT OF A MATHS SCHEME

For convenience three stages may be defined. *Stage One* is a preparatory stage. This is a period during which a basic number vocabulary is established, developed or strengthened. It is a time for experience, activity and the arousal of interest. Questioning and discussion are to be encouraged at the outset and must continue throughout all stages.

The *second stage* may be thought of as a time for the acquisition of general number knowledge, for a thorough grounding in a minimum programme of arithmetical skills and developing an awareness of social number usage, to include both a knowledge of the prices of common goods and services and arithmetic arising out of school events.

The *third stage* is largely based on a comprehensive social mathematics scheme which relies on the anticipated or determined needs of slow learners in adult life.

These three stages are by no means discrete. Obviously there are no real dividing lines between sections of a scheme. An understanding of number words and mathematical terms is a continuous and developing process. Early work needs revision and enrichment. Some concepts will be developed early, others will not be firmly established until later years.

1. THE PREPARATORY STAGE

A child's readiness to embark upon number work cannot be judged by an apparent facility in counting or jotting down simple 'sums'. Much more importance must be attached to children's ability to understand what numbers mean and to be able to relate them to practical situations. So, teachers of young children are more concerned to see that, for example, children know the 'story' of five rather than being able to repeat the 'number song'—i.e. counting to five in parrot fashion. To know the 'story' of five means that a child must appreciate that five is more than four and less than six. That five can be decomposed into 2 and 3, or 4 and 1, or can be formed from $3 + 2$, or $1 + 4$. Complete understanding demands a knowledge of the difference between fifth in a series and five as 5 units, irrespective of whether 5 stands for 5 elephants, 5 mice or just 5 as an abstract quantity.

It is a relatively simple matter to discover whether a beginner understands these first notions of counting. A few oral questions or the requirement to manipulate a small number of counters and to describe various arrangements numerically will reveal any inadequacy in understanding at this level. More teachers are beginning to appreciate that many older children, even some who can write down simple sums on paper, have still not come to grips with these simple notions.

With a little prompting most teachers can produce examples of children who are doing sums without any real understanding. At a simple level there are children who cannot count correctly. Even cursory observation reveals the pattern. John, faced with seven counters, touches them and, depending whether he touches one twice, or misses one out, makes the total eight or six. At a slightly more advanced stage, numerous children cannot 'count-on', i.e. when asked to find the sum of four and two, they are unable to say (or think) five—six, but return to count four before continuing. Observing a child solving the 'same' sum, which is expressed in different ways, can be revealing, e.g. $4 + 2 =$; $2 + 4 =$; $6 - 4 =$; $6 - 2 =$; $4 + 2 =$. A mechanical approach where there is obviously no appreciation of the complementary nature of addition and subtraction displays limited understanding. Working out the answer to the last sum again, having already solved it earlier, reveals further inadequacy.

Regardless of limitations which are so easily uncovered, many teachers of older slow learners still persist in teaching traditional arithmetic as though this marks the point to begin and a systematic programme of rote learning is going to produce a sudden flash of insight. If children are experiencing such basic difficulties with number then it is necessary to begin teaching at a much earlier stage. This is what is implied by the preparatory stage or period of number readiness, i.e. that before a child is able to begin to work with small numbers and to understand what he is doing, there are underlying concepts which he must have grasped. This is a fact which many adults find difficult to appreciate because it is a stage of learning which is, for them, far removed in time and because such simple notions were learned unconsciously.

Failure on our part to get down to the child's level of thinking may be bound up with a tendency to associate number and arithmetic with the writing of symbols on paper. For a child at this level primitive number concepts can only be expressed in language or demonstrated with concrete material.

Children cannot begin to conduct arithmetical processes with any understanding or to be able to apply mathematical skills to problem solving unless they have built up a considerable hierarchy of much simpler concepts or notions. These concepts are closely linked with language development and a network of generalisations extracted from a variety of activities and experiences.

Understanding is basic to further progress. Achievement depends first on not overestimating the present level of understanding and then on not underestimating the potential of slow learners.

AN ESSENTIAL MATHEMATICAL VOCABULARY

A vital element in every stage of mathematics is that children should be able to understand the words the teacher uses and that they should learn to use number words themselves. Over-estimating verbal understanding is always a danger for adults. They accept many concepts as being simple and self evident.

A distinction must first be made between receptive vocabulary (heard and understood) and expressive (or spoken) vocabulary. Unfortunately we have no guarantee that a child cannot understand a simple concept because he does not use the appropriate word. The contrary situation may arise that a child uses a word but does not understand it. He may be using a word as part of a 'verbal chain' or in a restricted sense by association with a particular object or situation.

Additional problems arise in deciding on an order of priorities in teaching words. It is a comparatively easy matter to decide that a knowledge of 'more', 'less', or 'the same as' precedes an understanding of terms like multiplication or division. Between these extremes it can become difficult to grade words for a systematic teaching programme. Attempts have been made to formulate 'initial' number vocabularies and perhaps the most promising list to date has been supplied by R. H. Nicholls.[3] Even this list contains some 200 words, and teachers of very young or dull children may wish to be more selective in coping with extremely limited concepts. This is clearly a question which each teacher must solve bearing in mind the limitations and individual differences of the children.

A teacher must be conscious of the whole range of mathematical words and phrases which children are likely to need. Obviously only a few words at a time can be presented and situations must be devised where appropriate words can be introduced and assimilated.

The following list for a suggested number vocabulary is, in part, derived by selecting 'number' words from studies of the oral vocabularies of young children[4] or severely subnormal children[5] and adults.[6] Other words have been added to make a well-rounded list.

It is only to be expected that there will be disparities in frequency of usage of vocabulary in populations so diverse in age, intelligence and environment. Variations resulting from experimental methodology are also to be expected. Nevertheless, it is apparent, on inspection, that some words are used frequently by all three groups and other words are seldom spoken. For example, 'big', 'some' and 'more' are used extensively whereas 'less', 'several', 'broad' and 'narrow' are not.

QUANTITY

big	same	full	both	load
some	different	enough	amount	plenty
lot	small	empty	several	short
more	great	tiny	huge	part
light	many	pair	least	single
all	any	few	sight	heavy
another	much	twice	pint	double
strength	most	weight	pile	heap
large	less	slim	weigh	spoonful

MEASUREMENT

long	square	foot	thick	depth
line	straight	tall	quarter	distance
fat	corner	deep	yard	rule
high	move	round	length	ruler
piece	part	size	shallow	thin
half	point	wide	height	sow
across	feet	width	broad	short
edge	shape	inch	fit	shorten
circle	narrow	space	mile	centre
	further	direction		

TIME

time	week	still	slowly	tonight
day	when	tomorrow	Friday	clock
night	Sunday	o'clock	always	past
morning	today	fortnight	till	after
fast	Monday	minute	since	second
yesterday	Wednesday	soon	sometime	quickly

year	Thursday	late	until	month
Saturday	afternoon	early	often	evening
daily	occasionally	hour	slow	quick
weekly	date	shortly	overtime	moment
speed	January	February	April	May
August	September	during	weekend	October
November	December	whenever	calendar	age
moving	March	June	July	never

POSITION

in	near	bottom	above	half-way
up	off	start	between	backwards
out	on	far	finishing	below
down	starting	middle	stop	separate
over	end	outside	back	towards
under	finish	nearly	by	sideways
where	side	underneath	right	upwards
somewhere	front	behind	apart	frontwards
ending	before	begin	close	nowhere
top	last	opposite	first	third
after	next	place	beside	forward
left	inside	beginning	second	

NUMBER

one	twelve	take	seventy	figure
two	thirteen	twin	hundred	add
three	fourteen	fifteen	twice	altogether
four	eighteen	sixteen	third	even
five	eighty	seventeen	second	odd
six	ninety	nineteen	fourth	count
seven	once	twenty	fifth	couple
eight	first	thirty	sixth	multiply
nine	eighth	forty	seventh	check
ten	number	fifty	ninth	share
eleven	sum	sixty	tenth	mistake

MONEY

buy	stamp	cheque	cost	grocer
sell	note	save	silver	greengrocer
spend	coin	pay	copper	poor
shop	earn	bank	price	salary
money	worth	bought	charge	change
	cash	dear	free	
penny	ten new pence	fifty new pence	one pound	

GENERAL

like	cold	red	fill	except
just	colour	blue	new	guess
about	wrong	green	reckon	alone
sort	hot	black	question	answer
score	each	white	sole	level
scale	none	orange	rough	plain
belong	sharp	brown	collect	copy
pattern	blunt	yellow	ounce	instead
nearly	shiny	pink	smooth	join
only	away	find	dull	lose
nothing	best	flat	missing	group
	better	every	chance	

Care must also be taken to ensure that comparative and superlative adjectives are introduced—i.e. bigger, biggest, longer, longest. Some words have more than one meaning and will need to be introduced in more than one situation. Practice must also be given in using phrases—e.g. 'one more than', 'nearly full', 'half empty'.

LANGUAGE AND SIMPLE CONCEPT FORMATION

Developing an initial number vocabulary is dependent upon the child's own actions. The teacher's job is to provide materials and apparatus which can be seen, touched, handled and manipulated in various ways. The child's own physical movements are also important in determining ideas about the world around as for example, space, weight, distance and rhythm.

Within the classroom a range of apparatus can be built up to extend the child's knowledge and to develop the appropriate language which he can use to think and to express his impressions. The present writer with the full co-operation of two colleagues* developed a series of assignments for a dull group of children in an E.S.N. day school. Twenty children between the ages of eleven and fifteen years were assessed as displaying a severe lack of number sense. Although many of the children were borderline ineducable, some were assessed as having I.Q's in the 60–70 range on the Stanford-Binet. Additional handicaps were evident—slight spasticity, partial sight, epilepsy, speech defects and maladjustment such as to suggest a high percentage of brain injured children. The group could hardly be claimed to be typical of many slow learners.

Nevertheless the approach and the activities may have significance for younger children and others with severe disability in number.

The programme had four major aims.
1. To promote number vocabulary.
2. To provide a precursor to the development of Piagetian concepts.
3. To lead up to the introduction of structural apparatus.
4. To develop activities which children could follow with the minimum of supervision and thereby free teachers for observation, individual help and essential discussion.

Apparatus was assembled from a number of sources. Hardware stores were combed for curtain rings of various sizes, nails, screws and other items which offered opportunities for sorting and grading. Additional items were made in the woodwork room, e.g. model wooden staircase, and ladder, giant series of rods (one to six feet in length), a series of cubes,

* With acknowledgements to Ian Raison and Stuart Sanders, Ashgate Croft School, Chesterfield.

houses of different sizes with separate matching roofs. Initially sense training apparatus was omitted where this was self-corrective and not easily observed in use. Materials from educational suppliers which could be classified by size, shape or colour were introduced (e.g. 100 plastic toys—approx. 50p. from E. J. Arnold).

The apparatus was arranged round the room on shelves and cupboard tops to allow ready access and choice for the children. The arrangement was such as to provide a group of activities with varied apparatus but with a common concept. Children were thus able to sort and grade items by colour, size, shape, or orientation. Seriation was accomplished with a variety of media, i.e. sticks, ribbons, rope of varying lengths, cubes, circles and shapes of increasing size. One-for-one correspondence was tackled through matching plastic spoons and eggcups, small wooden garages and cars, etc.

Children were free to select activities and a card (listing the number given to each item) could be marked by the teacher. A glance revealed which activities had been repeated and where a related series had been well practised. This left the teacher free for the vital role of observing and questioning individuals. From simple beginnings, asking 'what have you been doing?' questions led to 'which is the longest, shortest, etc.'. Other simple dodges, carried out while a child closed his eyes, involved removing part of a series, or reversing an arrangement. Responses indicated speed and quality of understanding.

Gradually work cards were introduced which introduced a limited vocabulary—'make one like this', 'find two more like this', 'put a longer rod under this'. To add interest to the lessons and to aid transfer, the physical movements of children were used to illustrate points. Grouping, comparing sizes, moving up and down stairs—(one more, first step etc.), running races, setting out the dining hall—large chairs for large tables, matching cutlery to places, were all exploited.

Activities of this type present opportunities for children to assimilate simple concepts at their own rate, they give the teacher a chance to see first if a child can respond to number language by manipulating objects and secondly if he can use vocabulary to describe qualities and quantities.

Vocabulary development need not be limited to work with apparatus. Story telling could be used to advantage. Finding suitable stories, poems or jingles for older children is difficult. 'Goldilocks and the Three Bears' is no longer suitable, but is an example of the repetitive introduction of comparative terms. Children's reading books are singularly devoid of number words. Teachers may be forced to make up their own stories. Further practice can be given if a teacher memorises a list of words and consciously introduces them into daily conversation. Studying the list of number vocabulary shows that many words have alternative meanings which are more frequently used and probably more easily understood. These words can be introduced to explain more difficult terms. The introduction of the written word can be both an aid to learning and a progression. Labelling objects in classrooms is a common feature of early stages in the teaching of reading. A welcome change would be to see the flash card 'door' removed and 'high' and 'wide' substituted with appropriate guide lines. A further aid to reading number words can now be seen in the belated production of number books with simple vocabulary and pictures.

Some recent publications which are worth inspection are:

Gale, D. H., *Number Readiness*. Four books and two workbooks, Hulton Press.

Lund, P., *Getting Ready for Mathematics*. Nelson.

McNally, J. and Murray, W., *Words for Number*. Four books in the 'Ladybird' series. Wills & Hepworth.

Coates, D. and McDonald, J., *Number Cards*. Methuen.

Randell, B. and McDonald, J., *Number-Story Caption Books*. Methuen.

PIAGET AND NUMBER READINESS

Little reference has been made to the contribution towards understanding the development of children's concepts attributed to Professor Jean Piaget and his colleagues. Yet his findings have been described as being of monumental importance in revealing stages in children's thinking. The present writer considers that it is impossible to interpret the massive writings of Piaget meaningfully in a few brief pages. The present position regarding confirmatory investigations specifically related to slow learners still leaves the onus on individual teachers to examine the relevance of his findings in relation to their own particular pupils.

Considerable help in interpreting Piaget's book *The Child's Conception of Number* (Routledge and Kegan Paul, 1962) can be gained by reading:

Churchill, E. M., *Counting and measuring*. Routledge & Kegan Paul, 1961.

Isaacs, Nathan, *New Light on Children's ideas of Number*. E.S.A., 1960.

Lawrence, E., *et al.*, *Some aspects of Piaget's work*. National Froebel Foundation, 1955.

Lovell, K., *The growth of basic mathematical and scientific concepts in children*. U.L.P., 1961.

Bunt, L. N. A., *The development of the ideas of number and quantity according to Piaget*. Wotters, Groningen, Djakarta.

2. DEVELOPING ARITHMETICAL SKILLS

This stage has been defined earlier as the time for the acquisition of general number knowledge, for a thorough grounding in a minimum programme of arithmetical skills and for strengthening awareness of social number usage. As this stage bears a closer affinity to traditional, mechanical arithmetic many teachers are happier teaching at this level and consequently it is easy to prolong the period unnecessarily.

A MINIMUM PROGRAMME OF ARITHMETIC

A crucial consideration is the recognition of a minimum programme for the development of arithmetical skills. A number of writers have outlined ideas on this theme and much of the impetus for drawing up these programmes comes from investigations into adult usage of arithmetic. The results of three surveys suggest that adults make only a very limited use of arithmetic and accordingly many of the processes learned at school have little value in later life.

ADULT USAGE OF ARITHMETIC

An early American study by Wilson[7] in 1919, examined problems which were met by over four thousand adults during a fortnight. He discovered that:

1. 83% of the problems dealt with buying and selling goods.
2. 11% involved the use of money in other ways.
3. 6% dealt with quantitative measurements.
4. Addition and multiplication were the main processes used.
5. There was some use of common fractions, and bills had to be made out or understood.

Surprisingly few other studies had been reported until Moore[8] realised that an out-of-date American survey might have little relevance to our problems. Accordingly he set out to examine the personal, social and business usage of arithmetic in a sample of eighty-eight men and women aged twenty-five to sixty years. Moore noted the following:

Out of a total of 2,837 problems encountered by eighty-eight adults in seven days, 1,512 problems were concerned with money—of which 1,208 involved only shillings and pence. 291 problems with £.s.d. were mainly (a) solved by addition or subtraction and (b) performed mentally. Other problems involving number made most use of addition, followed by subtraction, multiplication and to a lesser extent, division. Only 6% of all problems involved capacity, linear measurement and fractions (some use of logarithms and square roots were reported by three technical men). Fractions most used were halves, quarters and eighths.

There was a remarkable measure of agreement between Moore's small British survey and the American findings over twenty-five years earlier, although Moore[2] has since wisely observed that further changes can take place even in a decade and factors like television, high pressure advertising and economic facts presented in daily papers may make fresh demands on adults.

A further study by Thompson[9] was directly concerned with the use of arithmetic by E.S.N. boys of fourteen years of age and over, many of whom had left a special school for employment, several being married. Again, significantly, the use of money in buying goods and paying for services appeared of vital importance and accounted for 88% of problems met. It was also noted that:

(a) Most problems were oral. Exceptions were a very simple form of budgeting and the completion of time sheets.

(b) Number work was restricted to reading and understanding numbers and the use of addition and counting.

(c) Simple measuring instruments were used occasionally, mainly in the home, and only addition of length was required.

(d) Ability to tell the time was necessary and some needed to interpret timetables.

(e) The language of number was frequently required.

(f) Some general items such as Rent, Rates, Insurance and Hire Purchase were met without thoroughly being understood.

THE FUTILITY OF EXTENSIVE ARITHMETIC SCHEMES

Two or three studies might be considered as insufficient evidence to persuade teachers to scrap many cherished schemes and countless textbooks. However, common sense and a little reflection should convince us that this is one of those cases where very little research is needed to support truths which are already self evident.

Teachers of slow learners might conclude that not only is a drastic re-thinking overdue in primary and secondary schemes but that the consequent reduction in the arithmetic curriculum comes very near to providing a suitable programme for the less able.

A total of all the elements of the minimum programmes from a number of writers still provides a very limited scheme.

1. Notation and recognition of numbers to 100.
2. Number facts to 20 (+, −, ×) (mainly oral).
3. Addition and subtraction to 100 (mainly oral).
4. Money to £20 (written work using decimal currency).
5. Mental addition of money to 10 new pence, then 50 n.p. and £1.
6. Telling the time to nearest five minutes. If possible extend to nearest minute (an awareness of seconds).
7. Measurement in yards, feet, inches (metre, centimetre, millimetre).
8. Weight—mainly 1 lb., $\frac{1}{2}$ lb., $\frac{1}{4}$ lb. Awareness of ounces (kilogram, gram, 500 g., 200 g., 100 g., 50 g.).
9. Measurement with rulers to $\frac{1}{8}$ inch. Use of tape measure for yards (metres, centimetres, millimetres).
10. Awareness of values of tons, cwts., gallons and pints (kilograms, litres).
11. Familiarity with simple percentages, graphs, histograms, simple accounts, miles, m.p.h., m.p.g., the calendar (kilometre).

N.B.   Items 7 to 11 will be affected by changes to the metric system. From 1970 it seems likely that both systems of measures will need to run side by side for some time.

Much of the work should be mental and closely linked to practical situations. Some written work may be necessary but is probably best limited to addition and subtraction of £.s.d. to £20 and number to 100, and the recording of associated problems.

A realistic minimum programme should be within the grasp of most slow learners.

For a limited arithmetic syllabus to be most valuable several criteria need to be satisfied:

1. Children need to understand what they are doing.
2. They must be led to see the relationships between numbers and between the arithmetical processes.
3. The acquisition of basic number bonds and the four rules should be related to real-life situations.
4. Children may be guided to discover some facts themselves.

5. Frequent recourse to estimation needs to be encouraged.

6. The ability to check their own answers should be developed.

LINKS WITH OTHER SUBJECTS

Learning is more likely to be effective if it can be linked to an obvious and immediate need. Slow learners find it is difficult to sustain motivation for long term goals. It is advantageous therefore to consider ways and means of emphasising the arithmetical content of other lessons. Indeed many hardly need emphasis and specialist teachers should be particularly conscious of the contribution they can make. They should also maintain strong links with the class teacher who can adjust his work to take advantage of appropriate practical activities in the specialist subjects by preparation and revision.

Unfortunately it was common only a few years ago to find many cases cited of woodwork or domestic science teachers who did not expect, or relish, having to teach measuring or weighing. In fact these are precisely the situations where children can see the need for such skills and usually the real materials and tools are available for use. Woodwork and housecraft are not the only subjects which use mathematical terms. Art, for example, makes use of pattern and problems of size and shape come into painting and into the selection of appropriate materials. The distribution and collection of paper and paint, mixing paint, familiarity with colours and textures are all important. An awareness of subsidiary benefits in art lessons need not destroy informality, nor detract from its therapeutic, creative and expressive functions. Model making and craft work have obvious opportunities for discussion introducing appropriate mathematical terms.

TIME, MONEY AND NUMBER

The minimum arithmetic programme largely emphasises the teaching of time, money and number. It has already been stressed that it is a fairly simple matter to teach the rudiments of these topics but fail to impart understanding or transfer of skills to other situations. An outstanding example is in the teaching of time. Children can be taught to tell the time from a clock or watch by careful teaching. Beginning with the hours, then half and quarter hours, children soon reach the point of telling the time to within five minutes with little difficulty. This is particularly so if teaching is carried out systematically and use is made of the teaching apparatus which is readily obtainable (see list at the end of the section on Time). What is more difficult is to help children to get some idea of the passage of time or to anticipate and plan events where time is a factor. For example, John, aged fifteen years, could tell the time accurately from his own wrist watch. He could not cope with any of the following problems. 'I am busy now, come back in ten minutes.' 'If your mother expects you home at six o'clock, what time must you leave the football match?' 'How long have you been at this school?' 'What is the date of your birthday?'

Similar arguments could be advanced for money and number. A reasonable procedure seems to call for teaching along a broad front—so that time and simple work with money, should be taught alongside basic number work. Occasional projects might well include all aspects and some familiarity with weights and measures may be included. Any attempt to teach one aspect for a long period to the neglect of others is likely to produce a situation akin to the old rigid arithmetic syllabus.

TIME

Calendar work and telling the time should be part of the daily routine. Here, there is much to be said for some 'old-fashioned' school practices where every piece of work was automatically headed with the date. Perhaps 'routine' is the wrong word to apply to a system whereby we want children to become 'time-conscious'. It is for the teacher to acquire the habit of some daily reference to dates and times but, by varying questions, to encourage thinking and the crystallisation of experience. So, it is good practice to see that the date is written in various forms on different occasions and to help children to become familiar with (a) Wednesday, 6th March (b) 6th March, 1969, or (c) 6/3/69. Similarly a useful idea is to demand that children write down the time when they start a piece of work and again when it is finished. Not only will they become familiar with various forms of writing down the time but discussion on the length of time to complete the task ought to follow. Comparisons between time taken over different tasks may be made.

Far too many classrooms still lack a large clock. More than one would seem to be essential and an occasional 'exhibition' of clocks can arouse interest. The particular merits of children seeing or discovering the many varied ways of marking out clock faces are important. A stopwatch is also a useful piece of equipment in school. Activities with children running or walking round the school and both timing and guessing the passage of time are worth trying. Discussions based on common experiences using travel to school, lengths of T.V. programmes, and items from the news should all feature in trying to encourage the concept of time.

APPARATUS FOR TEACHING TIME

Leedham, J. F., *Telling the Time* (100 questions). E.S.A.

Ferrier, W. M., *Telling the Time* (sixty cards in five sets from *Real Life Number Scheme*). E. J. Arnold.

Hartnell, C. A., *Telling the Time*. Programmes from Weighbell Ltd., 27 Ridley Place, Newcastle-upon-Tyne 1. Weighbell teaching machine from E.S.L. (Bristol) Ltd., Mark Lane, Bristol 1.

Noel, J., *What's the Time*. Cards and work sheets, Philip & Tacey Ltd.

Nicholls, R. H. and Howarth, H., *Working with Time*. Three workbooks. Basil Blackwell.

MONEY

Ability to handle money varies enormously between different children in special schools. There are those who have part-time jobs and can discriminate between the rate for one job as opposed to another. They can be generous within sensible limits and may save money with a long-term goal. At the other extreme there are children who cannot spend sixpence on sweets or biscuits and anticipate the change.

Most teachers' schemes for practical arithmetic include some form of classroom shop. The value of many of these shopping activities must be open to question for it is evident that numbers of slow learners who have passed through several classes with 'shops' have gained little or nothing from the experience. Teachers are aware of some of the difficulties in running a shop. One frequent question is whether to retain the correct prices of goods or to adjust them to make transactions simpler. Real coins are more frequently used and even L.E.A.s encourage this practice. Now that the cost of plastic or cardboard coins exceeds the value of copper coins it is probably more sensible to use the real thing. Some still fear the temptation and risk of theft. This probably has to be faced and overcome. The use of trays designed to hold £5 in change helps to lessen the risk of loss by making for easy checking. The provision of small shopping lists or bills (printed or duplicated in school) has helped to guide the shopping activity from a purely play activity to a more directed learning activity. Yet, in spite of some modifications some dull children still seem to find the simplest money transaction difficult.

Here is another topic which would repay investigation. Perhaps even closer supervision of classroom shops is required. Observation by the teacher might be revealing. Probably many faulty learning situations can be surmised. Is this an activity which is carried on without much trouble, allowing the teacher to deal with other problems? If this is so, perhaps certain children are not receiving the guidance and questioning which the teacher should provide. Are the more able children dominating the shop and short-circuiting the 'thought-processes' of weaker members of the class who passively receive goods and change?

Running a real shop with children as shopkeepers, selling

sweets, biscuits and minerals at break and lunch-times has been successful in some schools. Change, daily and weekly totals, and banking are valuable exercises. The opposition of school dentists and some L.E.A.s are often quoted. Alternatives—selling apples and fruit, pose real problems at different seasons. Contact with a friendly wholesaler may make this a practical proposition.

There appears to be a very good case for providing more structured practical activities involving money. A scheme must be worked out which involves small carefully graded steps, with attention at various points to concepts which prove difficult for certain children. There are many ideas to be presented, each with associated difficulties.

1.   The notion of a monetary system with coins of increasing value, not always increasing in size. The recognition of coins.

2.   Recognition of written prices—price tickets. 'Reading' a price ticket and remembering the cost of an article. Comparing prices of two articles. Which one costs more?

3.   The concept of change. An article costs so much. Can it be bought with ten new pence? If so, will there be any change?

Simple work with coins may depend on a grasp of many of these notions. Thus learning that articles do not always cost an exact coin and that change is needed precedes questions about how much change.

There is no evidence to confirm that shop-play is a complete waste of time for many children appear to benefit from the activity, yet it may be as well to bear in mind the possibility that some children may only become confused by it. The social aspect plus buying, selling, weighing and even measuring are probably too complex at the outset for dull children. Where these comments seem applicable teachers will not be slow to devise methods of preparing a child for the more complex situation. Some ideas may be devised on the lines of activities outlined in the Preparatory Stage—e.g. sorting and grading— with coins, priced articles, price tickets, bus tickets, etc. Coins can be graded into a series according to value. Goods may be dealt with similarly or grouped, e.g. all articles costing less than five new pence, those costing between five and ten new pence. The permutations of such activities can be increased in accordance with the degree of practice which individual children need.

At this stage there is no harm in more able children recording the prices of goods, or doing simple shopping sums. There is, however, much to be said for encouraging them to look around and find out the costs of common goods and services. The spirit of enquiry and the habit of questioning are good preparation for later work in social arithmetic. The necessary arithmetic can probably wait and will be learned best in association with a social problem.

NUMBER

From the results of the investigations quoted earlier (Moore, 1956, Thompson, 1962) it is clear that the number requirements of adults are very limited. Some counting is required, the processes of addition and subtraction serve the needs of many and some ability to read and understand numbers seems vital. Extensive use of concrete material is essential and a careful selection should be made from the catalogues of the appropriate educational suppliers. Items must be bought to satisfy a particular need. In conjunction with varied material there seems to be considerable justification for making use of structural apparatus.

STRUCTURAL APPARATUS

Within the suggested limits there still appears to be a place for learning the basic number bonds and the arithmetical processes of addition and subtraction (possibly multiplication and division for brighter pupils). Experience suggests that some type of structural apparatus can be of value to slow learners. Many of these youngsters appear to have failed to grasp number concepts when presented with a multiplicity of number experiences through the motivational activity methods which we associate with infant schools. Structural apparatus seems to offer an opportunity for the teacher to focus their attention on important aspects of number through the notion of measuring rather than counting. It can be used to show clearly some of the essential laws of arithmetic ($a + b = b + a$) and the relationship between subtraction and addition. It is particularly valuable to the teacher demonstrating tens and units. A limited syllabus leads one to feel that a thorough mastery of simple number work is possible and using structural apparatus increases the chances of success.

As its use is still not widespread it has a more sophisticated appeal than a return to counters or shells.

There is a bewildering choice of apparatus on the market such as Avon, Colour Factor, Cuisenaire, Montessori apparatus, Stern, Structa, Tillich bricks, Unifix and Venture. Accordingly, suppliers are listed at the end of this section and a chart is included to make some simple comparisons possible at a glance. Teachers or even children can make their own apparatus using cards or strips of plywood. Some interesting variations, constructed in Haworth County Primary School, Keighley, were illustrated and reported by the headmaster, P. Wilding.[10] One is a bead bar (different numbers of wooden beads mounted on stiff wire) and another is an attractive set of small wooden ladders (various lengths with appropriate numbers of rungs).

Few attempts have been made to evaluate the use of structural apparatus with slow learners. This may be partly due to the difficulty of finding schools which are using the materials consistently in several classes. No doubt some promising experiments have foundered due to staff changes. The departure of a headteacher or an enthusiastic member of staff can lead to an enterprise being abandoned. Dusty sets of rods on display and unused boxes in cupboards are as much a feature in schools as is apparatus in active use. Attempting to investigate the merits of structural apparatus as used with normal children has proved fruitless. J. D. Williams[11] reports that many teachers depart from the proper use of the material, particularly when faced with difficulty, through not fully understanding its theoretical basis, and gradually return to their old methods. He has been led to examine this phenomena which he has aptly described as 'Method Reversion'.

Observation supports the view that structural apparatus has been used very badly at times, and it has become clear that it can be used by children in such a mechanical fashion that many of its benefits are squandered. The need to train teachers in the proper use of any chosen apparatus becomes paramount. Arguments about personal preferences for particular apparatus usually centre on questions of size, colour and the presence or absence of markings. The writer would question the advantages claimed for apparatus which posits 'colour families' as aids to seeing number relationships like 3, 6, 9, or 2, 4, 8. (This does not upset the other claims for the use of Cuisenaire or Colour Factor rods.) Others suggest that small or clumsy children find small rods (and the assembly of Unifix) hard to manage. The use of a box lid or small square of plywood edged with beading, seems to counter this objection by (a) limiting the tendency of small rods to slide about, and (b) providing a firm edge to keep one end of rods in alignment.

Serious debate seems to be about markings. Unmarked rods appeal to the writer because they help children to learn processes algebraically, i.e. $a + b = c$, or, as is recommended, by using initial letters of colours $r + g = y$ (red and green is the same as yellow). This seems the right way to begin for it opens the way to an understanding of arithmetical laws before counting is introduced—when processes can be obscured or neglected. The absence of markings is also directly helpful for children who habitually resort to finger counting and particularly those who are also inaccurate in this pursuit.

Having considered these points there still remains a strong possibility that more than one type of apparatus may be used to advantage in a school. One set might be used to ensure continuity of learning and another might well act as a safeguard against the danger of over-reliance and undue association of concepts with particular rods or colours. This is another instance where we desperately need guidance from teachers willing to experiment consistently over a period of time.

Teachers contemplating using particular apparatus would be well advised to study the appropriate manuals and further guidance can be gained from numerous articles which have appeared from time to time in the journals—*Teaching Arithmetic* (1963 to date) and in *Mathematics Teaching* (1961 to date). Careful reading from these sources reveals that some apparatus has special merits for certain stages of arithmetic and other structural material may suit particular children. For example, the Unifix (plastic interlocking 'bricks') can be composed out of, or decomposed into, smaller units, and this allows for a great variety of configurations, and for many kinds of counting activities which may be related to real life situations. The Avon apparatus is particularly suitable for learning about odd and even numbers. Cuisenaire and Colour Factor are both sets of unmarked rods with the attendant advantages already outlined above, because no particular value need be assigned to a rod, also, if needed—fractions (and decimals) can be introduced.

When structural apparatus is in constant use it is advisable to seek frequent opportunities to relate the use of the rods to other practical activities, or to use the structures when established to interpret the environment. So, for example, instead of writing a sum a child would describe the number of boys and girls in the class, and the total, using rods. Standing rods on end, or placing them in a simple frame can produce histograms to depict various school activities with a number content, e.g. attendance, milk numbers, pocket money, etc.

3. SOCIAL MATHEMATICS

Social adequacy has been consistently put forward as a major factor in the life success of slow learners. The mathematical components for social competence have been recognised, being determined in part by investigation, partly by intuition and anticipation of social change.

Therefore, in contrast to the previous stage, with an accent on restriction of computation, this final stage is open ended and its boundaries are marked only by the imagination of teachers

Apparatus	Basic Pieces	Containing and Measuring Material	Number Tracks
AVON ... ... (James Galt Ltd., Brookfield Road, Cheadle, Cheshire)	Flat pieces, 2 units wide, bearing one dot per unit 1–10	Number Tray	Number Channels to 20 and 100
COLOUR-FACTOR ... ... (Colour-Factor Ltd., 72 London Street, Reading, Berks.)	Unmarked coloured blocks 1–12		
CUISENAIRE ... ... (Cuisenaire Co., 40 Silver Street, Reading, Berks.)	Unmarked coloured rods 1–10		
DIENES M.A.B. ... ... (E.S.A., Harlow, Essex)	Grooved wooden blocks to bases 3,4,5,6 and 10		
MATHEMATICS DISCOVERY MATERIAL ... (Taskmaster Ltd., Leicester)	Red strips with engraved white lines. 1–10 inch tablets		
MONTESSORI ... ... (M. Montessori Training Org., 26 Lyndhurst Gardens, London, N.W.3)	Large marked blocks 1–10 and small bars of beads 1–10		
POLEIDOBLOCS ... ... (E.S.A.)	Mathematical shapes		
STERN ... ... (E.S.A.)	Larged scored blocks 1–10	Counting Board, Twenty Tray, Arith. Board, Number Cases	1–100 Track
STRUCTA ... ... (J. Galt)	Interlocking cylindrical pegs. Vertical number pegs. 1–10	20–Base	Bases can be joined
TILLICH'S BRICKS ... (E. J. Arnold, Leeds)	Plain or scored number sticks 1–10		
UNIFIX ... ... (Philip & Tacey Ltd., Fulham High Street, London S.W.6)	Interlocking cubes—bars 1–10	1–10 Channel Stair 1–10 Value Boats 10 x 10 No. Tray	1–20 Notation Ladder and 1–10 Track. 100– Track
VENTURE ... ... (Taskmaster Ltd.)	Scored number rods 1–12		Tracks to 10, 12, 20, 36

Reproduced by kind permission of the author, P. C. Johns. *Choosing a Structural Apparatus*, unpublished dissertation, Institute of Education, University of Nottingham.

Positional Notation Material	Number Boards, Charts, etc.	Number Pattern Material	Material Illustrating Powers	Teachers' Manual	Pupils Books
Notation Tray—9 tens and 9 units		Patterns on number pieces		Very brief Leaflet	
				Comprehensive	Two series with teachers' handbooks
				Comprehensive	Series of 7 books—1 about basic number
			Grooved wooden blocks to bases 3, 4, 5, 6 and 10	Comprehensive	Individual work cards
				None available	
Abacus	Addition Chart. Multiplication and Divsn. Brds.	Peg Board and Board with counters	Interlocking bead bars to base 10	Comprehensive	
				Manual for Infant Teachers & Part I for Junior Schools	
Dual Board— 10 tens, 9 units. 1–10 St. No. Game		1–10 Pattern Boards	Grooved blocks to base 10	Comprehensive	Workbooks, with teachers' handbooks
Hundreds, Tens and Units Card	Multiplication Chart 100 Chart	100 and 400 Peg Board		Brief Pamphlet	
			Grooved blocks to base 2, 3, 4, 5 and 10	None available	
1 Tens and Units, 5 Tens & Units and Hundred, Tens & Units Tray	Century Brd. Building to 100 Tray	1–10 Pattern Boards		Fairly Comprehensive	
		100 and 144 squared trays		Brief Pamphlet	

and the curiosity and industry of children. Due to the scope of a comprehensive programme of social mathematics the work cannot be left to the last few months of school life. The success of the scheme depends on the attitudes and habits of work which have been developed. Involvement in a great deal of practical work, especially with time and money, paves the way to recording experiences as opposed to merely copying sums. Attitudes of enquiry, habits of observation and a growth of number consciousness cannot be cultivated overnight, yet are essential to the outgoing nature of a social mathematics scheme.

SOCIAL ARITHMETIC CONTENT

Research, which was quoted earlier to support the case for a minimum programme in arithmetical computation, also supplied clues to the social situations linked to arithmetical usage.

Areas of study, under which more detailed topics can be introduced, can broadly be classified under headings of Home, School, Leisure, Employment and ultimately Citizenship or Community Living. Subsidiary groupings may involve items such as budgeting, shopping, time, clothing, wages, subscriptions, contributions, etc. Some of these topics can be viewed 'horizontally' as extending across the major headings. For example, the relevance of time, and appropriate calculations can be studies under Home, School, Leisure or Employment. Train and bus times and timetables enter into leisure pursuits, holidays and going to work. Topics can also be considered 'vertically' as increasing in difficulty and interest level appropriate to various ages. Thus, budgeting for younger children may involve pocket money, spending and saving, payments for bus fares, cinemas, comics, etc. Older children with larger amounts to spend may have part-time jobs on newspaper rounds, odd jobs on farms, etc. Increased spending power and savings for long-term goals can form topics for discussion as will useful comparisons between earnings, rates per hour, tips, and acceptance of growing responsibility to a degree of self sufficiency through small purchases of clothes, presents or the maintenance of a bicycle.

Approaching school-leaving, budgeting will be more closely concerned with (*a*) anticipated wages for the young worker, clothing (including appropriate clothing where necessary for the job—i.e. donkey jacket, overalls, boots), dinners, travelling expenses, union dues, 'keep' or 'digs', savings, personal insurance, miscellaneous items—sweets, cigarettes, entertainment. Discussions with examples from older brothers and sisters, simulated examples of various budgets will encourage the sorting out of priorities into 'needs' and 'wants'. Former pupils returning to school are often willing informants not only regarding wages and conditions but also how they spend their money. Activities of this kind make a greater impact than a teacher and usually lead to a lively and sensible discussion.

Further ideas are well developed in Thomson's article and the special needs of children in residential schools are considered. His approach is descriptive but valuable. Moore[2] tabulates clearly a scheme which lists topics considered appropriate for children in the age ranges (A) 10–12 years, (B) 12–14 years (C) 14–16 years.

For older children some distinctions are made between topics suitable for boys or girls separately. Examples from each section are as follows:

Section A (10–12 years) *Recreational*	Section B (12–14 years) *Sport and Leisure*	Section C (14–16 years) *Travel*
Going to the Cinema	Darts and table tennis scores	Holiday Travel
Swimming baths	Football league tables	Train timetables
Football and sport	Visit to football match	Running a motor cycle
Fairground visit	Cricket scores	Car Licences
Books, magazines, comics	Scout and Guide activities	Road Tax
	Purchasing records	Insurance
		Petrol consumption
		Speed and speed limits

SUITABLE TEXTBOOKS

Few suitable textbooks are produced specifically for slow

learners. In some cases the older products display an excessive emphasis on useless computation and the problems are unrelated to real life. All arithmetic books create difficulties for the child of limited reading ability. One good series is specifically designed for older slow learners and carries a social arithmetic theme. Used judiciously with practical work, these books have merit. The series is entitled *Arithmetic at Work* by N. A. Moore and A. A. Williams (Oxford University Press).

The scheme is progressive and consists of three series of booklets. Vocabulary control is exercised and the use of individual work assignments is linked to a discussion approach to social problems.

'*A*' *Series*.   Reading level $7\frac{1}{2}$ years.   Age levels 10–12 years.
    A.1   Rodway Road.   A.2   High Park School.
    A.3   Half Term Holiday. A.4   Shopping in Branton.
         16 pages.   Set of 4 books—6s. 6d.
'*B*' *Series*.   Reading level $7\frac{1}{2}$–$8\frac{1}{2}$ years.   Age levels 11–14 years.
    B.1   Spare Time activities   B.2   The weekend.
    B.3   Going shopping again. B.4   Around the house.
         16 pages.   Set of 4 books—6s. 6d.
'*C*' *Series*. Reading level approx. 9 years. Age levels 14–16 years.
C.1 Money Matters. C.2 Going to work. C.3 Keeping House
         32 pages.   6s. per book.

Another recent series is the *Outward Bound Arithmetic* by E. Scriven and D. D. Abraham (Pergamon). The books are designed for below-average pupils in the eleven to fifteen age groups, and take the view that social necessity is a fundamental aim. An indication of the coverage given may be gained from the titles:

Red Series. Book 1a. Sport and Leisure; Myself; Money; School. Book 1b. Time; Travel; Post Office. Book 1c. Garden; Shopping; Jobs at home; Payments.

Blue Series. Book 2a. Sport and Leisure; Myself; Pocket Money; School. Book 2b. Garden; Shopping; Jobs at Home; Heat and Light; Rent and Easy Payments. Book 2c. Time; Travel; The Post Office; Weather and Compass Points.

MEANS AND METHODS

A programme of social arithmetic demands an almost complete reversal of traditional procedures. Formerly, following instruction in computation, attempts were made to devise problems which would give practice in the mechanical processes. Our concern should be to discover real problems which are either within the children's experience or close enough to make them meaningful. The question of calculation must come last. Here, too, there is no necessity to establish a right and a wrong way of solving a problem. Much the best procedure is to permit the children to find their own solutions and to use these as a basis for discussion and comparison. Sometimes it may be worth while to draw attention to an 'official' method or to demonstrate a short cut. In most cases different methods, where effective, should be given equal praise. A recent example, noted in a special school, concerned a problem with four widths of 54 in. Different solutions were proffered by four children: (a) addition, $54 + 54 + 54 + 54$; (b) 54 doubled, 108 doubled again; (c) 50×4 and then add 4×4's; (d) 54×4. The comparison of methods seemed to hold the interest of the children.

Fact finding by the children is essential. Many children seem totally unaware of arithmetical data about their own families and homes. Ages of parents, brothers, sisters, and relatives should be known. Parents' occupations and earnings might be sought—without causing offence. Some idea of the mother's weekly household bills and a breakdown of expenses can be discovered. Then to find out about rents, rates, household repairs, etc. Beginning with the home creates a meaningful basis for extending a survey to look at the costs of new council houses, flats, mortgages and the expenses of living in digs, hostels or 'bedsitters'.

A great deal of other work demands that we move out of school. Window shopping, visits to furniture showrooms at slack periods, cafes, big stores, and auctions both of second-hand furniture and at cattle markets, broaden experience and provide valuable material for discussion back at school.

As a substitute for first-hand experience, or by way of recapitulation, simulated situations can be presented by the teacher for children to dramatise. A classroom shop is the familiar technique, a cafe could be another, and there are endless permutations of situations whereby children can be placed in situations calling for ability to deal with incorrect change or the return of faulty goods.

Over a period of time teachers will see the need for building up a stock of charts, assignment cards, forms (and duplicated replicas of forms). Projects or units of experience offer opportunities for children to collect and collate information according to their individual capabilities. The resultant display forms a basis for individual lecturettes and discussion which should draw together the findings and present a complete picture to the whole group. The special opportunities created by lessons in the housecraft, woodwork and craft rooms have already been mentioned. Measurement, weighing, costing, budgeting, estimating are best learned in these practical lessons. An awareness of work already covered in the specialist rooms is necessary for the maths teacher who can use these experiences as starting points for further work.

It should be apparent that we have now become less concerned with formal training in the setting down of sums. Recording of experiences may take many forms, and charts, graphs, or histograms may often prove the most effective way of portraying discoveries. Setting down of sums neatly in column form may be appropriate where untidiness and lack of system seems to lead to confusion and error.

Throughout this section the importance of discussion and the mental and oral solution of problems has been stressed. During this last section it should be clear that the vocabulary of mathematics has increased in frequency and complexity. Although terms will need explanation, no attempts should be made to substitute 'easy' words for terms which are generally used. This will only lead to difficulties later. Words like discount, guarantee, deposit, instalments, and value must be met and interpreted. To ensure understanding and transfer to new situations, they must be introduced many times and children must begin to use them too. These words must also appear in written form. The importance we give to the revision of vocabulary should be no less than that we gave to the traditional revision of mechanical computation.

REFERENCES

1. Williams, A. A., 'Arithmetic at the Crossroads' in *Special Education*, Vol. LIII, No. IV, Winter 1964.
2. 'Mathematics for Slow Learners'. Symposium in *Remedial Education*, Vol. II, No. 1, March 1968:
    Nicholls, R. H., *Programmed Preparation for Number*.
    Bell, P., *Developing Arithmetical Skills*.
    Moore, N. A., *Teaching Social Arithmetic to Slow Learning Children*.
    Marshall, J. J., *Modern Mathematics for the Older Slow Learner*.
    Williams, A. A., *Organisation and Assessment*.
3. Nicholls, R. H., 'Programming Piaget in Practice' in *Teaching Arithmetic*, Vol. I, No. 3, Autumn 1963.
4. Burroughs, G. E. R., *A Study of the Vocabulary of Young Children*. Monograph No. 1, Institute of Education, Univ. of Birmingham, 1957.
5. Brook, J. R., 'Spontaneous Spoken Vocabulary of a Group of Severely Mentally Subnormal Children', *Brit. Jo. Disorders of Communication*, Vol. I, No. 2, 1966.
6. Mein, R. & O'Connor, N. J., 'Study of the Oral Vocabularies of Severely Subnormal Patients', *Jo. Ment. Def. Res*, No. 4, 1960.
7. Reported in Kirk, S. & Johnson, G. O., *Educating the Retarded Child*. Houghton Mifflin, Boston, 1951.
8. Moore, N. A., *A Survey of the Usage of Arithmetic in the Daily Life of Adults*. Unpublished dissertation, Inst. of Educ., Univ. of Birmingham, 1957.
9. Thompson, G. E., 'What Arithmetic shall we Teach our Educationally Subnormal Children?' in *Special Education*, Vol. LI, No. 3, 1962.
10. Wilding, P., Bancroft, C. & Scarborough, J., 'Counting in Keighley' in *Teaching Arithmetic*, Vol. I, No. 2, 1963.
11. Williams, J. D., 'Method-reversion, the Problem of Sustaining Changes in Teacher Behaviour', in *Educational Research*, Vol. 8, No. 1, 1966.

CHAPTER 9

Units of Experience

THIS chapter is concerned with the possibilities of utilising project methods with slow learners. The idea is not new to special education but it does not seem to have gained widespread acceptance. Activity methods have been variously described as projects, centres of interest, units of work or correlated activities. The present writer prefers to use the term Units of Experience. This is an American term and has filtered into this country through the writings of Ingram[1] and Kirk and Johnson[2]. Basically it has been developed with the needs of slow learners in mind. The choice of this particular term seems to offer advantages in stressing the need to provide experiences for less able pupils and in its emphasis on the unity of learning whereby artificial subject divisions are broken down and work is seen to be related to everyday life.

Even casual contact with slow learners soon reveals the paucity of their experiences. Some lack experiences due to poor home background or inadequate schooling. Others have not made the most of experiences they have had. It is common to find children who have never been to the seaside or the nearest big city. Railway stations, theatres, stores, farms, are foreign to many children from the back streets, the council estates, and rural areas. A day's outing to the seaside is the only practical acquaintance of holidays or travel for many children. Even then the fairground or the entrance to the bingo hall is all that seems to be remembered. Some do not even know the name of the resort on their return. Distance, direction and time are abstractions too profound to plumb! How can schools expect to build any reading or writing schemes on such limited experiences? Colourful and apparently interesting reading books dealing with topics such as the circus, zoo, camping, or the seaside may present unexpected difficulties to this kind of child due to their unfamiliarity with the topic and their ignorance of the associated vocabulary. Examples of deprivation of experience can be repeated many times over. E.S.N. children in special schools may be cut off from even the most simple and everyday experiences of the locality. Not trusted to go shopping or to travel on buses, they can be over-protected at home and sheltered by the educational system. Transported from the fireside and the T.V. set by special bus to a special school in an unfamiliar setting, fed and looked after conscientiously, guarded from danger, separated from neighbourhood friendships and cut off from the outside world. Is this preparation for life?

Compensatory devices such as the annual trip to the zoo, the circus, the day trip, or the weekend camp are mere palliatives for this condition. Only by good general planning over a long period of time and the careful selection of topics can a series of units of experience be devised to prepare these youngsters for citizenship.

SELECTING A UNIT

Choosing a topic for a Unit is no easy matter. A consideration of activities and experiences which are appropriate to the age and interests of the children is an obvious starting point. Discouragement sets in when the school is in a depressing neighbourhood (e.g. a featureless housing estate) and there are difficulties in arranging or paying for transport. Many teachers of dull children claim that their pupils have few interests and that these are often transient and trivial. There is some justification for such pessimism for, as already suggested, many of these children have a home background which is either overprotective or unstimulating and equally they may have been 'non-participants' in their early educational activities. Intelligent and more independently minded children seem to absorb interests at second-hand through books, films or T.V. Duller children appear unable to anticipate the enjoyment and satisfaction to be gained from activities which they have not experienced personally. Rather than inhibiting action this provides an additional reason for striving to uncover latent interests or to engage in activities which may kindle interest and enthusiasm for the first time.

The real problem is not so much one of interest but more one of sorting out priorities and discarding topics which are trivial as opposed to those which are relevant to life out of school. Thus a unit on a circus or zoo may well be interesting and entertaining for children but a teacher will see more value in topics like 'Using the Library', 'Healthy Habits' or 'Child Care'. In cold print, a teacher's choice of topic may look as dull as these titles, and this selection would hardly seem capable of engaging the interest of children. In practice it is often the way the topic gets off the ground which is important. So, one may start from some unusual school or local event or an item of topical news, which has excited comment. The way the topic is followed up may continue to breathe life into it. For example, a visit to the children's section of the local library, with a short talk from the librarian and an opportunity to browse amongst a wide and colourful selection of books is eventful for most youngsters. If this is followed by the loan of boxes of books, the establishment of a class or school library, the training of child librarians, issuing of books which can actually be taken home, and visits to printers or bookshops, then a small unit of work can be developed which will hold a great deal of interest for children.

Genuine differences can still exist between teachers' ideas about children's interests and children's real interests. Often the teacher may be misguided in her choice by thinking of desirable interests which are related to the cultural and leisure activities she has developed from her own educated, middle class background. An instance of teacher and children operating on different wavelengths is given in a recent book by Ablewhite.[3] He gives an account of a teacher's attempts to encourage children to describe things which interest them. The results are disappointing until, following an opportunity to observe the children watching men operating a pneumatic drill in the road near the school, the teacher discovered that the children had been trying to recount only those incidents which they thought appropriate to the teacher's expectations.

Teachers can always learn from children, and, by observation and through talking to children, some interest will emerge which can be used as a starting point. An alertness to seize an opportunity when children show interest is important. In the back of her mind the teacher should have some framework of areas of study to which she can relate the unexpected interest and which will guide her in planning units along most profitable lines. With older children, it is much easier to select important topics for time is short and the problems of transition from school to work are brought sharply into focus. So we see that many schools place considerable emphasis on a school leavers' programme which includes preparation for employment, attention to leisure activities, home making, budgeting, etc. Many of these are in the best tradition of project work and might well be classed as Units of Experience. There is still room for development in leavers' programmes for the possibilities are enormous and the work to be carried out can hardly be covered in the last few months of school life. So, in one sense, it could well be useful to examine all the areas of study opened up by a leavers' programme. The need to begin work at a much earlier age will be realised and can be planned for.

Goldstein[4] in a curriculum guide for American teachers, defines areas of study in terms of 'Life functions'. He envisages correlated studies being carried out under broad headings: citizenship, communicating, home and family, leisure time, management of materials and money, occupational adequacy, physical and mental health, safety, social adjustment, travel. Each of these 'life functions' is described more fully and detailed guidelines are set out for teachers to show how each major topic may be developed at primary, intermediate, and secondary levels. It seems likely that attempts to produce other curriculum guides would have much in common with this list from Illinois.

PLANNING A UNIT

As well as having an appreciation of the place of a particular Unit within the broader framework of an overall plan teachers should consider how far a particular unit will satisfy certain basic criteria. Essential aims and purposes have already been outlined, but for convenience they will be listed:

1. Is it of real and vital interest to children?
2. Will the unit create a need for the use of tool subjects— spoken and written English, reading for information and pleasure, number work or legible handwriting?
3. Is it possible to devise activities which will involve children of different attainments?
4. How many real, concrete, first-hand experiences will be involved?
5. How far will children be working together or participating with people outside school?
6. Will opportunities arise which may help to develop qualities of self-reliance, self-confidence, independence?

The value of any particular unit will increase in proportion to the extent to which these criteria can be satisfied.

Other aspects of planning are not so important. The period of time which a unit occupies is not fixed. Some units may be quite short. Others may extend over a term or a year. Some units might well reappear at different stages of a child's school career. Children at different ages may well acquire different concepts or benefit at a more advanced level when topics are repeated. For example, a topic which is centred on the home might well be suitable at various ages.

For young children it has the merit of being within their immediate experience, they may look at different types of houses and families, learn about relationships, being helpful in the home, ages, sizes, roles, occupations, interests of family members, etc. Children who are older and near to leaving school would be concerned with a different range of activities and concepts in studying the home. With increasing maturity, concern about personal relationships might lead to discussions about adolescent/adult conflicts, marriage and sex education. Young people should be more interested in practical aspects of building up a home—house purchase, rents, rates, budgeting, furniture, painting and decorating. These are only limited suggestions as the topic is capable of further development at each level.

Flexibility is required, both in the allocation of time to unit work and in the development of a topic. Some units may be brief because a teacher has seized an opportunity which came up at short notice. For instance, the delivery at school of stock, large quantities of fuel, sand, etc., might be utilised. It may well be that such an experience, briefly discussed, may serve as a common reference point in some later study.

At times it is possible to envisage more than one unit in progress. Some units lend themselves to repetitive activities (e.g. recording data, feeding animals) and extend over a long period of time. The day-to-day work is limited and larger blocks of time are required mainly in the early stages when planning or carrying out work to establish the unit (as for example the construction of huts or pens in a poultry unit). Later, lengthy periods of time may only be necessary occasionally as when data is summarised, reports are presented or the unit is completed. When a unit follows a pattern of this sort it is quite reasonable to introduce another unit alongside the first study.

TYPES OF EXPERIENCE

One of the most important points to consider in planning a Unit is the number and nature of experiences to be provided. It is not unusual to find that work is centred around an interesting topic but experiences for children are limited. Three types of experience may be isolated—the first-hand experience, second-hand experience and the experience of expression. In practice, of course, these mingle and overlap but the teacher ought to see that they are part of each unit.

First-hand experience is to be sought wherever possible whereby these youngsters can see, handle or have some contact with real things. Contact with real things means either that children must be going out of school on visits and excursions or else objects may be brought into school for children to handle or see. Direct contact with actuality is essential for slow children as they often find it difficult to imagine real things from only a picture or a description. Discounting the obvious increase, in recent years, of school travel, Duke of Edinburgh awards, and many out-of-school activities, there is still a lamentable reluctance on the part of many teachers to move out of the school into the local neighbourhood frequently. Nor are children trained and trusted sufficiently to go out in twos and threes on expeditions. To break with habit needs effort and a modicum of courage to face the prospect of taking unruly or backward children out of the security of the classroom. But more than conviction is required, for, children must be trained and visits must be planned carefully, if anything of value is to be gained from the experience. They must be prepared for the visit, to have some idea of what to look for, what questions to ask, what to bring back in the way of information or materials. No sensible teacher undertakes a school journey without trying to anticipate and plan for all kinds of eventualities. Additional benefits will accrue to children from their training out-of-school, by learning how to conduct themselves in public, on buses, in the factory, the cafe or the supermarket. Movement outside the classroom could well be introduced gradually by exploring the school, its immediate neighbourhood or taking a short bus journey.

Bringing objects into school is practicable. Some local education authorities support a school museum service which provides many exhibits for loan to individual schools. Factories, national and public enterprises often supply display materials and samples of products for schools. Children themselves, are encouraged in most schools to help in the collection of articles, products and particularly objects for a Nature Table. These things which are so commonly brought into schools are an essential part of lessons and should not be undervalued. It is surprising to find how many people are prepared to come into school to talk to children and to bring along objects related to their own special interests or hobbies. Enterprising schools can make contacts with interesting adults through scanning the local press, studying the surprisingly varied list of local organisations and clubs, or enlisting the aid of people who lecture to adults at local evening institutes.

A multiplicity of *second-hand experiences* should always be included, particularly if first-hand experiences are limited. So, pictures, stories, films, film-strips, books, tape-recordings, radio, T.V. and models are all useful. Many teachers have collected pictures over a period of years from magazines and educational publications. These are difficult to classify and catalogue but a combined effort by a school to build up a library of pictures can be a permanent asset. There has been a gradual increase in the supply of simple books of the information type and it is much easier to find reading material to go with many units. Firms specialising in the supply of wall-charts and film-strips now have a very wide range of materials. Their catalogues should be studied for film-strips may sometimes be available for hire or inspection before making a firm decision to purchase. Films and film-strips on many topics are also available either free or at a small charge from many sources.

Experience through expression is not to be overlooked. This is the outlet for children to show the impressions they have gained from first- and second-hand experiences. Every unit should give opportunities for children to summarise their experiences or express their reactions in a variety of ways. In this respect most Units offer more opportunities for oral work than are usually provided in teaching the basic subjects. Oral expression may indeed be an end in itself, to encourage conversation, correct speech, discussion, questioning and giving explanations of models or other parts of their work. Units will often also show the need for making notes, writing letters, keeping accounts, making illustrations, plans, maps, or local timetables.

Expression may also be given through a variety of media in art and craft. New materials and experiments may be called for in efforts to recreate some experience. Dramatic activities and written work of various kinds will naturally be used at appropriate points.

SOME EXAMPLES OF SUCCESSFUL UNITS

Some children are very knowledgeable if their out of school interests can only be uncovered. Animals interest most children and many have first-hand experience of caring for them. One enterprising teacher discovered that every pupil (in a very dull group) had at least one pet. Several had three or more animals. This sort of interest can readily be turned to advantage. Children can write about their own pets or give lecturettes. A collection of information books about the care of pets is relatively easy to assemble. According to the age of the children a Unit can be developed to include social, moral and vocational aspects of this topic which is clearly linked to adult interests. Work may explore the problems of keeping pets in school, training of dogs and their nuisance value in towns. Visiting speakers from a vet or P.D.S.A. are possible. Newspaper clippings will lead to the discussion of ill-treatment of animals, the R.S.P.C.A., leaving money to dog's homes; sporting animals— horse racing, dog racing and blood sports.

Some youngsters may be entering pets at shows and pedigrees, breeding, feeding costs, will be covered.

Other units could have a geographical bias looking at pets in other countries, unusual pets—snakes, monkeys, and parrots. Attention can be focused on T.V. programmes to some purpose, and hibernation, animal habits, and the life span of various animals may be studied.

Many residential special schools place a particular emphasis on animal husbandry and children rear a variety of animals. Some have poultry units or rear pigs and keeping records of feed, egg production, pig weights provides valuable, practical number work. Other schools keep more exotic animals. The associated activities of building and constructing huts, cages and pens gives purpose to practical work. This topic offers scope for continuing study, and interest can be kept high by regular visits to farms, cattle auctions, horse-riding schools and places concerned with animal products.

Two very different Units were undertaken by older pupils in an E.S.N. day school. The children made surveys of the T.V. viewing habits of the school population, and of the newspapers and magazines taken in the homes. Both studies led to a considerable amount of repetitive arithmetic and the making of charts and histograms. The results were interesting to staff and pupils alike. The T.V. census identified the numbers of T.V. sets and radios in homes. The youngsters interviewed other pupils daily and established which channels, and which programmes were most popular. Individual and class, daily and weekly viewing habits were charted. Spontaneous comment came from the children regarding the excessive number of hours that young children spent watching television. The arithmetic of time differences was quite involved and well worth while.

The following list is a brief indication of some ideas for younger children:

Farm	Postman	Holidays	Fishing
Policeman	My Home-School	Food	Road Safety
Bread	Fireman	Myself	Danger

Some of these topics could be repeated, extended or given different emphasis with older children. In addition there are:

Our Town	Houses	World of Work
Post Office	Finding Out from	Gas, Electricity and
Fire Extinguishers	Books	Water Supplies
Clothes	Weather	Local Government—
How Eyes Work	Holidays	elections
School Magazine	Games and Sports	Rates and Taxes
Budgeting	Running a Home	Child Care
Appreciating Music	'Do it Yourself'	Cycling Proficiency
	Balanced Diet	Keep Fit

REFERENCES

*1. Ingram, C. P., *Education of the Slow-Learning Child*. Ronald Press, New York, 1935.
*2. Kirk, S. A. & Johnson, G. O., *Educating the Retarded Child*. Houghton Mifflin, Boston, 1951.
 3. Ablewhite, R. C., *The Slow Reader*. Heinemann, 1967.
*4. Goldstein, H. & Seigle, M., *Curriculum Guide for Teachers of the Educable Mentally Handicapped*. Interstate Publications, Danville, Illinois, 1958.

FURTHER READING

Books marked * above and also the following:
    Holt, J., *How Children Fail*, Pitman, New York, 1964.
    Holt, J., *How Children Succeed*, Pitman, New York, 1968.
    Mackenzie, R. F., *A Question of Living*, Collins, 1963.
    Mackenzie, R. F., *Escape from the Classroom*, Collins, 1965.
    Ministry of Education, *Half Our Future*, H.M.S.O., 1963.
    Goldsmith's College Curriculum Laboratory (Univ. of London).
Reports of the Pilot Courses for Experienced Teachers.
    No. 1. *The Role of the School in a Changing Society*.
    No. 2. *The Raising of the School-leaving Age*.
    No. 3. *Education of Children under Social Handicap*.
    No. 4. 14–18: *The School and the Young School Leaver*.
    No. 5. *New Rules for the Learner*.
    Ideas – a bulletin available from the same source.

CHAPTER 10

Social Education

ONE of the main aims of special education is to help slow learners to become socially adequate. At a simple level this takes the form of social training to develop acceptable habits and to encourage attitudes which will enable children to make satisfactory social relationships. At a higher level, through social education, it is desirable to foster the growth of good citizenship, to help young people to take their place in society having some knowledge of their rights and responsibilities at work and in the community.

Social adequacy is closely bound up with personal and vocational adequacy. Many aspects of the curriculum contribute to the attainment of social competence and some facility in language, reading, writing and number can play a part in achieving these aims. Although general aims should permeate the whole curriculum it is helpful to try to isolate certain aims and to devise various activities to encourage their fulfilment. Many schools seek to further social development in a number of ways; by attention to personal relationships, through the cultivation of an informal atmosphere, by arranging social groupings for activities and by social training.

SOCIAL TRAINING

Training in simple social skills is a feature of many special schools. Beginning at the level of establishing personal good habits, children are gradually led to an awareness of the requirements of a complex society which demands such varied skills as budgeting, using the telephone and employing leisure time wisely. To date there is little evidence of consistent attempts to evaluate progress in this area.

Considerable benefits might well be obtained in guiding and training the social development of individuals if greater use were made of the Progress Assessment Charts (P.A.C.) devised by Dr. H. C. Gunzburg. There are three versions of this form and the senior form (P.A.C. 2) is particularly appropriate for slow learners in the I.Q. range 55 to 80+.

The Progress Assessment Charts of Social Development are not tests in the usual sense but are report forms which provide a visual check of progress in four main areas of social development: Self-Help, Communication, Socialisation, and Occupation. There are 120 items which sample behaviour and they are arranged systematically and graded in difficulty. The main areas are subdivided. Self-help includes items referring to table habits, mobility, toilet, washing and dressing. Communication includes language differences, number, paper and pencil work. Socialisation examines play and home activities. The Occupational sector relates to dexterity (fine finger movements) and agility (gross motor control).

The prospect of being able to assess specific strengths and weaknesses should help teachers to direct attention to those areas where competence is clearly below the average achievement levels. Recent work[1], which has led to the introduction of a Progress Evaluation Index, enables useful comparisons to be made between children of similar chronological age and intellectual level.

SOCIAL EDUCATION

A significant development in combating social inadequacy has been made by the sociologist, Richard Hauser. He is concerned to note that education places excessive emphasis on intellectual and technical 'intelligence' and largely neglects the social and creative abilities of young people. Hauser envisages 'social education' as a means of restoring confidence in less able pupils, by enabling them to acquire a sense of social responsibility and to realise that they have something of value to offer to society. Thus the concept of social training, which emphasises a minimum programme of social skills to help children to become socially acceptable, has been extended to social education, which seeks to convert children from passive spectators to active co-operators.

The following programme has been used in a day special school for E.S.N. children. A number of other special schools and remedial departments in secondary schools have successfully operated similar schemes. The writer wishes to acknowledge a considerable debt to Richard Hauser for many stimulating and exhausting hours spent in discussion, and not least for his kindness in giving permission to print a large number of his practical suggestions for a social education scheme. It is impossible to give adequate coverage to the underlying philosophy but the interested reader might profitably read *The Fraternal Society* by R. and H. Hauser[2] and can look forward to a publication dealing with the education of the socially handicapped.

SCHOOL SYLLABUS FOR SOCIAL EDUCATION

I. OBSERVATION, ACTIVATION, CRITICAL EVALUATION

Initially, the problem with backward children is to stimulate them to be more observant and later to appreciate the part they have to play in society and to come to understand how their own actions impinge on other people. The first stage of the programme is best attempted through mime, acting and a variety of games.

(*a*) *Observation and Perception* may be increased by devising activities or tests which involve children in noticing details about their friends or their environment, or by remembering various incidents. Examples of this are: asking children to describe the clothing of a child who has left the room, to name the person sitting behind them, or the colours of items of clothing they are wearing.

Children also enjoy copying the actions of another member of the class, for example, a boy knocks at the door, comes into the room, makes his way to a chair and sits down. Another pupil has to copy this action exactly.

Another form of perception test which has proved successful in a number of schools, is one involving the assessment of strangers. A visitor to the school can be used as a guinea pig for this activity and the class is encouraged to assess age, occupation and other details. A class of twelve to thirteen year old E.S.N. boys and girls, after only three attempts at this activity noticeably improved their powers of observation and assessment. They began to notice details such as footwear and soft hands which gave some clues to the type of occupation.

Observation and assessment can also be increased by simple mime and acting situations which are familiar to children. Many of these activities are already commonly used in school drama, e.g. miming people at the dinner table, mending a puncture, carrying a heavy basket, etc. This might then spill over into acting simple dialogues or social situations within the child's own experience, for example, trying to persuade a parent to buy a pet, or pleading to be allowed to stay up late to watch a television programme.

Experience shows that children enjoy this type of activity and put a lot of energy into it. Taking into account the range of ability in an E.S.N. school, it should be obvious that some children will get more out of an activity than others. To involve them all at various levels it may be necessary to allow weaker members of a group to act or mime a situation first, then, after discussion and criticism, encourage others who have more ideas to come forward and act the situation again. This may be followed up by further discussion and suggestions.

(b) *Identification*. A number of plays can be devised whereby a child can readily see a link with real life situations. Examples can include the miming of everyday incidents such as receiving visitors, serving tea, helping a small child across the road. This can be extended to include miming of emotion, anger, surprise, fear (in a dark room) etc. Further work may introduce dialogues where two children talk about a common experience such as a television programme, a football match or some school event. After some practice with simpler activities of this kind, acting of other situations where a degree of identification is necessary can be undertaken. For example, acting a parent dealing with a naughty child, or an owner of a motor cycle catching a boy fiddling with it, or an action between a mother and a child wanting pocket money.

At this stage, the class should begin to criticise each small play freely. By questioning, the teacher should explore many aspects of the situation to draw out from the children information about the emotions and feelings of the different characters in the plays.

(c) *Social Situations* involving self assertion and unforeseen situations. As children get older and they become more experienced in miming and acting simple plays, it should be possible to tackle impromptu plays where children must assert themselves in a social situation, such as acting the part of a person returning faulty goods to a shop. Further work might be undertaken by acting out unforeseen situations which are outside the children's experience but which will help them to deal with incidents which might arise when they have left school and taken up employment. A good example is in seeking accommodation, either lodgings when working away from home or holiday accommodation. Many other incidents such as accidents, emergencies, being interviewed for a job, etc. will readily come to mind.

(d) *Lectures and Discussions* to arouse social awareness. Towards the end of school life, children seem able to take advantage of lectures about community life and will take part in simple discussions on suitable topics such as smoking, the care of old people, school activities and their relevance to life, Youth Clubs or anti-social behaviour.

(e) *Useful Social Activity and Community Service.* Ultimately it is hoped that a number of pupils will be brought to the point of wanting to make a positive contribution to society and to do some form of simple social service. To do this they must become aware of the problems involved and what part they can play in helping to solve them. Outside visits must be made. Lecturers should come in to talk about the problems of people who are in need of help. The early part of the programme should have prepared children to be able to ask questions and then to see what wants doing. An example of this type of activity followed on from a talk by a Welfare Officer about old people. The pupils found out where there were Old People's Homes in their own district, whether there were any old people in their own street who were not aware of welfare facilities which are open to them, e.g. the provision of hot meals. This work is carried on in the pupils' own time and may be followed up in school by discussions to decide what help young people can give, such as collecting and distributing magazines, visiting old people in their own homes, running errands for them, or persuading a parent or relative to take an old person for an occasional outing in a car.

ACTIVATION AND OBSERVATION

Begin with observation of familiar surroundings.

1. Copy a simple action of another class member, e.g. entering a room.

2. 'How observant are we?' Who is sitting behind you? What is he wearing? What is the colour of . . . ?

3. List clothing of child who has been sent out of the room. Check on return.

4. Name children, pictures, objects in room (oral or written).

5. Play games—children leave room—on return guess which objects have been removed or re-arranged, etc.

6. How many clocks in the school? Where are they?

7. Which teachers have cars? Make? Colour?

8. What is . . . . (teacher) wearing today?

9. Where is the medical room? Secretary's office?

10. Mark the names of children in proper places on a plan of the classroom (duplicated). Do this in another room.

11. Draw views of the school from different standpoints, from memory. Check.

12. Where is the nearest fire alarm, extinguisher, 'phone box, police station, etc?

13. Telephone numbers—school, doctor, ambulance?

14. What is the name of your own doctor? Where is his surgery? Your nearest hospital? Fire Station? Chemist's Shop?

15. Recall items from bus journey to school—churches, prominent buildings, etc.

16. Name films, T.V. programmes showing today.

17. Recall T.V. programmes, in more detail—titles, stars, tune, etc.

18. Memory tray—six objects exposed and covered. Write or draw from memory.

19. Progress to noting more details about classmates, colour of hair, kind of hands, etc.

Exercises in observation should become more penetrating, demanding powers of perception and deduction.

20. Introduce a stranger into the classroom. After leaving—describe him—clothing, etc. How old do you think he is? Is he neat and careful? What is his job? Is he kind, generous, happy? Is he married? Does he smoke? Children to give reasons for answers.

21. Repeat 'entering a room' game. Expect more notice to be taken of walk, mannerisms. Discuss ways in which people enter a room, sit, stand, walk, talk.

22. Perhaps move out of the classroom at this stage.

   (a) Observe items on simple journey round school.
   (b) Observe vehicles and people passing school gates. Return and discuss.
   (c) Make a bus journey to town, note details—recall.
   (d) Note differences in buildings, details of windows, doors, chimney pots, gates, door knockers (in neighbourhood).
   (e) Local walks, noting plants in front gardens, identify trees.

MIME OR DRAMA

1. Crossing the street; (a) old man, (b) careless child, (c) proper way.
2. Washing, cleaning teeth (others criticise).
3. At dinner table, cleaning shoes, or brushing hair.
4. Carrying a very heavy basket for an old lady.
5. Helping blind man across the road.
6. Putting a dog out at night.
7. Changing a flat tyre.
8. Greeting and receiving a visitor.
9. Serving tea, refreshments to visitors.
10. Mother calling in a disobedient boy.
11. Mother asking boy to clean windows.
12. Deaf mute brings message that building is on fire.
13. Explain to an Italian who cannot speak English, that your lorry has backed into his parked car.

UNFORESEEN SITUATIONS

1. Seeking accommodation from landlord.
2. Seeking employment from employer.
3. Asking way to station from policeman.
4. Explaining to bus-conductor that you have no money.
5. Booking seats or tickets.
6. Trying to buy something from a shop, when it is either not sold there, or is out of stock.
7. Accident—street, procedure.
8. Helping a boy having an epileptic fit.
9. Father, and daughter who has stayed out late.
10. Daughter telling mother she is going to get married.
11. Boy asking girl for a dance or a date.

IDENTIFICATION TESTS

1. Boy persuading father to buy him a bike.
2. Asking mother for more pocket money.
3. Persuading caretaker to retrieve ball from roof.

4. Asking an old lady if she needs any help.

5. Persuading mother to allow own choice of T.V. programme.

6. Mother persuading boy/girl to look after younger child when boy/girl wants to play outside instead.

7. Asking permission to stay out later.

8. Father asking unwilling son to clean car.

9. Owner of motor cycle catches boy fiddling with it.

10. Molested by gang of boys from other school.

11. Being ragged by others for catching special bus to 'daft' school.

12. Shopkeeper catches boy pilfering.

13. Blackmailing smaller boys to get sweets from them.

14. Persuading another boy to do a 'swop'.

15. Caretaker cleaning an unnecessarily dirty room.

16. Motorist knocks down a careless cyclist.

17. Father beats up mother.

18. Parent dealing with an unruly child.

Criticism to be encouraged after each episode. Gradually introduce questions 'What do you think he feels?' 'Would he be angry?' 'How would you feel in this situation?'

ACTING FOR SELF-ASSERTION

1. Boy/girl takes back a pair of shoes to a shop asking for a refund. Assistant tries repair, exchange and finally refund.

2. Seeking accommodation. Expect level of examining room, facilities, value for money.

3. Interview for job.

4. Falsely accused of damaging property.

5. Dealing with door-to-door salesman.

6. Asking for rise in pay.

7. Seeking service in restaurant, complaints about food.

8. Returning bad fish, being served with bad apples, or goods from the back of the shop not the window.

9. Dealing with a bully but avoiding a fight.

SITUATION TESTS

At first, present fairly straightforward situations where no moral conflict arises, but only a consideration of appropriate actions is involved, e.g.

1. What would you do if you were left alone in the house with your baby brother and the heater fell over, setting the carpet alight.

2. What would you do if you were left alone in the house with your baby brother and there was a gas leak?

3. What would you do if the electric iron started smoking?

4. What would you do if you were sitting alone in a car, and it started to move?

5. What would you do if the hot water tap would not turn off?

6. What would you do if baby brother swallowed a sweet whole?

7. What would you do if you heard a noise at your window at night?

8. What would you do if you smelt something burning?

9. What would you do if you lost all your money a long way from home?

Next try to introduce situations involving motives and moral conflict. The situations can be enlarged by seeking different opinions and complicated by introducing another factor as the situation develops, e.g.

1. What would you do if you picked up a purse containing £6.

After answers, say that purse belongs to a friend's mother or a poor old lady. Enlarge by asking—How would you feel if it was your mother's purse or your purse?

The teacher must try to avoid giving moral judgements or children may not give their true opinion. Encourage all pupils to respond.

2. Taking and driving away a motor cycle.

3. Vandalism.

4. Staying out late.

5. Dating boys/girls.

6. Entering a cinema through W.C. window.

7. Peeping Tom.

This is a very useful approach, through small groups presenting solutions in dramatic form. Follow up by discussion (very much on the lines of sociodrama—see *Who shall survive*, Moreno).[3]

DISCUSSION GROUPS OR DIALOGUES

Encourage free talk about subjects in which children are involved or interested, e.g. smoking, film or T.V. programmes, local or national news, likes or dislikes in lessons, hobbies, Pop music, etc. Try to involve all children.

As with some of the dramatic work, the tape recorder can be useful. Play back for reminder, discussion/criticism. Later analysis by teacher can assess contributions and help her to see where her own questioning may be improved.

Useful discussions can follow a lecture, e.g. School Medical Officer— 'Smoking'; Headmaster—'Is Corporal Punishment Necessary?'; Welfare Officer—'Who should care for Old People?'; Magistrate—'Should boys be punished or put on probation?'; Youth Leader—'Why Youth Clubs?'

If these debates are able to stimulate action, through some strong feelings which have been aroused, then this may lead to asking further questions.

(*a*) What is the nature and extent of the problem?

To answer this question children must go out of school and make a survey.

(*b*) What can we do about it?

Children should be encouraged to suggest answers. They should become personally involved in the problems of the neighbourhood. Any voluntary social work which is undertaken should be carried on mainly out of school hours. Some social responsibilities in school may be accepted by children if they are able to take the initiative in identifying problems and suggesting remedies. Some simple instances of this are to be seen where older children take an interest in caring for younger children, or running a school club, collecting litter, etc.

At this stage in the scheme, which will be reached towards the end of what is planned to be a four year course, children can profit from talks and discussions about themselves, other people and social groupings. They are anxious to understand themselves and interested in other people's actions. They respond to talks about matters which seem both adult and relevant to real-life situations. A number of the following topics have proved interesting in practice. Intelligence, individual differences, the value of creative and social ability to personal development and society at large. Social groupings—the family group, the class, the crowd, the democratic group. Personal development and social responsibility. The problems of adolescents, the school leaver. The young worker.

Parents might well be drawn into projects. They must be kept informed about them because the work will involve children in activities out of school, after four o'clock, during weekends, holidays and, eventually, when they leave school. It has been noted that some parents have taken a fresh interest in their children at a time when interest in their school activities had begun to flag.

REFERENCES

1. Gunzburg, H. C., 'Assessing Social Competence' in *Special Education*, Vol. 57, No. 2, June 1968.
*2. Hauser, R. & H., *The Fraternal Society*. Bodley Head, 1962.
3. Moreno, J. L., *Who Shall Survive*. Beacon House, New York, 1953.

FURTHER READING

Books marked * above and also the following:
Department of Education & Science, *Education under Social Handicap*. Leaflets No. 17 (Dec. 1964), No. 20 (March 1965), No. 22 (June 1965).
Department of Education & Science, Schools Council Working Paper No. 17, *Community Service and the Curriculum*, H.M.S.O., 1968.
Hauser R., 'Social Education' in *Forward Trends*, Vol. 8, No 3, Summer 1964.

Paterson, N., 'Community Service – A Place on the Timetable', in *New Education*, June 1968.

Surrey Educational Research Association, *The Older Non-Academic Secondary Pupil*, S.E.R.A., 1963.

Cave, R. C. & O'Mally, R., *Education for Personal Responsibility*, Ward Lock Educational, 1967.

CHAPTER 11

Practical and Artistic Activities

A POPULAR fallacy assumes that children who are academically deficient possess compensatory practical abilities. So, the saying runs, 'if he's not good with his head, he's good with his hands'. Unfortunately, this is far from the truth, for many very dull children seem to have an all round deficiency. In the lower ranges of the intelligence scale it is common to find children whose practical gifts are extremely limited. Every E.S.N. school has its quota of boys who are approaching the limits of achievement when they are knocking a nail into a piece of wood. Irrespective of intelligence there are children who are naturally awkward. It is becoming increasingly evident that there are also a number of children with minor brain injury who may have very poor motor co-ordination and/or spatial and perceptual difficulties. Clumsiness associated with diminished mental powers presents a very poor prospect in every aspect of their education.

At the same time, there are a number of E.S.N. children whose practical ability, as displayed in woodwork for example, more nearly approaches standards in normal schools. A smaller percentage of dull children show special aptitudes or abilities.

It follows that any programme of practical activities for slow learners should take into account a wide range of individual differences in practical ability. The justification for giving practical activities a significant place on the timetable should not be based on a misplaced notion of widespread ability but on the realisation that these children are going to depend more on practical skills than on intellectual capacity in later life.

Looked at from this point of view it is tempting to regret that backwardness is so frequently equated with reading failure and developments in remedial techniques have concentrated on improvement in reading. The lack of literature on 'Remedial Teaching in Woodwork' or 'Improving Practical Skills' suggests that an important aspect of special education has been neglected. A glance at the list of books, at the end of this chapter, suggests that interest in this area has developed only recently.

In addition to the needs of the 'practically handicapped' it is possible to conjecture that there may well be considerable reserves of unrealised potential in practical performance amongst many slow learners who have been given a very poor diet of activities. Far too frequently it appears that woodwork and housecraft are the mainstays of the practical arts. Occasionally gardening may be thrown in as make-weight. Where such situations exist there is a complete failure to appreciate that individuals can display skills in an entirely different range of occupations.

If we accept that practical and artistic activities can play an important role in the lives of slow learners, the status of these activities must be raised to being regarded as something more than mere educational frills. A full and carefully planned programme in the practical arts should not be conceived as being primarily vocational training. Patently, every child cannot be taught a specific trade for it is impossible to predict or guarantee his eventual employment. Nevertheless, where any child displays a considerable degree of competence in a particular skill he should be given every opportunity to make the most of his ability. Taking into account individual differences and interests suggests that a wide range of practical and artistic activities must be offered in an attempt to find something at which each child can gain skill and satisfaction.

The growth of feelings of personal adequacy which derive from the satisfaction of producing acceptable work in art and craft can have wider implications. The intrinsic values of these activities as a means of expression are also of special significance in the education of slow learners. Where written and verbal expression is limited, the arts offer not only a compensatory outlet but a desirable means of expression which can provide enriching experiences and may often lead to improved oral expression.

This is one area where special schools have greater freedom to organise a timetable which can both provide for those whose practical abilities are limited and allow a degree of choice in pursuing a particular bent. In theory the larger secondary or comprehensive school, with generous provision of workshops and specialist staff, ought to be able to offer a wider range of activities. In practice the remedial or special class teacher is expected to be mainly concerned with classroom work and may have an uphill task trying to persuade specialist colleagues to give proper recognition to other needs of the less able. It is all too easy for interesting work, such as building canoes or go-karts, to become the preserve of a few more gifted children. Every boy cannot build a canoe and in many practical activities materials are too expensive to allow for mistakes. A description of a desirable programme for special schools may give teachers in ordinary schools some ideas to adapt and a target to work towards.

The range of activities which can be mounted may appear to be unduly restricted by the abilities of staff and the problems of timetabling. The limits of teaching ability may be more imaginary than real, for staff, like the children, may have unsuspected talents. Most teachers have additional hobbies and interests which they are prepared to use for the benefit of the children. Indeed an opportunity to use these talents may unleash a flood of energy and enthusiasm.

As well as hobbies and interests, teachers may have acquired other skills, such as painting and decorating or bricklaying, which follow in the path of home ownership. Even a rudimentary knowledge, allied to common sense and a little reading, can be enough to guide a group of children. In subjects like woodwork and housecraft the trained specialist is usually to be preferred, but the specialist who is narrowly perfectionist is not necessarily the best teacher for the less able, for the niceties of dovetail joints or *cordon bleu* cookery are not the first essentials. The teacher who is also a good housewife, or the husband who knows the value of plastic laminates, glue and hardboard may be more in touch with the real needs of the children.

Parents might well be involved in all sorts of ways. Some will have a wealth of information, others can track down supplies of unusual materials or obtain gifts of offcuts of timber, plywood or plastic. Mothers might be prepared to help in school in the daytime and there is no reason why some fathers could not take a small group at an evening course in a specialist activity.

ORGANISING ACTIVITIES

Timetabling problems can be overcome. One plan is to arrange for most practical and artistic activities to take place at the same time. In this way every teacher can be available and those who might otherwise be deployed in a more academic instructional role can be released to take a practical session. If all staff are available, groups can be kept to a reasonable size and those activities which attract few children need not be eliminated.

One special school which followed this plan was able to offer a range of activities as diverse as—woodwork, motor mechanics, gardening, constructional work involving concreting, brick-laying and carpentry; arts and light crafts—including painting, printing, pottery, modelling, basketry, lampshade making, leatherwork and weaving, in addition to housecraft, puppetry and music, movement and mime. Activities varied from time to time with staff changes or when new ones could be introduced and others were thought to need a rest.

EXERCISING CHOICE

The children were allowed to make their own choice of activity at the beginning of each term but were expected to keep to this activity for a whole term. The opportunity to exercise choice was considered valuable and it was a new school experience for many. Not all children exercised their choices wisely and some were slow to assess their own abilities. This was not unexpected for some had very little ability in any activity, and many others tended to join groups with a friend. Many, quite sensibly, shopped around and enjoyed a variety of experiences. Every activity attracted a hard core of enthusiasts who firmly and regularly opted for the same activity (or teacher). Interest seemed to be high when there was freedom of choice. The willing gardener, for example, was able to devote more time to his chosen study and had a greater chance of developing some skill. An inviting by-product is the satisfaction which a teacher gains from teaching a willing and interested group of pupils. This, in turn, can easily lead to a more relaxed atmosphere which not only aids learning but can make for informality and the introduction of group work with leaders (or 'foremen') and later to unsupervised work. Thus, ultimately, children can develop greater social and personal adequacy.

A record of the children's interests and abilities shown over a period of time is helpful when discussing job placement with the Youth Employment Officer. An excess of deskwork (or 'seat-work'—an apt American term) gives a very poor picture of a future worker. A child can be virtually 'written-off' with a series of low ratings in basic subjects. No matter how limited his practical abilities may be, a more positive and informative picture can be built up from comments such as—'can work with a group', 'can be trusted to clean and replace tools and lock up after a job'.

ART AND CRAFT?

An overall programme which includes both practical and artistic activities has several advantages, other than as a time-tabling convenience. It should be conceded that the distinction between art and craft is often an artificial one. A fine piece of furniture has aesthetic appeal. The design of many products involves both fitness for purpose and beauty of line. The artistic and practical elements of some activities are finely balanced. It would not be surprising to find woodcarving, metal sculpture or pottery carried on in either the woodwork room or the art room. At the extremes one might more easily categorise music or painting as fine arts, and bricklaying or carpentry as industrial crafts. The distinctions can be over-emphasised with the consequent dangers of fine arts being associated with school and teachers and at the other extreme the element of craftsmanship being overlooked. Similarly, it is possible to consider particular activities as being either funda-mentally vocational in aim or classed as hobbies. It should be made clear to children that an activity can be both an occupation and a pastime. Gardening is a useful illustration.

Slow learners gain much satisfaction from completing a job but should learn to appreciate the quality of the finished product. Much depends on the teacher's skill in selecting projects which look well on completion when the young worker has little experience and limited ability. Good materials and the best tools available are essential for success, economical in the long-run, and a proper example for the young craftsman.

Encouragement should be given by displaying good work to best advantage. Some schools make a practice of exhibiting children's work once a week at a morning assembly. Paintings, a stool, rug or a product from the cookery room can be given equal pride of place and a brief reference to the skills involved and attractive features can be a useful lesson.

Although it is necessary to teach the separate skills of arts and crafts it is also important to integrate activities if children are to see the value and purpose of their efforts. There is considerable scope for practical and artistic activity in many Units of Experience. Discussing this approach in Chapter 9 it was stressed that arising out of many projects the need for reading and writing becomes apparent. The same claim could well be made for the practical arts, for slow learners do not always see that school activities are related to life experiences. Teachers may also begin to lose sight of their aims by becoming too closely concerned with the specialised detail of breaking down

7—BTFSL * *

tasks into simple steps and structuring the teaching situation. The broader and more outgoing activities developing from Units of Experience or a School Leavers' Programme provide a healthy corrective.

SUPERVISING INDIVIDUAL WORK

The organisation of a wide range of activities calls for a high degree of skill from the limited number of teachers available in a special school or those prepared to help in a remedial department. Teachers have to cope with individual differences and may well have to supervise different activities. Art teachers seem to be adapting well to conducting various activities in the same room. The range of work on display at exhibitions shows quite clearly that they are experimenting with many media in an attempt to provide individuals with the most satisfying and successful means of expression. Similarly the teacher of light crafts should be able to cope with individual choice. At times the gardening teacher may have to keep an eye on boys making a concrete path as well as directing the efforts of his own group. Even in traditional crafts, such as woodwork, it is rare to see class lessons. One boy will be making a stool, another a clothes horse, while yet another may be turning a lamp or a bowl. There is no special merit in every child being engaged in a different activity. Indeed it should normally be expected that some boys would want to make models which they see others doing. It is a healthy sign, however, that some account is being taken of individual differences and interests.

Progressive ideas can flounder without proper planning. Some traditional teaching practices need to be maintained to establish a system which children can understand and follow. To be able to cater for individual differences within groups, children must be given training in the care of tools and materials. Following this, they must be given responsibility for the distribution, care and collection of tools and materials. A woodwork teacher may have all tools on view in racks or hanging from pegboard. An art teacher may have stands which hold the exact number of brushes available. Each can check at a glance that tools have been correctly replaced at the end of a session.

Opportunities should be taken to draw a group together for a demonstration or explanation. One child's model may be used to interest others either as a means of suggesting ideas which may be taken up later or broadening experience. At certain stages a particular process which has general application may well be demonstrated to the whole class. Completed models may be discussed to bring out children's comments on cost or design.

FURTHER READING

Alvin, J., *Music for the Handicapped Child*, O.U.P., 1965.

Carlson, B. W. & Ginglend, D. R., *Play Activities for the Retarded Child*, Cassell, 1961.

Devereux, H. M., *Housecraft in the Education of Handicapped Children*, Mills & Boon, 1963.

Dobbs, J. P. B., *The Slow Learner and Music*, O.U.P., 1966.

Evans, H. T., *Woodwork for the Lower Stream*, Technical Press Ltd. (London), 1959.

Hartung, R., *Creative Corrugated Paper Craft*, Batsford, 1966.

Hartung, R., *Creative Textile Craft*, Batsford, 1964.

Linzey, Z., *Art is for All*, Mills & Boon, 1967.

Malcolm, I., *Puppetry for the Mentally Handicapped*, N.A.M.H.

Melzi, K., *Art in the Primary School*, Blackwell, 1967.

Morgenstern, M., Low-Beer, H. & Morgenstern, F., *Practical Training for the Severely Handicapped Child*, W. Heinemann (Medical Books) Ltd., 1966.

Rottger, E., *Creative Clay Craft*, Batsford, 1963.

Rottger, E., *Creative Paper Craft*, Batsford, 1966.

Rottger, E., *Creative Wood Craft*, Batsford, 1960.

Tritten, G., *Art Techniques for Children*, Batsford, 1964.

Walter, F., *Practical Handicraft*. 1. Working in metal, leather, clay, etc., 2. Working with wood, Mills & Boon, 1967.

CHAPTER 12

Training for Leisure

EDUCATORS who look into the future inevitably consider the advent of automation, the shorter working week, and the consequent need for schools to begin to prepare young people for an age of extensive leisure. Already many teachers have accepted that hobbies and leisure time pursuits should be part of the regular school curriculum. This is not something which should be relegated to out-of-school hours but needs to be allocated lesson time. Perhaps it is not too much to hope that subjects like art, craft and music will acquire fresh respectability and lose much of their former lowly status as some of the 'educational frills'.

Slow learners are not being left out of this movement. Indeed their teachers have long been committed to educating for leisure. They have had ample opportunity to see how often their pupils are at a loss what to do with their spare time. Recently a number of investigations have demonstrated clearly that leavers from special schools lead very restricted lives. Although the majority find little difficulty in finding employment the pattern of their leisure time is a drab one. There seems to be an almost total lack of lively interests to balance the monotonous hours spent largely in dull, repetitive work. Social contacts are limited, few belong to youth clubs or display any initiative in joining other organisations. The major time filler seems to be television, with a minority of adolescents making an occasional visit to the cinema or dance-hall. It is unusual to find many who are attending evening classes.

Response to current practices may be disappointing but

perhaps it is still too early to make judgements. Most of us had interests at school which we have not carried over into later life. We cannot be sure that some leisure interest may not spring up in later life which had its beginnings in school. Teachers, who are introducing young people to the pleasures of angling, sailing, rock-climbing and many other sports and pastimes should persist with such training and try not to become discouraged too early. It is possible that many youngsters are having their lives enriched in ways which are not readily observable. Surely the boy who has been a cross-country runner or a rock-climber will get more out of his passive television viewing because he can identify himself with the runner and climber. He knows the feeling of physical exertion and can appreciate some of the skills in a sport.

Is it easy to take up painting or canoeing in a home where dog racing, football and horses are the dominant interests? Living in a neighbourhood where sailing, rock-climbing or hiking may be regarded as unusual hobbies, may call for strength of character and initiative which these youngsters do not possess, to break through social pressures. Certainly many such sports will become more wide-spread. The growth of sailing in this country since the war has been phenomenal. Dinghy sailing and canoeing are well within the means of the working class. Perhaps in the future when the factory sports clubs widen their range of activities some dormant interest may be aroused again. Some benefits may accrue to the next generation. Today's slow learner who, in spite of parental indifference, turns up in the rain on a Saturday morning for a gruelling cross-country run, may well become tomorrow's parent who encourages his own children to take a full part in their school activities. Instead of being unco-operative he may be keen to provide the shorts, the football or climbing boots or perhaps the skis for the youth of 1980?

Let us not be deterred then by slow progress but rather take heart from some of the exciting ideas which are being demonstrated by enthusiastic colleagues. A number of outdoor pursuits like fishing, hiking, climbing, sailing and canoeing have already been mentioned. Some of these have arisen from successful work which less able pupils have undertaken in connection with the Duke of Edinburgh's Award Scheme.[1] Many are natural partners for more traditional camping expeditions. There seems little reason to doubt that most activities are within the capabilities of some slow learners. One enterprising special school even has go-kart racing. A track in the playground has been suitably laid out with bales of straw at strategic points. Staff and pupils enjoy the sport and skills are evident on both sides. At other times the building and maintenance of their vehicles provides a purposeful activity in a practical sense.

Many of the outdoor pursuits, mentioned above, are open to people from all walks of life. To be realistic one might claim that there is little purpose in introducing interests which in later life are either expensive hobbies or seem to be the preserve of a select class. Thus it might be claimed that sailing is expensive and golf is not a game for the working man. In fact, sailing dinghies cost no more than a motor cycle and the growing number of sailing clubs have low subscription rates for junior and non-boat-owning members. Agile youngsters are in great demand as crews and can graduate to helmsmen. Many municipal golf courses are open to the casual visitor at modest charges. Putting and golf are features of many holiday resorts and some skill can add to the enjoyment of holidays. If a sport is too expensive or exclusive one might suspect that it will be prohibitive for most schools to undertake.

This is a time for experiment, for traditional practices in secondary schools have ignored the needs of the mass of youngsters. Sporting activities have all too often been limited to major games like football and cricket and the energies of the staff have been directed towards the minority in the school first eleven. Probably only a minority of school leavers have continued to participate in either sport in later life.

Space, time and teaching staff are likely to be the limiting factors in the range of leisure pursuits which can be taught. Common sense suggests that some activities require a minimal outlay and do not demand a team to make a game feasible. On these criteria, swimming would come high on any list and, according to the availability of local facilities or clubs, tennis, badminton, judo, ice skating, cycling or hiking might appeal to the more active young people.

A study of local facilities might well prove to be a suitable starting point for settling on a range of leisure time pursuits. A strong link with youth clubs, evening institutes and voluntary associations might well have several benefits. Initially it may help children to see that particular activities are both adult and popular, and this is not just another school lesson with a novel gloss. Then children often need to be shown where the head-quarters of various organisations are, and details of meetings and subscriptions can be made available. Perhaps some interests, acquired in school fail to carry over into later life because of lack of awareness about the extent of facilities available in particular localities. A study of leisure facilities would seem to be an essential project for older children (see also Chapter 9— Units of Experience). A genuine interest from a school might easily arouse a willingness amongst experts from local clubs and associations to visit schools and give demonstrations or talks.

Although opportunities for further education for adults are increasing many of the subjects offered seem biased towards the more intelligent members of the community. Local colleges of further education have a bewildering choice of courses; language courses extending to Swedish and Russian, business and commercial studies, typewriting, music, current affairs, fencing, drama and educational courses leading to particular qualifications. Evening institutes offer more practical training in car maintenance, dressmaking, flower arrangement, physical education, and other courses at modest fees. Duller young people rarely seem to join. There is probably no single reason for this. Ignorance about available tuition may be one reason because they either cannot, or do not, read announcements in the local press. Shyness or reluctance to engage in something that smacks of school and failure, may be other factors. Perhaps some may start but drop out because many evening courses are steeped in class teaching methods and less able pupils easily fall behind.

Some national effort is called for in making provision for further education of less able members of the population.

Youth clubs, too, are sometimes selective in their membership. Undesirables and trouble-makers are quickly shown the door, but the dull and often inarticulate young person is not actively helped to stay and find a niche. He may not be discouraged from attending but, rather by default as he drifts aimlessly, and makes few friends, is he allowed to discontinue attendance. There are outstanding examples where this is not the case.

Success and failure in youth clubs is closely paralleled in those clubs based at E.S.N. day special schools. Some attract very few children. The difficulties of transport and the narrow range of activities which can be provided by one or two adults is restricting. They fulfil some purpose by demanding that children make the voluntary effort to travel unsupervised on public transport. Frequently they seem to have a therapeutic role, for young people come along mainly to have someone to talk to and share their problems and anxieties. The more successful youth clubs at some special schools are able to attract many of their older pupils and leavers and also provide a haven for many of the less able children from local secondary modern schools. Occasionally they admit children with other handicaps and those who have returned to the area after living away in residential schools.

The contrast between the best and the less successful of these clubs has to be seen to be believed. Part of the attraction of the more successful clubs may be in the design of the building where a youth club wing with facilities, such as a coffee bar, games room or dance floor are incorporated. The fundamental factor of the success of a club seems to lie in the quality and attitude of the adult staff. The mature and sympathetic leader will recede into the background and hand over most of the running of the club to the young people. The rejection of an authoritarian or even a paternal role is characteristic of many of the best run youth clubs for normal young people. There is now sufficient experience to show that slow learners can also respond with maturity when given responsibility and treated as adults.

Two approaches to training for leisure have been emphasised.

1. The necessity for putting leisure activities and hobbies on the timetable.

2. The possibilities for youth clubs.

Of course there are other ways of tackling the challenge. Club activities or societies can often be arranged to take place in school lunch breaks. In addition there will be occasions during the year for extended expeditions when the popular camping or holidays abroad come into their own. Schools are becoming increasingly more adventurous in these trips. Exchange visits between special schools in different areas have been very successful.[2] Cycling with light-weight camping has also proved worthwhile. Cycling or walking holidays which introduce children to youth hostelling are far-sighted, for this type of holiday offers an inexpensive and enjoyable way of seeing the countryside.

Many local education authorities are actively encouraging outdoor pursuits and have established premises and centres as a base for school expeditions. There is an increasing number of adventure holidays or courses offered by the C.C.P.R.[3] and many of their activities have a tremendous appeal for youngsters. The advantage of qualified instructors and training in appropriate safety precautions are particularly advantageous to the small school.

Considerable emphasis has been laid in this chapter, on sporting and outdoor activities. Obviously many of these need not be solely the province of the hobbies lesson but ought to be part of a truly well-based physical education programme.

INDOOR GAMES

Equally important is the possibility of developing interests in a number of games and indoor hobbies. To think in terms of chess and more 'academically' respectable games is both shortsighted and out of touch with reality. Many slow learners in special schools even find difficulty in managing the scoring in table tennis and take time to get used to playing cards. Every possible avenue has to be explored. Preliminary skills which have to be encouraged are common to most games. These include the ability to win or lose without excessive reactions, to play together in a group fairly, taking turns and observing the rules. Not only are social skills evident but some aspect of number seems to creep into most games.

Card games are an obvious choice where space is limited, and could usefully be encouraged in wet lunch hours. Ordinary playing cards can be used simply for snap, or pelmanism. Many other simple card games like Happy Families and other old favourites are popular and cheap to buy. Children should be given responsibility for checking that the correct number of cards is replaced after games. Those who can read may enjoy card games like Scrabble or Lexicon.

Many other games like draughts, ludo, snakes and ladders, Monopoly, Chinese Chequers, and Pegity, have held the interest of children and adults over many years. With training some can enjoy a game of chess. Then there are many games which involve a greater degree of movement—darts, billiards, snooker, bagatelle, table tennis, quoits, skittles. These have proved to be very popular in a number of special schools.

Perhaps a further group of hobbies might be classified under the heading of constructional and model making activities. Here there is a vast range of commercial products ranging from the traditional Meccano to modern plastic building sets. Model making can begin very simply with inexpensive prefabricated kits. Weaning away from reliance on commercial products can follow. With model planes, for example, progression from simple gliders in balsa wood can easily proceed to making more advanced models from plans.

Some school subjects like art, reading, music, drama or gardening and woodwork have pleasurable as well as utilitarian aims. There ought to be opportunities in a well balanced hobbies and leisure programme for individuals to choose to enjoy these activities in a less formal atmosphere, emphasising the links with adult leisure pursuits.

Parties and dancing are two activities which can be arranged with a minimum of adult guidance and supervision. They can be a means of giving young people some measure of responsibility in the planning and conduct of social gatherings. They are a real and vital means of encouraging social contacts in a natural way. Girls seems to find little difficulty in dancing to popular music. Boys need a chance to become accustomed to the idea. They can be helped to feel more at home in an awkward situation if they are given some dancing lessons. Girls and boys also enjoy some instruction in old-time and ballroom dancing.

There are bound to be objections and difficulties in the way of providing a purposeful and enjoyable 'training for leisure' programme. Cost and staffing are obvious limitations. On both counts this seems an appropriate occasion to enlist the support of parents.

RESIDENTIAL SCHOOLS

Residential special schools seem to have a special responsibility for the leisure time activities of their pupils. In an unpublished dissertation, Wilson[4] pointed out that probably only twenty-five hours are spent in the classroom out of approximately ninety hours of wakeful time per week. One might well ask how far residential schools are planning leisure hours constructively or whether the time is being occupied by social training—washing, tidying, bed-making, shoe cleaning and routine domestic help. Experience of institutions suggests that it is easy to extend these chores to fill the hours which have to be supervised by adults. Television also offers an easy way of passing time.

Those residential schools which offer a wide range of evening activities resemble miniature evening institutes. Children can choose from P.E., woodwork, metal-work, model making, art, basketry, rug-making, needlework, puppetry, listening to records and playing indoor games like snooker and table tennis. Voluntary help from outside school is sometimes forthcoming and assistance has been given by students from Colleges of Education. Additionally, pupils are encouraged to join village youth clubs, scouts or evening class.[4]

Where conditions are not so favourable, staff already jaded after a day's work, may have to supervise leisure time activities in an unsuitable building which is also remote and isolated. A situation can easily arise where youngsters are being denied experiences which they might have had at home. It is worth remembering that even children in day special schools do join in some neighbourhood activities by attending local football matches and cinemas, and are able to go cycling or swimming with friends. At home many show a keen interest in animals. Finally, one of the major drawbacks to segregated special education is still the tendency for authorities to operate single sex schools. Normal youngsters and their duller peers are beginning to form boy and girl friendships in their own neighbourhoods long before they leave school. This poses problems for the residential school. They are problems which ought to be faced and overcome.

REFERENCES

1. Duke of Edinburgh's Award Office, 2 Old Queen St., London, S.W.1.
2. Henderson, J. & Hoose, L. A., 'Residential Exchange Holidays' in *Special Education*, Vol. LII, No. 3, Autumn 1963.
3. Central Council of Physical Recreation, 6, Bedford Square, London, W.C.1.
4. Wilson, L., *Out of School Hours in the Residential School*. Unpublished dissertation, Inst. of Educ., Univ. of Nottingham, 1967.

FURTHER READING

C.C.P.R., *Sport and the Community* (Report of the Wolfenden Committee), 1960.

Disley, J. (ed.), 1964 *Expedition Guide*, pub. Duke of Edinburgh's Award Office.

Know the Game series – Educational Productions Ltd., 17 Denbright St., London, S.W.1.

Ministry of Education, Pamphlet No. 41, *Camping and Education*, H.M.S.O., 1961.

CHAPTER 13

Preparation for Employment

TRANSITION from school to work may prove difficult for many slow learners. Many teachers accept the need to provide some kind of course to bridge the gap between school and work. Inevitably ideas vary from school to school as to the nature and extent of a school leaver's programme. Some are content to plan a limited number of industrial visits whereas others devote the final year in school to an integrated course which seeks to introduce their pupils to three aspects of adult life—the world of work, the community world and the world of leisure. An extensive programme of this type could well be tackled along the lines suggested in an earlier chapter as a 'Unit of Experience'. Some of the approaches outlined in 'Training for Leisure' and 'Social Education' would also be appropriate for a comprehensive course.

There is a noticeable trend in some special schools for more realistic forms of work experience to be undertaken. In some areas attempts to place children in real working conditions have been hampered by problems of insurance and union regulations. Some ingenious attempts have been made to surmount these difficulties. Knight[1] describes a *Factory Day at School* where, in addition to a programme of industrial visits and classroom study, work under factory-type conditions is simulated in school. One day a week, the woodwork room adopts production line methods and boys work a longer day, clocking in and out, and learning to observe safety and other factory regulations. Other schools have been able to arrange for 'day release' courses for small groups of pupils at technical colleges. Perhaps the most ambitious scheme has been described by Jerrold.[2] This takes the form of a 'sheltered' workshop sited away from the 'parent' day special school. This unit is under the supervision of a manager/teacher who has had industrial experience and provides training and workshop experience for E.S.N. boys who are unsuited for immediate employment or who have failed in open employment.

The development of a wide variety of leavers' programmes has led to a considerable number of 'follow-up' studies of E.S.N. school leavers. Investigators have attempted to evaluate job success, reasons for failure and the need for after-care services. Jackson[3] has questioned the value of many such studies. He points to the limitations of studies which

(a) examine only the initial period of employment,
(b) confuse employment adjustment with social adjustment,
(c) equate stability in one job as a positive factor when it may be due to lack of initiative or parental pressure.

Whilst a number of studies suggest that many E.S.N. leavers experience a period of settled employment in the early, post-school years, we have yet to discover what happens to these young people in later life, when parental support may be removed. The effects of marriage and family commitments, particularly in the case of unskilled workers on low wages, has yet to be examined.

In the interim period we must encourage those courses which are preparing children for a wide range of difficulties which they may encounter in both social and vocational aspects of life. Indeed there is some evidence from investigations (notably Matthew, 1964) that many slow learners do not fail in employment because of inability to do the job but through social and personal inadequacy. Common causes of failure include lack of punctuality, absenteeism, failure to adjust to fellow-employees, or to the employer, inability to take responsibility, indifference, unreliability and emotional instability.

There are many indications pointing to a particular need for an efficient system of after-care which should have strong links with the schools. The provision made for the severely subnormal by enlightened care as instanced by the Slough and Pirate Springs experiments[4] should stimulate work with E.S.N. children.

Research and experiment by Dr. H. C. Gunzburg[5, 6] suggest that many handicapped children might benefit from a directed programme based upon the use of Progress Assessment Charts.

A SCHOOL LEAVER'S PROGRAMME

It seems clear that there are so many aspects to the world of work that any determined attempts to prepare slow learners must embrace a wide range of activities. The contributions of other activities in the curriculum has been stressed in other chapters. Where these are not adequately provided for in other ways a good leaver's programme should include leisure, health, travel, family affairs and community studies. When associated activities are separately timetabled a School Leaver's Programme may provide a focal point to make the purpose of these activities clear to the children. Some vital points may be summarised.

1.   Communication skills must be emphasised.

2.   Social arithmetic particularly with a bias towards budgeting and Hire Purchase may be singularly important for the lower paid workers.

3.   A practical bias to the curriculum is needed.

4.   Social adjustment must be encouraged.

5.   Special attention may have to be given to cleanliness, smartness, punctuality, accepting responsibility and working with a minimum of supervision.

As many of these aspects are considered elsewhere in more detail, this particular chapter emphasises the vocational side of a leaver's programme.

An integrated scheme should include many visits which are not always confined to industry. Theatres, shops, restaurants, museums, hospitals, etc., may be visited as an introduction to the adult world and as an essential part of social training.

VISITS

Industrial visits should aim to give a wide experience of many different types of working conditions and also be representative of possible occupations in particular areas. Thus, pupils should be made aware of indoor and outdoor work, heavy industry, large, noisy factories, small firms, service industries, etc. Girls should visit laundries, bakeries and see something of catering and domestic work as well as those local factories which employ female labour.

Visits require preparation and follow-up. Children can be directed to note particular features on their visits and be encouraged to ask the right questions. Back in the classroom they can discuss whether they would like to work in a particular place, if there were any jobs which were within their capabilities, what wages and conditions were like. With increasing experience a teacher will discover many other points whereby children's observation can be directed to make the visits worthwhile. Canteen facilities, safety regulations, protective clothing and many other facts can be gleaned in addition to the more obvious questions about hours of work and prospects.

CLASSROOM ACTIVITIES

A considerable amount of work needs to be carried out in the classroom. Maps of the district, with coloured pins to mark factories visited and the homes of individual pupils will lead to problems of transport, time and cost involved in getting to work. There are many useful wall-charts which can supplement visits and focus discussion. A series of 'Career Wallcharts', with supporting pamphlets, has been available from H.M.S.O. for a number of years. Occupations are grouped under various headings suitably illustrated, as for example, 'Catering and Domestic Work', 'Work in the Open Air', 'Work with Machines'. Specific local industries can often be illustrated with charts from other sources, e.g. 'Down a Modern Coal Mine' (N.C.B. Public

Relations Office). Some useful aids are obtainable from Educational Productions Ltd., East Ardsley, Wakefield.

Opportunities for written work will arise which will be seen to be purposeful. Letters of thanks can follow visits. A copy of teachers' own letter arranging a visit can be displayed. Samples of time sheets and forms may have been obtained and practice in basic form filling can be given.

SITUATIONS VACANT

Discussion should be directed at some point to the various ways of finding employment. Individuals may have few ideas but collectively a group should soon name:

(a) Youth Employment Officer.

(b) Labour Exchange (for over eighteen years of age).

(c) Advertisements in Local Press.

(d) Notices outside factories.

(e) Personal contacts through parents and relations.

These different avenues can be explored. The functions of the Youth Employment Officer can be explained and the addresses and times of opening of local offices discovered and recorded. Mock interviews can be held in preparation for the visit of the Y.E.O.

The 'Situations Vacant' column in the local newspaper can be used or a duplicated substitute supplied by the teacher. Selecting possible jobs and writing letters of application can be useful activities. This can be followed up by 'short-listing' suitable applicants and conducting mock interviews. These can be purposeful and enjoyable occasions and illuminating situations will arise for teacher and pupils.

Opportunities for making independent visits and using the telephone may arise naturally and can be followed up by practice and discussion as necessary.

OUTSIDE SPEAKERS

It is sometimes difficult to find suitable people who can come into school and talk on topics related to employment. Some guidance and preparation is usually necessary if they are to talk briefly and simply to less able pupils. There is usually no difficulty in finding people who are willing to help in this way. An outside visitor provides a welcome change for the children but only experience can reveal the most suitable local speakers. The Youth Employment Officer is an obvious first choice not only so that he may become known to the children but because he may lead to further contacts. Youth leaders, policemen, fire brigade officers can all make useful contributions. Shop stewards and foremen are often most successful as speakers and the interest shown by the school is often repaid later by help in placing a young person in employment.

Former pupils who visit the school are often very willing victims for an informal 'question and answer' interview in the classroom. Their early experiences at work seem more relevant to the same generation. Stories of 'leg-pulling' and their personal reactions are just as valuable for young people to hear as the accounts of working life given by adults.

THE USE OF DRAMA

The benefits of dramatising interviews have already been mentioned. Drama can also be used to considerable effect in exposing children to social situations which they are likely to meet in employment. The ability to get on with other people is important and situations can be presented where children act out problems involving dealings with foremen, workmates, or in following instructions, seeking time off from work, apologising for mistakes or misconduct, strikes, etc. The teacher can often play a part in these dramatic activities where children cannot anticipate adult behaviour. The reversal of roles where the teacher is not always the authoritarian figure can bring in elements of humour and create an atmosphere where boys and girls are more at ease and willing to take part.

OTHER AIDS

From time to time programmes on the radio or television are

devoted to the 'World at Work'. Tape recordings of selected parts of radio programmes have been used successfully in a number of schools. A number of suitable films and film-strips are available and catalogues from the main suppliers of films should be examined for recent productions. Sources of suitable material are listed at the end of this chapter. Many films sponsored by large industrial undertakings (Dunlop, Ford, Unilever, etc.) are well produced and can add to the experience of visits.

The spread of work preparation schemes in special schools and classes and the growth of 'Newsom' courses has not passed unnoticed amongst educational publishers. A number of useful publications have already been produced and others are planned. An early production to meet this need is the *School Leavers' Handbook* by Tansley and Brennan.[7] In addition to providing ideas for teachers, this makes a useful present for a school leaver. A *School Leavers' Workbook* is also available from the same source and this may be suitable for individual children and may well prompt a teacher to duplicate additional material to meet the particular requirements of his own class. Other books present situations which young people may meet after leaving school. Some are factual, others use a story form presentation. Most are written in simple language and can be read by pupils with reading ages of eight to nine years and above. They can also be read to a class by the teacher to provide talking points or a stimulus for dramatisation. *Spotlight on Trouble*[8] and *Out with Tom*[9] are two series of books of this type which have been edited by Gunzburg. Another useful series is *The Websters of Welford* by Uncles[10] and book 4, *Sorting Things Out* and book 5, *Looking Ahead* are particularly appropriate at this stage. Young people in various occupations are featured in Anderson's series *Adventures in Work*[11] and North's *Just the Job* books.[12] The special interests of girls are provided for in the *Ann and Jenny* books[13] and the Bradleys' *Between Ourselves*.[14] Aspects of work and leisure, such as safety and money matters, are catered for by the *Safe and Well* series,[15] *Better Buying*,[16] and the *Pathway Books*.[17] A selection from the titles of the latter series gives some indication of the topics covered: *Money in Your Life*; *Danger—Watch Out*; *Hobby—Nothing to Do*; *People and Jobs*. The final books have recently been published to complete the series, *The Working World*.[18] This seems to have much to offer older slow learners on many aspects of preparing them not only for the world of work but also for the personal and social problems of adolescence.

Most enterprising teachers will make their own charts and displays from collected material such as National Health Insurance Cards, Income Tax Forms, wage slips, pay packets and time sheets. Familiarisation with clocking in may be achieved with the aid of a time clock and many schools seem to have persuaded a local firm to donate an old model.

SOURCES OF SUITABLE FILM, FILM-STRIPS AND OTHER MATERIAL

Sound Services Ltd., Kingston Road, London S.W.19. An agency for films from many industrial and other concerns. Many films are on free loan. Their catalogue is well worth purchasing.

The Electricity Council. Free loan of general interest films and film-strips on safety at work, in the home, on the roads.

The Gas Council. Film Library, 6/7 Great Chapel Street, London W.1. Free loan of popular and humorous films. Much useful material for girls.

British Transport Commission. Film Office, 23 Saville Row, London W.1.

The National Coal Board. Film Library, Hobart House, Grosvenor Place, London S.W.1. Free loan.

The Industrial Welfare Society, 48 Bryanston Square, London W.1. Useful film-strips with records, e.g. 'Interviews', 'Fitting in with other People'.

'Choice of Careers' film-strips from local Youth Employment Officers.

Educational Productions Ltd., East Ardsley, Wakefield, Yorkshire. Film-strips, e.g. 'Meet your Neighbour', Careers and Work, Local Government series.

R.O.S.P.A. Film Library, 17 Knightsbridge, London S.W.1.

Dental Council, 44 Hallam Street, London W.C.1.

Ministry of Health, Public Relations Division, Alexander Fleming House, Elephant & Castle, London S.E.1.

Concordia Films, 117/123 Golden Lane, London E.C.1.

Pictorial Charts Unit, 181 Uxbridge Road, London W.7.

Educational Foundation for Visual Aids (E.F.V.A.), Brooklands House, Weybridge, Surrey.

REFERENCES

1. Knight, D. J. & Walker, M. A., 'A Factory Day at School' in *Special Education*, Vol. LIV, No. 3, Autumn 1965.
2. Jerrold, M. A. & Fox, R., 'Pre-Jobs for the Boys' in *Special Education*, Vol. 57, No. 2, June 1968.
3. Jackson, N., 'How Reliable are the Follow-Ups' in *Special Education*, Vol. LV, No. 1, Spring 1966.
4. O'Connor, N. & Tizard, J., *The Social Problems of Mental Deficiency*. Pergamon, 1963.
5. Gunzburg, H. C., *Progress Assessment Chart of Social Development*. N.A.M.H., 1963.
6. Gunzburg, H. C., 'Assessing Social Competence' in *Special Education*, Vol. 57, No. 2, June 1968.
7. Tansley, A. E. & Brennan, W., *School Leavers' Handbook & School Leavers' Workbook*. E. J. Arnold.
8. Gunzburg, H. C. (ed.), *Spotlight on Trouble* (8 titles). Methuen.
9. Gunzburg, H. C. (ed.), *Out with Tom* (14 titles). Methuen.
10. Uncles, J. C., *The Websters of Welford*. Nelson.
11. Anderson, J., *Adventures in Work*. O.U.P.
12. North, M., *Just the Job*. McGraw Hill.
13. Boyers, B., *Ann and Jenny Books*. Ginn.
14. Bradley, P. & J., *Between Ourselves*. Oliver & Boyd.
15. Appleton, J., *Safe and Well*. McGraw Hill.
16. Wright, C., *Better Buying*. Ginn.
17. Temple, S., *Pathway Books*. Weidenfeld & Nicolson.
18. Segal, S. S. (ed.), *The Working World*. Cassell.

FURTHER READING

Bloodworth, G., *Getting Ready for Work*, Darton, Longman & Todd, 1967.

British Council for the Rehabilitation of the Disabled, *The Handicapped School Leaver* (Elfed Thomas Report), 1964.

Carter, M., *Into Work*, Penguin, 1966.

Ferguson, T. & Kerr, A. W., *Handicapped Youth*, O.U.P., 1960.

Industrial Welfare Society, *Transition from School to Work*, I.W.S., 1962.

Ministry of Education, *Half Our Future* (Newsom Report), 1963.

Tansley, A. E. & Guilliford, R., *The Education of Slow Learning Children* (Chapter 12 – Education for Social Competence), Routledge & Kegan Paul, 1960.

CHAPTER 14

To Call In the Expert?

TEACHERS ought to be making much better use of a variety of social and welfare agencies than they appear to be doing at the present time. Not only will they benefit by gathering information which may lead to a better understanding of individual children's difficulties, but also they will acquire allies who can take action in the interests of a child in matters where teachers have neither the time nor the expertise to be effective.

In recent years there has been a demand for closer co-operation from the more progressive elements in every professional body concerned with the welfare of handicapped children. Traditionally, the medical profession has had a major role to play in the examination and assessment of handicapped children. At times they have been allowed to make decisions which have involved them in educational assessments about which their competence may be questioned. Their assumption of power rather than partnership has often alienated educational psychologists and teachers who have felt ignored and undervalued. Hostile attitudes have been hardened by the reluctance of some medical officers to make medical records available to teachers, and their practice of keeping confidential all information about their patients has often been too strictly interpreted where children are concerned.

Recrimination and counter recrimination cannot advance co-operation to the ultimate benefit of the children, who are the concern of all. It seems likely that many teachers are not fully aware of the functions of other services and the extent and limitations of the advice and help they may expect to receive from other professional workers. Perhaps a breakthrough could be achieved if teachers were more willing to approach co-operation in a better spirit and with a more sympathetic understanding of other people's problems.

PARENTS CAN HELP

The first expert we need to approach is the parent. In many schools there is too little contact between teachers and parents and often contacts are restrictive and unproductive. Parents normally see much more of their own children and have a more intimate contact with them in an entirely different setting. They should be a mine of useful information and might even be co-opted as substitute teachers for specific tasks both in and out of school.

Under existing parent-teacher contacts real exchanges of information are often denied. There should be opportunities for parents to be seen in a more relaxed situation where confidences may be exchanged. Instead of a one-sided questioning from parents—'How is John getting on with his reading?' perhaps teachers should be querying—'Well, how do you think he is progressing, does he show much interest at home in books, pictures, etc.?' 'Does he have many friends?' 'What are his interests?' 'Is his sister a better reader?' Does this cause any friction in the home?' 'Is he happy at school?' 'Does he help in the house, garden, run errands, etc.?' 'Is he interested in pets?' 'Has he got a bicycle?' 'Does he make his own way about the area on public transport?'

Other questions about his health and early school experiences will not only serve to give a teacher a better picture of a child, but may reveal how socially mature and independent he is for his age, or whether there are any home problems which may be affecting his school work. It is not unusual to discover that problems with school work are reflected in behaviour at home. Indirectly one will discover much about parental attitudes and any adverse environmental conditions. Further, one may be better able to suggest to parents how they may help in simple ways by encouraging independence, or providing experiences through taking children on trips and visits, or allowing more freedom in spending money, etc.

Every possible avenue of parental co-operation cannot be explored in a few words and the topic is of such importance that the next chapter will be concerned with some of the problems of parents. These brief remarks are made here because, in this particular context, where a team approach to child study is so essential, parents ought not to be overlooked.

THE FUNCTION OF A SCHOOL PSYCHOLOGICAL SERVICE

Misunderstandings of the role of an educational psychologist are only too common. There are complaints about the inadequacy of the service but there is often a failure to make use of the service to best advantage. It is well to appreciate that, just as we are short of teachers, so too is there a grave shortage of educational psychologists and psychiatric social workers. In Britain, since the war, there has been a remarkable expansion in the number of Child Guidance Clinics, but there has not been a corresponding increase in staff to man them. Added to staff shortage, this period has been marked by a tremendous increase in special school provision, particularly in schools for the educationally subnormal, and this has inevitably led to an excessive demand for psychologists to be occupied with routine tasks of intelligence testing as part of the ascertainment procedure. This is a task which may occupy the psychologist for long periods of time almost to the total exclusion of other duties, and there is a consequent reduction in time spent in ordinary schools.

Membership of a team at the Child Guidance Clinic makes demands on his time in testing, case conferences and administrative work. In addition the educational psychologist may be called upon to act in an advisory capacity to the Education Officer. He may also be involved in the promotion of curriculum development and in research or fact finding for those educational changes which are being considered by the Education

Committee. In many areas, selection for secondary education still takes place and the educational psychologist may be heavily bound up with some aspects of the selection procedure. Many have additional commitments at the Child Guidance Clinic, giving remedial teaching to retarded readers or play therapy to maladjusted children.

When one appreciates the full range of their responsibilities and the difficulties caused by shortage and movement of staff it is not surprising that ordinary schools may be neglected. Visits may be infrequent and reports may sometimes show evidence of brevity. Full consultation and discussion with heads and teachers may be impossible. Failure to give advice for educational treatment, or to conduct a battery of diagnostic tests, is rarely due to reluctance or inadequacy on the part of the educational psychologist. The excessive demands of routine testing and administrative duties in connection with selection procedures are often less satisfying than advisory work in schools or dealing thoroughly with problems of individual children.

Where a local service is under pressure it is difficult to suggest ways out of the impasse. In some cases it may be possible for local teachers' associations to encourage Local Education Authorities to increase their quota of educational psychologists, or to appoint remedial teachers or extra clerical help to free psychologists for other duties. Regrettably, what often happens is that schools cease to bring forward cases of backward and maladjusted children. This only hides the problem for, unless an attempt is made to secure full benefit from the psychological service, Local Education Authorities may remain unaware of a need in their area and provision, in one form or another, is unlikely to be forthcoming.

In areas where there is a well-staffed Child Guidance Clinic, teachers of slow learners should take full advantage of the service. Particularly in the case of special schools or classes it seems foolish to assume that the teaching staff are capable of dealing satisfactorily with every problem without recourse to outside help. An experienced and perceptive educational psychologist is often a source of information about a child's home background and previous school history for he has usually had contacts with home and school during assessment.

In cases where children are emotionally disturbed, or teachers feel that home circumstances are unfavourable and parental attitudes do not respond to school pressure, the full resources of a Child Guidance Clinic ought to be utilised. The Child Psychiatrist will see the child and parent and his medical status may have additional influence with parents. He can prescribe drugs and give therapeutic treatment which is beyond the scope of the teacher. Treatment may be extended to parents who are themselves disturbed and a Psychiatric Social Worker will visit the home and through her training and experience may gain additional insights into specific problems. She may then, following consultation with other colleagues, continue to visit the home and try to change conditions there.

THE CHILD PSYCHIATRIST

Psychiatry has a poor public image and some teachers have poor opinions of child psychiatrists. They hear garbled reports of treatment which appears to be so unstructured and permissive that badly behaved children are said to be out of control. Written reports are couched in unfamiliar jargon, treatment usually seems to have little effect and some psychiatrists are thought to be unwilling to take on disturbed children of low intelligence. If these ever were serious complaints they are less valid today. Psychiatrists, like teachers of slow learners, are having to deal with cases where others have tried and failed and they have not reached a position where it is possible to give guarantees of success in every case.

The child psychiatrist is often the leader of a team of professional workers at a clinic. Apart from exercising a general supervision over their activities, and co-ordinating and administering, he will often act as the chairman of the case conferences, which are called to discuss the assessment and treatment of individual children. Following reports by the psychologist and psychiatric social worker he will give his own assessment, and may suggest possible courses of treatment in which one or other of the team may take part. He has also his own professional expertise to apply in the examination and assessment of patients, interviewing parents, and by giving therapy and making periodical review of cases.

Assessment and treatment may take various forms depending on the age of the child. A young child may well be given a considerable amount of freedom to play with toys, sand, water, paint or small world apparatus. It is not the psychiatrist's job to teach the child, but to observe his reactions in these situations, and considerable freedom is likely to be more revealing that restriction. Indirect questioning and an opportunity to establish a relationship under relaxed conditions may be more productive than adopting an authoritative role. In addition to a medical examination, sensory and motor tests may be given, and personality tests. Treatment may often be best conducted through play therapy with young children.

With older children it is often possible to discuss their problems with them, and treatment may continue through discussion and counselling or sometimes through dramatic activities.

Procedures for reporting back to schools vary. In some clinics the psychiatrist may only send reports to the medical officer and the educational psychologist may be expected to keep schools informed. Where written reports are received, the psychiatrist may well be brief in writing to non-medical people and is often guarded in his comments. It should be appreciated that it is both difficult to ascertain and measure the degree of maladjustment in a disturbed child and progress may be slow and uneven. Technical terms may also lead to unfortunate misinterpretation.

Symptoms of maladjustment are sometimes classified under the headings of nervous disorders, habit disorders, behaviour disorders, organic disorders, psychotic behaviour and educational or vocational difficulties. The categories listed below are those used in the Underwood Report.[1]

1. NERVOUS DISORDERS
   Fears and phobias, anxiety, timidity, over-sensitivity.
   Withdrawal—unsociability, solitar ness.
   Depression—brooding, melancholy periods.
   Excitability—over-activity.
   Apathy—lethargy, lack of interest, unresponsiveness.
   Obsessions—rituals and compulsions.
   Hysterical fits—loss of memory.

2. HABIT DISORDERS
   Speech—speech defects, stammering.
   Sleep—night terrors, sleep-walking or talking.
   Movement—twitching, rocking, nail-biting.
   Feeding—food fads, nervous vomiting, indiscriminate eating.
   Excretion—incontinence of urine and fæces.
   Nervous pains and paralysis—headaches, deafness, etc.
   Physical symptoms—asthma and other allergic conditions.

3. BEHAVIOUR DISORDERS
   Unmanageableness—defiance, disobedience, refusal to go to
   school or work.
   Temper.
   Aggressiveness—bullying, destructiveness, cruelty.
   Jealous behaviour. Stealing and begging.
   Demands for attention. Lying and romancing.
   Truancy—wandering, staying out late.
   Sex difficulties—masturbation, sex play, homosexuality.

4. ORGANIC DISORDER
   Conditions following head injuries, encephalitis or cerebral
   tumours; epilepsy, chorea.

5. PSYCHOTIC BEHAVIOUR
   Hallucinations, delusions, extreme withdrawal, bizarre symptoms, violence.

6. EDUCATIONAL DIFFICULTIES
    Backwardness not accounted for by dullness.
    Dislike connected with subjects and people.
    Unusual response to school discipline.
    Inability to concentrate.
    Inability to keep jobs.

7. UNCLASSIFIED
    One has only to think of individual children to realise that
these categories overlap and may exist in various combinations.
Causes of maladjustment are hard to disentangle and heredity
and environmental factors, particularly early environmental
influences, may interact so that complexity confuses diagnosis.

THE SCHOOL HEALTH SERVICE

The School Medical Officer can often be a powerful ally.
Opportunities must be provided to see the doctor while he is
on the school premises. The class teacher who knows a particular child should be closely involved. She may give a brief
report about the child beforehand explaining, if necessary, why
sight, hearing or some suspected defect calls for a specially
thorough examination. Later the class teacher should meet the
doctor to hear the results of the examination. When an examination is inconclusive and suspicion remains that all is not
well, this may be the time to ask the doctor to suggest further
avenues of approach, or to question the need for examination
by a specialist. There are often advantages to be gained by the
teacher or head being present during a medical examination.
He may be able to help a shy or withdrawn child to respond to
questioning. He can ensure that non-readers are not given eye
tests using charts with letters of the alphabet.
    Frequently head and school medical officer together may be
better able to advise parents following an examination, and the
doctor will add weight to a headteacher's particular requests to
parents when such advice involves medical questions. Examples
of this are when teachers feel that children are short of sleep or

food. Indeed, many parents who will not normally attend parents' evenings may well come to the school for the medical inspection. Such opportunities should be taken not only to seek the doctor's support for a particular purpose, but perhaps to encourage the parent to visit the classroom and meet the child's teacher. The school doctor, in becoming aware of the incidence of defects in a school, may be instrumental in securing part-time assistance from a speech therapist or physiotherapist.

If many of these benefits are currently more typical of conditions in special schools there is no reason to believe that requests for similar consideration to be extended to slow learners in ordinary schools will be rebuffed. The main difficulty here is that the teacher of backward children rarely has enough free time to make contacts with other specialists in the ways described. A full appreciation of the nature and scope of his work may help the teacher to make a better case to the head for some free time or relief at the appropriate moments when medical officer or psychologists are in school.

SCHOOL NURSE

An obvious helper and frequent visitor to the school is the nurse. Usually she will have been present at previous medical examinations and can follow up pupils to see that prescribed treatment is being carried out. Often school nurses have special insights into a child's background and early history. Many have seen the children grow up during their school years and have already had frequent contacts with problem families. They are usually prepared to visit homes if necessary to encourage tardy or feckless parents to obtain spectacles or have them repaired. Often in the last resort they will see that a child is escorted to a hospital or clinic to keep an appointment when parents have failed repeatedly to do their duty. Occasionally they can help or advise when children seem to be in desperate need of clothes or food and official sources have dried up.

THE EDUCATION WELFARE OFFICER

Another servant of the local authority who is often under-valued is the Attendance Officer or 'school bobby'. Now, he is called an Education Welfare Officer and the change of nomenclature marked a change in his function. Their new duties place more emphasis on social work with problem families. Rather than being a punitive representative of the authority they are now expected to see what lies behind the persistent non-attender, the truant and the hypochondriac. Poverty, need and ignorance often go hand in hand with many of the problem families they meet and practical aid is often better than admonishment—so they now have some responsibility in indentification of families in need of free meals and clothing. They often transport handicapped children to residential schools at the beginning and end of terms. They have close links with other social workers so that they can secure home helps for children left to cope alone when mother suddenly goes into hospital, or find jobs for fathers who have lost employment due to family problems.

The Education Welfare Officer can become almost another member of staff to the special school or remedial department, for in classes of slow learners there will almost certainly be a number of problem families. A good Education Welfare Officer who has been in the area some time, will know more about a family than the teacher will ever find out. Some teachers of slow learners make a point of visiting the homes of all their children. There is much to commend this practice, but there is a limit to the extra work a busy teacher can accept, and not all can undertake this onerous task. The Education Welfare Officer, as a more frequent visitor to these homes, has ready access and is on friendly terms with parents. He is much more likely to be able to persuade parents to accept good advice. He can be helpful, for example, with parents who refuse to let a child be transferred to a special school, or in investigating cases of neglect.

MENTAL HEALTH OFFICERS

Special schools ought to have particularly close links with their local Mental Health Officers. These officers have responsibility for those E.S.N. children leaving school who have been recommended for voluntary supervision. Often they are engaged in After-Care work not only with these youngsters, but with others who break down under stress or repeatedly fail to find suitable employment. Like most social agencies they are overworked, but they often complain that schools fail to make use of them, and that there is a general lack of consultation which often seems to be due to teachers' poor knowledge of the services and expertise available. Some Mental Health Officers have never had any cases referred to them from schools. They would appreciate closer contacts with schools for they have to advise parents and occasionally information from teachers would be valuable. Frequently the social worker who is attached to a Mental Health Department is able to help parents of severely subnormal children to come to terms with their child's handicap. This service might well be extended to the parents of E.S.N. children. Occasionally Mental Health Officers are concerned at the apparent ease by which subnormal children are excluded from ordinary schools, special schools, or training centres. The subsequent contacts with the home lead them to feel that if they had been consulted earlier there might have been significant changes in children's behaviour through curative work in the home. During the course of contacts with parents Mental Health Officers become aware of problems which may affect school progress.

PROBATION OFFICERS

Probation Officers are visitors to most schools at some time. Though they often carry a heavy case load they prefer to emphasise the preventive aspect of their duties. In many cases of delinquency they feel sure that schools were aware of symptoms at an early stage, and action and advice might well have been channelled through the probation service before delinquent acts became serious or habitual. As with many other social workers they would prefer to meet a child's teacher in school. Usually their only contact is with the headteacher. Most would be prepared to visit at lunch-time or after school if they could meet the teacher personally and gain a better insight into a child's problems through first-hand contact with someone close to the child.

OTHER SOCIAL AGENCIES

There are other social agencies which are primarily concerned with problem families and frequently encounter handicapped children. Prominent among these agencies are the Children's Department of the local authority (with a staff of Child Care Officers and Family Caseworkers), the N.S.P.C.C. officers and a number of voluntary bodies such as church social workers. All these workers would welcome closer co-operation with schools and prefer to be involved at an early stage. More frequent visits to a school on an informal basis might be valuable. A chat over a cup of tea in the staff room could lead to mutual understanding. It is not unknown for a social worker to be called in by a parent, and she may then be bound by confidence and not permitted to see a teacher. If the school had made the first approach to the agency information might have been available to both sides.

Enough has been said here to underline the fact that schools ought to be making every effort to establish close and friendly contacts with all social agencies in their catchment area. Too often teachers are heard to complain in the staff room, 'What can I do with this child if he has such a bad home?' Social workers have a more positive approach by asking 'How best can this family be helped to improve the care of its children?'

REFERENCES

1. Ministry of Education, *Report of the Committee on Maladjusted Children* (Underwood Report). H.M.S.O., 1955.

FURTHER READING

Buckle, D. & Lebovici, S., *Child Guidance Centres*, W.H.O., 1960.

Burbury, W. M., Balint, E. M. & Yapp, B. J., *An Introduction to Child Guidance*, Macmillan, 1946.

Cleugh, M. F., *Psychology in the Service of the Schools*, Methuen, 1957.

Clyne, M. B., *Absent: School Refusal*, Methuen, 1966.

Kahn, J. H. & Nursten, J. P., *Unwillingly to School*, Pergamon, 1964.

Maclean, I. C., *Child Guidance and the School*, Methuen, 1966.

CHAPTER 15

Parents Have Problems

PARENT-TEACHER contacts have never been strong in Britain. Even the existence of a Parent-Teacher Association is no guarantee of close co-operation or mutual understanding and respect between teachers and parents. In fact the existence of a P.T.A. can be the means of maintaining a polite but formal barrier between the two parties. In this situation the organisation is tightly controlled by the school, a high percentage of meetings are social gatherings, and fund-raising is a major aim. A tidy, annual programme includes lectures on general, non-educational matters with a sprinkling of homilies directed at parents. Awkward questions from parents about the educational aims and methods never seem to arise. On the credit side, there are schools with teachers mature enough to move more than half-way to meet parents and to encourage suggestions and questions about educational matters. Reserve is broken down and friendly relationships are often built up through informal activities where parents and teachers join in some co-operative venture. Reports in the educational press, from time to time, give examples where swimming pools have been built with parents help or parents come in to learn about new teaching methods or help with repairs, sewing or small construction jobs. Improved relationships are inevitably noted and teachers' fears that parents will interfere with the running of the school prove to be groundless.

The desperate need for closer and better parent-teacher co-operation has been strongly spelled out in the Plowden Report.[1] The relevant section of the report takes its basic premise that parental attitudes greatly influence educational performance. Evidence is produced which suggests that as much as 24% of variation in a child's performance can be traced to the way parents help or hinder. Naturally the corollary follows that a closer partnership between teacher and parent is essential to educational advance. Rather neatly we are persuaded to consider a 'virtuous' circle where parental encouragement leads to better performance and better performance arouses more parental encouragement. There are many positive suggestions for teachers which make the Plowden Report essential reading for all teachers with any responsibility for slow learners. Of particular interest is the summary of an experiment which sought to evaluate the effects on educational attainments resulting from attempts to influence parental attitudes. This clearly showed that improvement was most marked amongst the least able children.

Such evidence will encourage many teachers who were already convinced that contact with parents of handicapped children is vital, not only for the benefit of the child but often to support and help the parent.

Special schools face up to this with varying degrees of success. Residential schools and day schools may find that a wide catchment area creates transport difficulties for parents. Nevertheless it is usual to find most parents supporting functions at a special school.

UNDERSTANDING PARENTS' DIFFICULTIES

Little chance of any real contact with parents will exist where teachers stand in judgement of parents and are needlessly critical of obvious shortcomings.

A teacher's first effort should be directed towards trying to understand the effect that a backward or a handicapped child can have on parents and family. Try to appreciate even a few of the trials, the disturbing and frustrating experiences which they have had to face over a period of years, sometimes even from birth. Parenthood is no sinecure. At least parents of normal

children have neighbours or grandparents to turn to and com-
pare notes and gain support and advice at times of stress.
Parents of handicapped children may have no such support or
guidance. The children of friends, neighbours and relatives may
be normal. At times there is no one to turn to. Advice from
medical practitioners is not always helpful. It is clear that the
bewilderment, and shock which parents feel when they are
made aware of their child's disability is intensified frequently
by ill-formed and conflicting advice.[2]

It is incredible to think that professional people can be so
insensitive to add to existing doubts in the ways reported in
Stress. There are several examples which could be quoted but
the following are sufficiently striking.

'One doctor told a mother, "mongols make nice pets about
the house", another told a mother to "put her away and forget
you ever had her". Yet another told the father of a two-month-
old mongol boy that "his mind will not develop beyond that
of an eighteen-month-old baby" and the father killed the
child.'

Anxiety often begins at birth. The first enquiry from mother
is to ask 'is the baby all right?' They want to know if baby is
normal. Sometimes discovery of backwardness is almost immediate if the child is noticeably defective. Some suggestion of
mental retardation can often be detected at birth because of
accompanying physical conditions (mongolism, hydrocephaly
(large head) or microcephaly (small head) are examples). Other
cases are harder to detect and suspicions are formed only when
a child's development is very slow.

At whatever point parents discover that their child is different
most will experience feelings of shock, fear, shame, guilt,
rejection or bewilderment. Some may pass through some of
these phases, and quite quickly come to a sensible acceptance
of the limitations of their child. Others may harbour feelings of
guilt and rejection for a long period. These feelings can often
be sustained and strengthened by the attendant frustrations as
the child grows up.

For the child who is obviously defective, and for the one who gradually reveals his inadequacies as he emerges from the cocoon of pram blankets, parents have to face unfavourable public attitudes. Tolerance and acceptance of physical and mental handicap has increased only slowly over centuries. Public sympathy still shows itself more ready to flow to particular handicaps. Thus blindness calls for more charitable responses yet the handicap of deafness is not always understood and can be the subject of ridicule and humour. Severe epilepsy, physical deformities and mental handicaps often arouse fear and revulsion.

Public attitudes are soon conveyed to parents, and, being members of the public themselves, they may easily share these feelings subconsciously towards their own child. Even the kindliest of neighbours and friends can be hurtful. They may be unable to cope with the situation and respond by either ignoring a disability, or by being either tactless or over-tactful. Every blundering contact, however well meant, can upset a sensitive parent. Unfortunate experiences can lead to parents keeping children indoors and avoiding social contacts. In extreme cases parents themselves may withdraw from social life.

It takes only a small step to keep a child who is developing slowly in a protracted state of babyhood. Over-protection, and over-possessiveness are followed by over-indulgence and a reluctance to give independence. When this happens the child has an additional handicap. This is often difficult for a teacher to penetrate before she can get to grips with a child's underlying learning difficulties.

OVER-PROTECTION

Many special school teachers can quote examples of children who are still being treated as babies by misguided parents. Boys are often the target for mothering and even at secondary ages it is not unusual to find some being dressed, washed and even sleeping in mother's bed. The effects on the family can be disturbing, father may receive scant attention from his wife, and other siblings may be neglected and made to feel unwanted.

The effect on the handicapped child can be even more devas-
tating. Stephen Jackson[3] summarises some of the effects of these
tragic phenomena in a short and readable article. He draws
attention to characteristics which may develop in an over-
protected child. There may be aggressive behaviour, dislike of
P.E. and games, over-weight and a tendency to a stiff, formal,
rather adult mode of speech lacking in childish vigour and
spontaneity. This adds to the problems of one who is already
unable to make friends and the lack of experience may also
depress intelligence and particularly show up by slow progress
in arithmetic.

CAN TEACHERS HELP PARENTS?

Over-protection is only one of a number of parental shortcomings, which teachers can air in staffroom chit-chat. Thought-
less criticism is far from helpful. It may be salutory to consider
that teachers and professional people with handicapped children have the same problems to face and do not always come
to terms with them. Parents of handicapped children need all
the help we can give them. The question is how best this may
be done. Sympathy and understanding are needed but a realisation of the magnitude of the problem must lead to some
realism. Teachers of slow learners accept many commitments
in the interests of their pupils. Demands on their time through
after-care, and out-of-school activities, can become excessive.
There must be a limit to the extent to which they can reasonably
extend their educational role to include therapy, social work,
youth leadership and ultimately to guidance and counselling
for parents as well as children.

The most profitable time for parent guidance is during the
pre-school period. But this is clearly a time when teachers can
have little contact with parents they have yet to meet. Nor can
we reasonably expect them to extend their efforts to pre-school
training. Teachers can only lend support to individuals or act
through their professional organisations to encourage parental
pressure groups who seek to obtain nursery school provision for

handicapped children. Authorities should be encouraged to make use of the 'at risk' registers which list children who, because of abnormal conditions before, during or after birth, seem in danger of becoming handicapped in some way in later life. Teachers have neither the time nor do they possess the expertise of the social or psychiatric social worker who may best help the families. They should at least be aware that these agencies may well give early help to families which may ease the tasks of educating some youngsters at a later date.

Nursery education is so woefully inadequate that many parents are starting playgroups and these might well be of real help to slow youngsters. One or two parents' self-help groups are already beginning to upset the predictions of experts by demonstrating the remarkable progress which they have achieved with seemingly dull children. Needless to say these efforts are usually the result of an aggressive initiative from intelligent, middle class parents. Some other agency may have to act as a catalyst for a group in poorer areas. Perhaps this might arise from the Welfare Clinic, for, many of these already provide facilities for mothers to continue attendance for discussions and lectures beyond the stage of post-natal care for the baby.

SCHOOL-HOME RELATIONSHIPS

From the general tenor of earlier remarks in this chapter it should be self-evident that once a slow learner is in school every effort should be made to help parent as well as child. The importance of a sympathetic attitude on the part of the teacher has been stressed. Though teachers may be willing to approach parents in the best spirit and full of good intentions, it is well to anticipate the possibility of suspicion and rebuff. Parents with their own memories of school, may find it difficult to be relaxed in the presence of a teacher. They can be shy or reluctant to visit the school and, in some cases, feelings of inferiority may be enhanced by their own poor educational attainments.

Many teachers of slow learners make a point of visiting the

homes of their pupils. Those who are committed to this approach speak highly of the benefits. They begin to understand problems at first-hand and tend to outgrow shallow criticism of bad home management and child care which may show up in school through poor clothing or lack of sleep. Most parents welcome visits and are much more approachable to a teacher who is prepared to come out of school and meet them on their own ground.

Some teachers may not find home visiting possible for various reasons. Nor are home visits justified too frequently. There is a need to supplement visits with varied activities in school. Parents should be made welcome and headteachers particularly should set aside times when parents know they will be seen. They must also be prepared to put aside other work to see a parent who arrives unexpectedly. There are many occasions when all parents can be invited to the school. Some events may best be managed during the evening but opportunities for parents to visit when the school is in session often prove most popular. The mass meeting of parents has limitations. Most parents want opportunities to talk to particular teachers and head and class teachers can be so overwhelmed by numbers that the fixed outcome is exhausted staff and disappointed parents. Parents need more than a few brief minutes chat at the head of a queue of other parents. Time is too short and the situation too public to be able to relax and loosen the tongue and allow the real problems to be aired.

There is something to be said for selective parents' evenings, or afternoons, when smaller groups of parents visit the school, to meet the staff in a more relaxed situation, perhaps over a cup of tea. Sometimes they may need to meet two teachers together.

Other forms of small group parent activities can be rewarding. An interesting account of the possibilities of parents gaining support and understanding from group discussions is given by Frances Lloyd.[4] She arranges for small groups of selected parents to meet together in school. Thus parents with a common problem may come together. Parents of children with epilepsy, or speech defects or those with very dull children can meet others who share a like burden. Questions are more easily encouraged in a small group. Advice can be offered directly and helpful suggestions can come from other parents.

Such a promising approach does not need elaborating in detail. A sensitive teacher will seize a good idea and adapt it. From small beginnings, there may well develop a pattern for the counselling service which is badly needed for parents of handicapped children.

SOME PROMISING PRACTICES

The following suggestions form an outline programme for the promotion of good parent/teacher relationships. They are drawn from a number of schools.

1. Anticipation and preparation. Established special schools often have a waiting list and parents of future entrants should be invited to see the school as early as possible. The child, too, should have a preview of his new school. Some authorities provide pamphlets to explain Special Education to parents. A simple leaflet, obtainable from the N.A.M.H. is entitled *Why Special Schools*. Some schools produce their own brochure outlining some of their aims and activities.

2. Parents should always be made welcome.

3. Any parents who do not come near the school should either be invited personally at a specified time or visited, annually, by a teacher, educational psychologist or education welfare officer.

4. Keep parents in touch with school affairs. Encourage children to tell parents about interesting school events. Supplement this with duplicated newsletters from time to time.

5. Make sure that parents have opportunities for regular private talks with teachers.

6. Consider carefully how best to make use of written reports. Standard forms with restricted comments can become meaningless and repetitive. Plowden has some sensible suggestions to make about more descriptive reports.[1] Reports can become a burden to teachers and the end product in turn is

stereotyped and dull. Selective reports may provide one solution, whereby reports are issued only when a child has suddenly made progress or if he is passing through a difficult phase.

7. Build up a stock of books and pamphlets for parents. These may be loaned to parents or used by teachers as references for discussion and guidance. Some suitable titles are recommended below.

8. Try to involve parents in educational matters. Send homework or school books home so that they keep in touch with day to day progress. Guide them in ways in which they can help their children at home. For example, in a reading book taken home by a child, an instruction slip to the parents might read:

(*a*) Try to hear your child read every day.

(*b*) Five or ten minutes is enough. Do not overdo it and force or upset the child.

(*c*) If the child cannot read a word ask him to sound it out. If he still cannot read it tell him the word and move on fairly quickly.

(*d*) Ask one or two questions about a page he has been reading. Point to one or two words at random and ask him to read them.

(*e*) Look at any pictures, talk about them, ask the child to tell you about them.

(*f*) Try to give praise wherever possible.

REFERENCES

1. Ministry of Education, Central Advisory Council for Education (England), *Children and their Primary Schools* (Plowden Report), Vol. I. H.M.S.O., 1967.
2. *Stress in Families with a Mentally Handicapped Child.* National Society for Mentally Handicapped Children, 1967.
3. Jackson, S., 'The Over-protected Child' in *Special Education*, Vol. XLIX, No. 1, 1960.
4. Lloyd, F., *Educating the Sub-normal Child.* Methuen, 1953 (p.31).

SOME RECOMMENDED BOOKS FOR PARENTS

Where magazine, published monthly, from A.C.E., 57 Russell St., Cambridge.

Books and pamphlets obtainable from the National Association for Mental Health. Address – N.A.M.H., 39 Queen St., London, W.1. For example:

Another Kind of School – a leaflet for parents of children who are not accepted for school.

Wing, Dr. L., *Autistic Children.*

Molloy, J., *Teaching the Retarded Child to Talk*, U.L.P.

Your Mentally Handicapped Child.

All About Asthma. B.M.A.

Linsey, Z., *Art is for All.* Mills & Boon.

British Epilepsy Association, *Epilepsy and Education, Epilepsy and Employment*, and other titles.

Matterson, E. M., *Play with a Purpose for the Under Sevens.* Penguin.

Morse, M., *The Unattached* (youth clubs). Pelican.

Kahn, J. H. & Nursten, J. P., *Unwillingly to School.* Pergamon.

Hunt, N., *The World of Nigel Hunt.* Darwen Finlayson.

Prince, Dr. G. S., *Teenagers To-day.*

A similar service supplying publications is provided by the National Society for Mentally Handicapped Children. Address – N.S.M.H.C., 86 Newman St., London, W.1. For example:

Parents' Voice – a quarterly magazine.

N.S.M.H.C. Holidays.

The Needs of Mentally Handicapped Children.

Stress in Families with a Mentally Handicapped Child.

Training and Employment of the Mentally Handicapped.

The Child with Mongolism – leaflet.

Home Care of the Backward Child – leaflet.

CHAPTER 16

Making a Career in Special Education

FOR the ambitious teacher, service in almost every branch of special education offers good career prospects. Many new special schools have been opened since the end of the war and promotion to headships and posts of responsibility has often been rapid. There are also many residential schools offering appointments for heads, deputies and housemasters. The extra pay for residential duties, plus accommodation, often in pleasant surroundings, can be attractive for the young married man.

Work in recognised special classes in ordinary schools often carries extra allowances. In secondary schools there should be several classes with one post as Head of Department. Regrettably the development of remedial departments in comprehensive schools has often been slow. Whether this is due to an initial anxiety to demonstrate academic standards is a matter for conjecture. It hardly seems possible that 'non-academic' children can be neglected indefinitely. The growth of 'Newsom' type courses and larger remedial departments should be followed by the creation of graded posts and Heads of Departments offering a reasonable career structure at secondary level.

A wide variety of posts exist associated with a complex of remedial teaching, diagnostic and advisory work. Peripatetic remedial teachers, remedial teaching at Child Guidance Clinics and remedial advisory posts all offer prospects for advancement and additional remuneration.

Posts as lecturers in special education, and particularly many such posts created in recent years for training teachers of the severely subnormal, are mainly filled by appointment of teachers with experience in some field of special educational treatment. Some of the larger education authorities employ local advisors, inspectors or organisers in special education. Another outlet for teachers with an administrative and advisory bent is in H.M. Inspectorate which has a Special Schools Section with appointments at various grades.

Work with slow learners can therefore not only be challenging and offer real personal satisfaction to able teachers but it is extremely varied and offers a promising career structure in many ways.

ADDITIONAL TRAINING

Many teachers towards the end of their training or after a first encounter with a 'backward' class on leaving college, become interested in the possibilities of making a career in Special Education. They wonder what qualifications are needed to be able to work in a special school or how they might best equip themselves professionally to work in other branches of special education.

Although posts of responsibility tend to go to teachers with additional qualifications, it should be clear, from the position outlined earlier, that there are not enough trained personnel. Lack of training is no bar to a first appointment. Some headteachers and L.E.A.s do not appoint teachers straight from college to posts in special schools. They feel that some experience of normal children is desirable. Not all headteachers share this view. They would welcome young men and women with fresh ideas and enthusiasm. The negative approach is clearly mistaken if a young teacher is barred from a special school, where he may get help and advice, yet may be given a backward class in a downtown school and left to flounder.

The following advice is intended for those who wish to further their study of the education of backward children or gain an additional qualification. Self-help is an obvious step.

1. *Reading.* There is a growing number of books and journals for teachers of slow learners. Some books have been

recommended in each chapter and a cumulative list is given at the end of this book. A number of journals emanate from professional organisations and are mentioned below.

If a local library does not stock particular books, they will often buy them on request or obtain them on inter-library loan. Some local education authorities operate a library of books for teachers. A postal supply is also available from stocks maintained by teachers' unions.

A comprehensive stock of books and journals is likely to be held by the library of an Institute of Education. Membership is normally free to serving teachers in their area, lists of books on particular topics are normally available (e.g. maladjustment, backwardness, reading) and books may be borrowed by post. The College of Special Education, 85 Newman Street, London W.1, will supply guided reading programmes to suit individual requirements.

2. *Join a professional organisation.* Both the N.U.T. and N.A.S. have sections for teachers of handicapped children. Some branches form local sections and support for new ones can be given. The N.U.T. through its Advisory Committee on Special Education has been prominent in making recommendations to Government departments and Royal Commissions on educational matters and teachers' conditions of service and has published a number of documents and pamphlets.

A number of other organisations are more specifically concerned with educational topics. The *Association for Special Education* (A.S.E.) is a long established body and membership is open to teachers and many others concerned with all types of handicapped children. So, one will meet doctors, speech therapists, psychologists, health visitors, teachers and many other professional people at their meetings. They have branches in most parts of the United Kingdom, who organise local programmes. A small subscription covers the supply of quarterly issues of the association's journal *Special Education* and three issues of *News-Letter*. National and International Conferences are held and these are highly recommended. An Advisory Service and Research Committee are active assets to members.

The *Guild of Teachers of Backward Children* has been established for over ten years and from small beginnings has gained international recognition. Membership is not restricted to teachers, although teachers who work with slow learners in ordinary schools are well represented. Like the A.S.E. it has a network of local branches, a small subscription, and a quarterly journal *Forward Trends*. The annual National Conference is a friendly, lively and informative gathering. The Guild has been the moving spirit behind the establishment of a *College of Special Education* which is intended to provide advice for teachers and eventually provide training and award qualifications possibly by a combination of correspondence and short residential courses. Already the College is producing pamphlets containing advice for teachers. Their first booklet—Guide Line for Teachers No. 1 entitled *Training to teach the backward child*, deals with many of the points raised in this chapter. Other pamphlets produced are No. 2 *Vocational Guidance, Employment and After-Care*, and No. 3 an introductory handbook *The Severely Subnormal*.

Initially the College is acting as an advisory and information centre. In addition to bibliographies and books it also provides lecturers, short courses and exhibitions.

The *National Association of Remedial Teachers* has been formed more recently but is already gaining support mainly through the excellence of its quarterly journal *Remedial Education*. Like other organisations there is a small membership fee and benefits from courses and conferences.

3. *Visit other schools.* Teachers who have attended courses or conferences appreciate the benefits to be gained from discussions with colleagues. Teachers who are new to special education, or even experienced teachers, would be well advised to make a point of visiting other schools. Not enough is done in this way to draw on the experience of other teachers.

4. *Special Courses.* Reference has already been made to many short courses, or conferences organised by various bodies. These are usually well advertised in the weekly educational papers. Some vacation courses run by the Department of

Education and Science and several Summer Schools are annual events and provide a good introduction to the extended courses, which lead to specialist qualifications.

A full list of approved courses is given in a handbook, *Programme of One-Year Courses and One-Term Courses for Qualified Teachers*. This is an annual publication obtainable from the Department of Education and Science, Teachers Branch II, 83–91 Victoria Street, London S.W.1. Copies find their way into many schools or can usually be inspected at local education offices.

In a recent programme, thirty-one one-year courses were listed dealing with the education of backward or E.S.N. children. One term courses were being offered at five centres. Serving teachers may be seconded by their L.E.A.s on full salary, or grants are available to other teachers who intend to work in England or Wales.

In addition to full-time courses, four Institutes or Colleges of Education offer two-year or three-year part-time courses. Most courses are advertised in the educational press and 'specialist' journals mentioned above.

An additional qualification is recognised by payment of an allowance under a Burnham Award. Teachers in Special Schools or recognised special classes will also receive a 'Special School Allowance'. Some authorities only make this payment to special class teachers if they have a qualification.

There are, then, both financial and personal rewards to be gained from serious study. Additional qualifications are increasingly being expected from candidates for promotion. There is, however, a great deal to be gained from a course by increasing one's professional competence.

Selecting a course to suit your own needs may be difficult from such a wide choice. Many will naturally choose the nearest one. Differences between courses are not always as important as they appear on paper. Some courses are designated as Advanced or Diploma Courses (usually at Universities), others are called Supplementary or Certificate Courses. Advanced courses usually specify that a teacher must have a minimum of five years' teaching experience, possibly with some experience of slow learners. Supplementary courses may only demand two years' teaching experience. It has been claimed that a Diploma is of higher standing than a Certificate. This may only assume importance where a teacher wishes to go on to take a higher qualification at a university (for example, M.Ed.) for university entrance requirements demand some advanced qualification. For all practical purposes, as, for example, amongst applicants for headships of special schools, either qualification would be acceptable. Other benefits, as to the 'quality' of the course are more likely to be the result of the student's personal effort and study rather than the content of the syllabus. Some account may be taken of the fact that some courses do appear to place an emphasis on specific handicaps and are more geared to special school work. Others are more general or may particularly stress work with slow learners in ordinary schools.

Considerable responsibility is placed upon mature students for making a success of their studies on these courses. The benefits which accrue to teachers, children and schools make the enterprise well worth the effort.

Association for Special Education

> L. J. McDonald Esq.
> Secretary
> 19 Hamilton Road
> Wallasey
> Cheshire

National Association for Remedial Education

> S. W. Ashton Esq.
> Secretary
> 26 Shrewsbury Road
> Clay Mills
> Stretton
> Burton-on-Trent
> Staffs.

Guild of Teachers of Backward Children

> Minster Chambers
> Southwell
> Notts.

FURTHER REFERENCES

A comprehensive list of professional and voluntary organisations which are in any way concerned with handicapped children is supplied in Part Two of *No Child is Ineducable* by S. S. Segal, published by Pergamon Press, 1967.

This not only provides a concise account of the history and purpose of these organisations, but gives details of membership, facilities, publications and films.

A SELECTED LIST FOR FURTHER READING

Ablewhite, R. C., *The Slow Reader*, Heinemann, 1967.

Blair, G. M., *Diagnostic and Remedial Teaching*, Macmillan, New York, 1956.

Boom, A. B. (ed.), *Studies of the Mentally Handicapped Child*, Edward Arnold, 1968.

British Council for the Rehabilitation of the Disabled, *The Handicapped School Leaver* (Elfed Thomas Report), 1964.

Cheshire Education Committee, *The Education of Dull Children at the Primary Stage*, U.L.P., 1956. *The Education of Dull Children at the Secondary Stage*, U.L.P., 1963.

Cleugh, M. F., *The Slow Learner*, Methuen, 1968 (2nd. edit.).

Cleugh, M. F., *Teaching the Slow Learner in the Primary School*. Methuen, 1961.

Cleugh, M. F., *Teaching the Slow Learner in the Secondary School*, Methuen, 1961.

Cleugh, M. F., *Teaching the Slow Learner in the Special School*, Methuen, 1961.

Clarke, A. M. & A. D. B., *Mental Deficiency – the Changing Outlook*, Methuen, 1958.

Collins, J. E., *The Effects of Remedial Education*, Oliver & Boyd, 1961.

Department of Education & Science, *Slow Learners at School*, Educational Pamphlet No. 46, H.M.S.O., 1964.

Dolch, E. W., *A Manual for Remedial Reading*, Garrard Press, 1945.

Duncan, J., *The Education of the Ordinary Child*, Nelson, 1942.

Erickson, M. J., *The Mentally Retarded Child in the Classroom*, Macmillan, New York, 1965.

Fait, H. I., *Adapted Physcial Education for those with Physical and Mental Deviations and Low Physical Fitness*, W. B. Saunders, 1960.

Ferguson, T. & Kerr, A. W., *Handicapped Youth*, O.U.P., 1960.

Gaitskell, C. D. & M. R., *Art Education for Slow Learners*, Ryerson Press, 1953.

Goldstein, H. & Seigle, M., *Curriculum Guide for Teachers of the Educable Mentally Handicapped*, Interstate Publications, Danville, Illinois, 1958.

Gray, W. S., *The Teaching of Reading and Writing*, U.N.E.S.C.O., 1956.

Gunzburg, H. C., *Social Rehabilitation of the Subnormal*, Baillière, Tindall & Cox, 1961.

Holt, J., *How Children Fail*, Pitman, 1964.

Ingram, C. P., *Education of the Slow-Learning Child*, Ronald Press, New York, 1935.

Jackson, S., *Special Education in England and Wales*, O.U.P., 1966.

Kephart, N.C., *The Slow Learner in the Classroom*, Merrill Books, 1960.

Kershaw, J. D., *Handicapped Children*, Heinemann, 1961.

Kirk, S. A., *Teaching Reading to Slow Learning Children*, Houghton Mifflin, 1940.

Kirk, S. A. & Johnson, G. O., *Educating the Retarded Child*, Houghton Mifflin, Boston, 1951.

Kirk, S. A. *et. al.*, *Early Education of the Mentally Retarded Child*, Univ. of Illinois Press, 1958.

Lloyd, F., *Educating the Subnormal Child*, Methuen, 1953.

Morris, R., *The Quality of Learning*, Methuen, 1951.

National Association for Mental Health, *The Handicapped Child in the Family*, N.A.M.H., 1952.

O'Connor, N. & Tizard, J., *The Social Problems of Mental Deficiency*, Pergamon, 1963.

Peter, L. J., *Prescriptive Teaching*, McGraw Hill, 1965.

Pritchard, D. G., *Education and the Handicapped*, 1760–1960, Routledge & Kegan Paul, 1963.

Queensland University Faculty of Education, *Remedial Centre-Report*, 1953–1957.

Sarason, S. B., *Psychological Problems of Mental Deficiency*, Harper, New York (3rd. edit.), 1959.

Schonell, F. J., *Backwardness in the Basic Subjects*, Oliver & Boyd, 1942.

Segal, S. S., *Teaching Backward Pupils*, Evans, 1963.

Segal, S. S., *No Child is Ineducable*, Pergamon, 1967.

Sheridan, M. D., *The Handicapped Child and His Home*, National Children's Home, 1965.

Stevens, M., *Observing Children who are Severely Subnormal*, Edward Arnold, 1968.

Tansley, A. E., *Reading and Remedial Reading*, Routledge & Kegan Paul, 1967.

Tansley, A. E. & Gulliford, R., *The Education of Slow Learning Children*, Routledge & Kegan Paul, 1960.

Thomas, J. E., *Hope for the Handicapped*, Bodley Head, 1967.

Vernon, M. D., *Backwardness in Reading*, Cambridge Univ. Press, 1957.

Wall, W. D. *et. al.*, *Failure in School*, U.N.E.S.C.O., 1962.

Williams P. & Gruber, E., *Response to Special Schooling*, Longmans, 1967.

INDEX OF PUBLISHERS AND SUPPLIERS OF APPARATUS

Pitman, Sir Isaac & Sons Ltd., 39 Parker St., Kingsway, London W.C.2.

Reader's Digest Assoc. Ltd., 25 Berkcley Sq., London W.1.

Schofield & Simms Ltd., 35 St. John's Road, Huddersfield.

Science Research Associates (S.R.A.), Reading Road, Henley-on-Thames, Oxon.

Thorpe, F. A. (Pub.) Ltd., Artisan House, Bridge, Anstey, Leicester.

University of London Press Ltd., St. Paul's House, Warwick Lane, London E.C.4.

Ward, Lock & Co. Ltd., 116 Baker St., London W.1.

Warne, Fred'k. & Co. Ltd., 1 Bedford Court, Bedford St., London W.C.2.

Weidenfeld G. & Nicolson Ltd., 5 Winsley St., London W.1.

Wheaton, A. & Co. Ltd., 143 Fore St., Exeter.

Wills & Hepworth Ltd., Derby Sq., Loughborough, Leicester.

Index